THE SECRET LIFE OF THE
Gold Coast

Brendan Shanahan is twenty-seven and was born in Sydney. He has an honours degree in Art History and Curatorship from the Australian National University, Canberra, and has written a popular rock music column for Sydney's *Sunday Telegraph* since 2000. He avoids 'proper' jobs and has travelled in South-East Asia, North America, western Europe and southern Africa. He has no permanent place of residence. This is his first published book.

THE SECRET LIFE OF THE
Gold Coast

Brendan Shanahan

VIKING
an imprint of
PENGUIN BOOKS

VIKING

Published by the Penguin Group
Penguin Group (Australia)
250 Camberwell Road, Camberwell, Victoria 3124, Australia
(a division of Pearson Australia Group Pty Ltd)
Penguin Group (USA) Inc.
375 Hudson Street, New York, New York 10014, USA
Penguin Group (Canada)
10 Alcorn Avenue, Toronto, Ontario, Canada M4V 3B2
(a division of Pearson Penguin Canada Inc.)
Penguin Books Ltd
80 Strand, London WC2R 0RL, England
Penguin Ireland
25 St Stephen's Green, Dublin 2, Ireland
(a division of Penguin Books Ltd)
Penguin Books India Pvt Ltd
11 Community Centre, Panchsheel Park, New Delhi – 110 017, India
Penguin Group (NZ)
Cnr Airborne and Rosedale Roads, Albany, Auckland, New Zealand
(a division of Pearson New Zealand Ltd)
Penguin Books (South Africa) (Pty) Ltd
24 Sturdee Avenue, Rosebank, Johannesburg 2196, South Africa

Penguin Books Ltd, Registered Offices: 80 Strand, London, WC2R 0RL, England

First published by Penguin Group (Australia), a division of Pearson Australia Group Pty Ltd, 2004

10 9 8 7 6 5 4 3 2 1

Copyright © Brendan Shanahan 2004

The moral right of the author has been asserted

All rights reserved. Without limiting the rights under copyright reserved above, no part of this publication may be reproduced, stored in or introduced into a retrieval system, or transmitted, in any form or by any means (electronic, mechanical, photocopying, recording or otherwise), without the prior written permission of both the copyright owner and the above publisher of this book.

Design by Miriam Rosenbloom © Penguin Group (Australia)
Cover photograph by Cal MacKinnon
Typeset in 12/17.5 pt Granjon by Midland Typesetters, Maryborough, Victoria
Printed and bound in Australia by McPherson's Printing Group, Maryborough, Victoria

National Library of Australia
Cataloguing-in-Publication data:

   Shanahan, Brendan, 1976– .
   The secret life of the Gold Coast.

   ISBN 0 670 04049 5.

   1. Shanahan, Brendan, 1976– – Journeys – Queensland – Gold Coast.
   2. Gold Coast (Qld.) – Description and travel. 3. Gold Coast (Qld.) –
   Social conditions. I. Title.

   919.432

www.penguin.com.au

For my mother: whose 'life-style' has always had a great deal of the former and very little of the latter

Contents

★

	Acknowledgements	ix
	Prologue	xi
1	In Paradise	1
2	Barefoot and Pregnant	10
3	Trouble in Paradise	24
4	Enter the Dragon	40
5	Nowhere to Run	49
6	1-800 G-E-T O-U-T N-O-W	61
7	The Garden of Earthly Resort Features	72
8	Lifestyles of the Rich and Childless	78
9	Schoolies: When Munchkins Attack	97
10	The Fourth-largest City of the Future	109
11	I Put a (Sexy) Spell on You	118
12	The Kraken Wakes	125
13	All the Lonely People	132
14	Clan of the Cave Bear	152
15	Porn to Run	158

16	Swing Party Down-under!	168
17	Don't Hit Mummy	185
18	Flip Out On Level Eight	193
19	Escape from Pleasure Island	211
20	I See Dead People	226
21	Bonito Sees Death	238
22	Kane and the B3 Nightclub Spectacular	241
23	Rod and Todd	249
24	Fish Roulette	259
25	Kane Rane	270
26	Farewell to Paradise	274
	Epilogue	283

Acknowledgements

★

I would like to thank the following people for their support: Rachelle and Phil; my 'journalist friend' Amy; Joyce Pallister for help with research; Alexander McRobbie and Paula Stafford for all the historical information; Chloe for suggesting the direction for this book; Annabelle and Jeremy for indulging my itinerant habits, and Carrie and Greg for the same. Thanks to Greg Stolz and the *Courier Mail* for permission to reproduce the story '"Torture" Mistaken for Bondage Ritual' on page 12. Thanks also to Mark and Clare and Luke and Pants for rescuing me in Brisbane.

Prologue

★

INSIDE, THE APARTMENT was like the set of a Beckett play: no furniture, no television, no light globes in their sockets; not a single object that might indicate that this was a place of human habitation. The only visible source of life was a tiny, old-fashioned electrical heater that sat in the middle of the room issuing a low, sinister buzzing noise. Its grubby orange blush crept out to coat the bare, grey surfaces of the room in which the curtains were drawn and everything else was dark.

My friend, a journalist, had arrived to interview a heroin addict who, after having injected a large amount of the drug, drifted off into an opiate slumber on a windowsill eight storeys above the ground. A few minutes later the girl rolled over and fell straight out the window with nothing but concrete paving to break her fall. Thanks to the effects of the drug, she hit the ground as slack as a dead cat and walked out of hospital an hour later with barely a scratch. It was the kind of story the magazine was looking for these days.

The addict's boyfriend led the journalist and the photographer into the kitchen while he disappeared into the bedroom. There were no utensils or food, just a giant pile of clothes, like a termite mound, standing in front of the refrigerator. In the manner of a mountaineer negotiating a precipice, the journalist shuffled past the clothes and was left to stand outside the bedroom door, waiting. From within she could hear the boyfriend attempting to rouse the

Prologue

sleeping girl. He soon reappeared, alone, apologising, before disappearing to try again.

After a matter of some minutes the girl appeared, groggy and listless, her eyes heavy, her jaw set in a slackened death mask. Before the journalist had had a chance to introduce herself, the girl fell over. The boyfriend picked her up off the floor and shook her with urgent reminders that this was the journalist from the women's magazine – the one that had come to do the story – the one who had come to *pay* her. The boyfriend was keen to reassure the journalist that everything would be all right.

After the second collapse, the journalist disappeared out the door and into the sunshine to call her editors and propose that this story be canned. They agreed and the journalist, trailed by the photographer, made her way across the lawn towards her car. The sight of her leaving was enough to wake the girl from her stupor; she began to scream, staggering her way to the front gate. 'You fuckin' bitch!'

The boyfriend, too, became aggressive, making a lunge for the journalist and forcing the photographer to intervene. The journalist made a run for the car. Together she and the photographer locked the doors and sped away. In the rear-vision mirror they could see the pair running after them with a disjointed junky-jog, shaking their fists and screaming obscenities, like unhappy zombies hungry for a meal of brains.

The journalist's name was Liz and she relayed this story to me as we drove. It had happened some months earlier but it had made a big impression upon her, as it did now on me. 'Up there is where the girl fell out of the building,' she told me, pointing to a cluster of towers in the distance. It was my first visit to the Gold Coast and I was seeing the city from what I was to later learn was its most spectacular vantage – the southward approach across the Southport Bridge, the bridge that traverses the Broadwater, the mouth of the Nerang River, and connects

Prologue

the north and south of the city. All around us stood buildings – they seemed to run forever into the blue haze as we sped along the highway. Tall, white and crystalline, they gathered in apparently arbitrary fungal clumps, as though they had sprouted in the last rain.

'That palm tree is fake,' said Liz. 'It's actually a radio antenna.' I looked up. Beneath the foliage hung loaf-shaped transmitters like deformed coconuts. The Broadwater sparkled to our left. Across its expanse floated a little wooden church, its pointed spire rocking gently in the wake of a boat shaped like a duck cutting a white gash through the blue.

Further we drove. I wound down the window and felt the breeze against my face. The buildings grew in density; there was the Aegean, the Marrakesh, the St Tropez, the Biarritz, the Phoenician, Xanadu. The names seemed to spring direct from the subconscious, the triggers of a psychiatric test: 'I want you to tell me your associations with the following words: Kasbah, Atlantis, Copacabana, Monte Carlo...' The variety and absurdity of their manufacture was endless: a postmodern extravaganza complete with hot-pink pyramids and mock classical pillars in baby blue; a soaring devil-horned tower in emerald glass; a spiky, lopsided structure bristling with Bavarian turrets; a jagged Art Deco monolith; white Mediterranean domes that left purple circles on the retina; a swimming pool in the form of an Aztec temple. Standing at the edge of the ocean the buildings turned their outlandish ornament to the sea, often revealing on their western aspects little more than soaring blank walls, giving the highway spectator the sense of an actor behind the proscenium. Here these buildings stood to face... what? Arriving armies? Or the inevitable future when sea levels would rise and flood the city, leaving in their wake nothing more than the teetering spires of a thousand ruined civilisations artfully reproduced in fibreglass?

Prologue

And it was big, huge in fact: the sixth-largest city in the country, and its growth outstripped all else. Yet who even thought of it as a city? A city was a place with a subway, a natural history museum and a park downtown with a bronze statue of the founding father staring benevolently through wire *pince-nez*. Who had founded this place? Nobody. No one had written a declaration or found gold in a creek or dumped a boatload of criminals or spied a strip of trees off the port bow and cried 'Land!' Yet, despite this, half a million people, as though victims of the same subliminal message spliced into one evening's soap opera, had picked themselves up and moved here, most of them in the last twenty years. I might not have believed it, had not all around me stood the evidence: hundreds of towers stretching in every direction, new ones rising up every day, miles upon miles of piles upon piles of little boxes, all of them with tiny balconies on which to stand clutching a cocktail while staring out at the ocean. What had all these people come to find, I wondered, and – perhaps more importantly – had they found it?

Here, surely, was the city of the future – if only because it had no past. But the future was not *1984* or *Metropolis*, it was not some dank dystopia of rain and reinforced concrete; the future was bright, full of light and absurdity and a message that here on earth man was building paradise: Paradise Sands, Paradise Gardens, Paradise Island, Paradise, Paradise, Paradise . . .

One

★

In Paradise

BY THE TIME of my first visit to the Gold Coast, my life had stagnated to such a point that to the casual observer it may have been mistaken for a particularly earnest Polish film: which is to say, slow, joyless and poorly funded. My previous book (my first), a biography of a well-known Perth eccentric, had met with legal problems and had, after almost eighteen months of work and indecision, been shelved by the publishers. My disappointment and frustration were acute, and now depression, that ever-looming threat, had drawn its veil across my countenance.

My mental state was possibly not helped by a life of inveterate transience. Since starting my last book I had been more or less continually on the road. By taking advantage of Australia's newly competitive airline industry and the generosity of friends, I had managed, for more than two years, to exist without any permanent abode. Partially this was a nominal gesture lending some thin veneer of legitimacy to my new-found ambition as a travel writer, but mostly it was just another form of procrastination. By the time I arrived on the Gold Coast, therefore, I was thoroughly lost; my misery had become a cocoon, layered and hard to the point that it seemed it might be with me forever. So when I headed over the Southport Bridge for the first time it seemed quite a happy coincidence that I had arrived in the city of the lost; a city where seemingly everyone had come from somewhere else and where 'running away' was a box you ticked on the emigration form. My arrival also coincided neatly with some new revelations about the nature of travel.

'Why are you travelling?' a confused African villager once asked me – a man who had never ventured further than his neighbouring hamlet. I said it was to see the world. 'No,' came the bewildered reply, '*why* are you travelling?' At the time I might have said something like, 'To better know the world.' But now, after several more journeys and a little more thought on the subject, I have come to understand that the only reason I travel is to better know myself. That travel is a fundamentally selfish act was a disturbing but inescapable conclusion; with a white face and a Visa card there are very few problems that cannot be solved; and as you are airlifted to safety and the locals left to be massacred in some gruesome medieval pogrom, so slips away the illusion that you were ever anything more than a tourist. The heart of darkness is a luxury for those who can reasonably expect to live beyond their fifth birthday. Perhaps this is why I find myself drawn to the 'fake', the 'inauthentic': Tijuana, Kuta Beach, Sun City, Ibiza; like prostitution, the transaction here is transparent. The idea that these places represent a fundamental cheapening of the travel 'experience'; that they are a debased and shabby product of the naïve tourist yearning for a preconceived notion of their destination, seems to me not merely a rather touching statement of the obvious, but an exoneration of all those 'travellers' who have hacked their way into the jungle, full of a misguided atavistic enthusiasm for the 'primitive', the 'simple', the 'other', and found only their own egos.

That one could love Venice but not Las Vegas's Venetian (a hotel and life-sized fibreglass replica of the Doge's Palace at which one can experience the thrill of floating in an imported gondola down a canal smelling strongly of chlorine) when the two were virtually indistinguishable, right down to the number of crass Americans and sneering Euro-trash perched on iron lawn chairs at expensive outdoor restaurants, was beyond me. How much more 'real' than its new world simulacrum is a Venice shored-up by pneumatic pumps and in which the only residents own hotels?

For the seeker of 'authentic' experience, the tourist city is nothing but an imagining, a mirage, an inconvenient hallucination on the way to something more sustaining, more *authentic*. People talk about Mikonos as if it wasn't Greece, about Pattaya as if it wasn't Thailand. 'That's not the *real* Africa,' the dedicated 'traveller' (never 'backpacker' or 'tourist') will tell you, as though what *was* African – or Greek or Thai, for that matter – was something external, something that might be pointed to or eaten or photographed (always for the benefit of the *traveller*), rather than something that came from within; as though the man selling T-shirts outside Planet Hollywood in Kuta Beach had less right to be Balinese than the Hindu priest at the volcano shrine.

On a more immediate level, the Gold Coast seemed to offer the ideal subject for a book in which I could combine my love of the grotesque with a diet of two-for-one tequila slammers. If I was tired of worthy travel then it was time to write a gloriously worthless book; something light and disposable; something middle-aged ladies could buy at the train station without embarrassment. It has always been my secret ambition to be a second-rung chat show guest; the emergency guy they ring when this month's Hollywood ingénue is in rehab –

Peter Ustinov or Stephen Fry. After the disaster of my first book I had become as hungry for success as I was for diversion. No more youth hostels full of fragrant Germans in lycra trousers telling boring stories about crawling across China! On the Gold Coast there were meter maids who had scratched one another's eyes out in a vicious bikini-clad turf war; developers who had owned whole governments and Japanese surfers who walked all day with a board under their arm but couldn't swim a stroke. Whether these things were any more than clichés hardly seemed to matter: as we drove over the bridge I might as well have been a lucky contestant from a 1986 episode of *Perfect Match* off on a romantic, all-expenses paid holiday to the sunny Gold Coast. And this city and I had a compatibility rating of 93 per cent.

Consistent with my new philosophy of indulgent middle-class travel, there seemed no better way to familiarise myself with my intended home than to take, as so many millions had before me, a discount package holiday to Surfers Paradise. I scanned the brochure at the travel agency in Sydney. A thousand towers with a thousand names lay before me in a brimming cornucopia of swimming pools, spa baths, water views, ensuite bathrooms and room service massages. Unfortunately my budget and my fantasy had yet to meet any sort of consensus, and when I told the travel agent that I would take the cheapest deal on offer, she looked genuinely disappointed.

My hotel was on Orchid Avenue, a nightclub row of strip clubs and cavernous, pounding meat markets in the centre of Surfers Paradise. Orchid Avenue is the kind of place where the producers of reality TV shows go to find couples who want to test their fidelity by having topless models smear them in chocolate sauce. My hotel shared a foyer with a strip club and had clearly taken some decorating tips from its neighbour. The entrance hall looked like a brothel, complete with pink cursive neon sign (some of the letters broken) flashing

'Reception'. At night the cats in the alley below sounded disconcertingly like screaming children and for some time I simply sat in my room in the dark, watching the people in the tower block opposite, or stared at the handle of the giant glowing guitar that rose from the Hard Rock Café over the rooftops, listening to the screams and feeling lonely. My vision of swingin' debauchery had been somewhat deflated by the mediocrity of my accommodation and the unseasonably empty bars downstairs.

The business of finding a base on the Gold Coast was one that had occupied me for three frantic days. At the time of my arrival it had seemed impossible that among the seemingly endless piles of little boxes there might not have been one for me. But now I knew that the market was tight. The approach of summer had slimmed my chances and I had grown weary of the supercilious looks I was receiving from real estate agents who clearly regarded me as little better than a vagrant. I stared at the big guitar outside. The walls were closing in. I needed to go for a walk.

From Orchid Avenue I wandered to the sea, along the beach and then to Cavill Avenue. Cavill Av (pronounced phonetically, as in 'have'), as it is known to the locals, is the centre of Surfers Paradise. Prior to 1933, the area was known as Elston but after lobbying by a group of locals led by hotelier Jim Cavill, it was named after Cavill's pub, the Surfer's Paradise Hotel. (The apostrophe was dropped in the 1950s when the Gold Coast began a campaign to establish itself as an international destination. Tourists apparently have an aversion to punctuation.) Cavill Avenue runs from Marine Parade (the road parallel to the beach) to the Nerang River in the west, the two roads forming a disjointed shantytown of takeaway joints, souvenir shops, nightclubs and shopping malls. (On the beach sits a yellow shopping centre that had once been a waterslide; the developers retained the framework of the slide and simply built around it, connecting the building to the beach by a pedestrian overpass designed merely, it would seem, to add insult to injury and create what might be the single ugliest structure in Australia.)

In recompense for its general dowdiness, Surfers Paradise has a certain ratty plebeian charm, an English seaside naughtiness of novelty beer hats, wet T-shirt competitions and trick pens with naked ladies; a charm that belies any substance to the moniker of 'Australia's Vegas'. Comparisons of the Gold Coast to Las Vegas are as perplexing as they are frequently cited, credible surely only in the minds of those who have never actually seen that cosmic explosion in the desert. The timid, decorous kitsch of Surfers Paradise resembles not in the least, certainly in any physical sense, the infinite grotesqueries of Vegas, a city whose scale and sensual might would defy the descriptive powers of any great writer in history, living or dead, chained to a desk and threatened with the execution of a loved one.

Yet any beguiling dagginess Surfers may have once possessed was now in the process of being ruthlessly expunged. In the wake of its most recent population explosion, the Gold Coast was adopting, holus-bolus, the vernacular of international capitalism. Where once stood the Chevron Hotel – the first modern luxury hotel on the Gold Coast and an institution that marked the beginning of what we know as Surfers Paradise – now grew the Chevron Renaissance, a monolithic trinity of skyscrapers – one sixty storeys – teeming with Starbucks outlets and Irish theme pubs. It wasn't any more attractive than the old Surfers – the Renaissance had more in common with Puff Daddy's beach house in Malibu than it did with the principles of Brunelleschi – it was just newer and bigger; the kind of thing local councillors talked about as 'setting new standards of international excellence'.

Walking from Surfers Paradise to Broadbeach one is continually reminded that as an instrument of urban planning the skyscraper makes a very good beach shade and wind tunnel. In spite of being a confirmed enthusiast (there are few sights more thrilling than the bristle of distant needles rising from the horizon) one must concede that there are few logical reasons to build them. Skyscrapers are highly inefficient buildings; they consume a shocking amount of resources and become exponentially more expensive the higher they grow. Other than the possibility of a view, there seemed no good reason, therefore, to build the Q1, a ninety-storey residential tower in southern Surfers and the largest of its kind in the world. It was to be almost double the height of the surrounding buildings; even in drawings it looked absurd, like a child in a yearbook photograph who had gone through puberty at the age of ten. When I would later question the creator of the Q1 on his motives for building such a structure, he would tell me that the building was an exercise in the efficient use of scarce land, before noting in the same breath that the actual tower took up less than a quarter of the site. In other words: with some imagination one might have built exactly the same number of units using buildings of a much lesser height, all with equal access to ocean views. The delusion that tower blocks were invented to combat urban overcrowding, however, is fundamental to the skyscraper myth. The skyscraper was never a device for the clever utilisation of space: at the time of their invention in the late nineteenth century, there were still farms on Manhattan. The Q1, likewise, was clearly not an exercise in exploiting scarce land resources; it was a physical demonstration of the Gold Coast's ambitions as the City of the Future, an assertion of civic pride in a town with little sense of civics.

Another disadvantage of apartment blocks is their tendency to suck life off the streets, leaving the abandoned and bewildered pedestrian to flounder, disoriented, through barren chasms of concrete, wondering whether he is on the road that will bring him to Broadbeach. At night you can walk a kilometre among the towers that stretch silently north and south from Surfers Paradise and see no one but lost tribes of Chinese tourists wandering dazed and hot, grabbing at your clothes imploringly and pointing to their hotel keys as they mutter plaintively, 'Per-ease... Sunc-tory Cov?' And all you can do is look at them apologetically and wave them in the direction of the endless highway in the hope that the pantomime taxi you are steering will wend them back to safety.

From Surfers Paradise the beachside suburbs spread south along the highway in an unbroken chain of development: tower blocks, strip malls and a scattering of squat 1960s motels with names like the Montego and the Mayfair. These southern suburbs – Broadbeach, Mermaid and Miami (in that order) – face beaches with different names, but they're all on the same bit of sand. To the north, across the mouth of the river, the suburbs spread from the town centre of Southport until they reach a national park. The coast-hugging 'strip' structure of the Gold Coast is one of the city's especial peculiarities. The highway runs down the middle of the suburbs, sometimes only a block west of the beach, creating an arbitrary Maginot line between rich and poor, dividing the beachfront houses from the western developments (although anything on an inland canal is likely to be pricey) in a ribbon of exclusivity that is sometimes no more than 50 metres wide and often several hundred thousand dollars more expensive. It seemed a lot to pay for the privilege of being on the right side of a 20-metre strip of tarmac.

At Burleigh Heads the beach reaches it first geographical obstruction, and it is here that the character of the city undergoes a change. This is where smaller communities have been swallowed up by the Gold Coast and a few houses from the 1920s and '30s still survive, studded among the towers and the endless marina developments. Here too is a distinct air of poverty, especially in places like Palm Beach and Tugun (the former featuring a sign at its boundary: 'Welcome to Palm Beach, a warm place for warm people'), suburbs with some of the highest unemployment rates in Australia, full of dowdy weatherboard houses, their curtains drawn like those of suburban drug labs.

It is a ride of well over an hour on a city bus before the Gold Coast reaches its official but somewhat unceremonious conclusion at a roundabout in Coolangatta. It is an arbitrary geographic delineation, however, for the Gold Coast is not a city of limits; it is a city of the imagination, of aspirations, of ambitions, and these, as a glance at the new developments stretching further and further into the southern horizon will confirm, know no bounds.

After giving up and following the Chinese tourists to the highway, I arrived, exhausted, in Broadbeach, an unremarkable 'family oriented' version of Surfers Paradise. After a brief rest I crossed to the other side of the highway to begin the journey back to my hotel. Unfortunately, the streets of the Gold Coast were not, to paraphrase Nancy Sinatra, made for walkin'. Like almost all the Hyper Republics, or anywhere where the Hard Rock Café is still a hip nightspot, the Gold Coast is not foot-friendly. This was an unfortunate state of affairs because I have never owned a car, and even if I did, would be unable to drive it. Spying a bus stop in the distance, I decided to cease my trudging. Walking past a dark and lonely strip of nature reserve, I arrived at the stop. The highway traffic was heavy and the sidewalk devoid of life. The screeching of bats was deafening as they swooped down from the trees to cut across my path. The air smelt of rotten figs.

After some wait among the shrieking bats the bus arrived and I left this small patch of primeval veldt to return to my shrinking room and the great big guitar that shot up over the roofs like an excited exclamation mark to proclaim my arrival.

Two

★

Barefoot and Pregnant

THE NEXT DAY I ditched my plan to find my own apartment and went to a share-house agency providing accommodation seekers with the contact details of those with rooms to rent. The man who ran the agency was an imperious high-camp uranist by the name of Trevor who sat behind his desk and stared at me blankly whenever I made a joke, adding that he preferred to 'focus upon the situation at hand' before swivelling round in his chair to tap with a thin wooden pointer several pieces of paper pinned to a corkboard on the wall behind him, much in the manner of a 1950s school teacher armed with an especially favoured new map of the Commonwealth. After I paid the $80 membership fee, Trevor began to run through some available properties. 'Now this one,' he said, gesturing at the corkboard, 'is in a beautiful building: very centrally located' – there was a dramatic pause to impress upon me the gravity of what was to come – 'full resort features.'

Full resort features was a term with which I had become familiar; real estate agents on the Gold Coast were constantly talking about them. The emphasis was always placed, almost conspiratorially, on *full* as though to reassure the potential occupant that the problem of resort feature theft that had seen some tenants wake up to mere *half* resort features was unlikely to afflict this complex. The definition of full resort features, however, could vary wildly: from a swimming pool that looked as though it had last been used to bathe elephants to a series of exotic recreation chambers with incomprehensible European names full of faddish American exercise equipment. I told Trevor that I was especially interested in finding high-rise accommodation. He regretted to inform me that there was none currently available but he would let me know the moment it came to his attention. In the meantime, I was presented with a long list of potential housemates and by that afternoon was arranging a series of appointments to visit an array of promising-sounding properties.

All the promise was on paper, however, for the next two days were spent tramping up and down the length of the city visiting a series of increasingly depressing low-rise units in distinctly slovenly parts of town. Most were hot brick boxes centred around oily green swimming pools, complete with crying babies and men in deck chairs lounging on the lawn, sipping bourbon and following my entrance to the building with a slow, silent trailing of their slitted eyes. In one apartment I was met by a girl clearly under the effects of heroin who, in response to my question about the length of the lease, just blinked her glassy eyes and said that she did not know how long she expected me to stay and that it didn't matter, before staring blankly at the refrigerator. I said my goodbyes and backed out the door. The girl did not move from her position at the fridge, but merely closed her eyes, slowly.

It was now Thursday; I had to leave my hotel in two days and my Gold Coast fantasy of sunset daiquiris and midnight jacuzzis was falling far short of expectation. The same day over my morning coffee I read the following item in the *Courier Mail*:

'Torture' Mistaken for Bondage Ritual
Greg Stolz

For more than two weeks, sounds echoed through the Gold Coast's oldest high-rise building in what residents thought was some sort of bizarre sex ritual.

It was only when a battered Dayn Robert Ross fled his flat in the heart of Surfers Paradise on Tuesday afternoon that alleged torture was revealed.

Mr Ross, 23, was recovering in Brisbane's Princess Davidandra Hospital yesterday with severe wounds to his back. He had allegedly been held captive in his rented first-floor unit in the 35-year-old Kinkabool building for more than a fortnight and repeatedly beaten with a bamboo stick and metal pole.

Police raided the unit on Tuesday afternoon and arrested a suspected illegal immigrant. Neighbours told yesterday of hearing what sounded like beatings coming from the unit since the accused man suddenly moved in with Mr Ross about two weeks ago. 'We could hear him being hit but we thought they were into bondage or something,' Kinkabool resident Milly Winkelbauer said. 'My bedroom's right near their front door so I heard a lot of weird stuff.'

Ms Winkelbauer's cousin, Andrew Doncaster, said he heard flogging sounds, arguments and grunts. 'We just heard all sorts of weird stuff going on there like yelling and screaming and someone getting whacked,' he said. 'We saw him (Mr Ross) limping across the road and we thought that was a bit strange.'

Gold Coast police inspector Ken Bemi said Mr Ross told detectives he had invited the man to stay at the unit, only to suffer two weeks of alleged beatings. 'He (Mr Ross) attempted to escape the unit on several occasions but was prevented from doing so,' Insp Bemi said.

On Tuesday, Insp Bemi said, Mr Ross had 'seized the opportunity' to escape. He crossed the road to the Surfers Paradise police post where he told of his alleged ordeal.

Singaporean national Eng Hou 'Thomas' Mah, 25, appeared in Southport Magistrates Court yesterday charged with deprivation of liberty, torture and assault occasioning grievous bodily harm. The alleged offences occurred between September 19 and October 8.

Wearing a Buffy the Vampire Slayer T-shirt, a barefoot and handcuffed Mah sat impassively in the dock as the charges were read.

Police prosecutor Jacki Hart told the court that Mah was an alleged illegal immigrant. Duty solicitor Michael Gatenby said Mah had been interviewed by Immigration Department officials and a bail application had been ruled out. He said the case could be referred to the Mental Health Tribunal.

Mah was remanded to appear on December 10.

The story was interesting not merely for its narrative but for the suggestion that the Gold Coast was the kind of town where someone might be tortured for more than a fortnight and the locals, inured to such goings-on, would simply dismiss the screams as yet another couple that liked it rough. The trials of Mr Ross had all the qualities of a bad omen; a certain sense of resignation had begun to take hold in me. There was a definite possibility I would have to delay my intended starting date in the city and return to Sydney and find accommodation from there. Then, that afternoon, I received a phone call.

'Hello, Brendan.' It was Trevor. 'You wanted a high rise – I have one.'

The building was good, very good, or so I was assured: located in the middle of town and virtually drowning under the weight of its own resort features. 'This one will go *very* fast, Brendan,' Trevor lisped portentously. Something in his tone told me he was telling the truth, that this would be an improvement on the demoralising excursions I had thus far undertaken at his recommendation. Without delay I hung up the phone and rang the contact number, only to be greeted by voicemail. I persisted all that afternoon and, after several attempts, finally reached the woman who was offering the room. She introduced herself as Krystal. We chatted briefly and I explained my writing project and my requirements. She said they needed someone very quickly and so we arranged to meet that evening after she had finished work.

The apartment was in a hotel complex called the Moroccan, half a block west from the beach on Elkhorn Avenue. The street was lined with scraggly, smooth-skinned palm trees and a series of up-market boutiques – Gucci, Prada, Cartier – selling, for the most part, accessories: golf shoes, scarves, belts and handbags, handbags, handbags. In the dark, the round white tower loomed above me. The building felt like a self-conscious attempt to create an atmosphere of luxury. It was not the sort of place I was accustomed to living, and I wondered whether I had found the correct address.

I buzzed the unit number and introduced myself to the voice of a woman over the intercom. The glass security doors slid open. Passing through a foyer of fat couches and gilded mirrors, I entered the lifts and rose to the eighth floor. I knocked and the door was opened by a short, barefoot Maori girl with a pleasant but unremarkable face and a swollen pregnant belly filling out her tropical print cotton dress. I guessed her age at about twenty-eight and her stomach at six months.

'Heyyyyy,' she said. 'Howww ya goooinng.' Krystal had a slight New Zealand accent coupled with a drawling stoner intonation that stretched all her words to great length only to dispatch them at the end in vicious inflexive spikes. The effect was strangely relaxing. I introduced myself and entered the triangular foyer. The unit was shaped like a segment of pie. 'I'm in there,' Krystal said, pointing to a door at my immediate right. 'I have my own apartment kind of thing 'cause I have a two-year-old kid. But don't worry or nothin',' she added hastily, 'he stays in there with me and he's at day care during the day. He won't be any trouble.'

I assured her that it was of no concern.

Krystal said there was one other housemate, a student: 'Norwegian . . . or Swedish . . . or Spanish . . . or some shit.'

'What does he study?' I asked.

'Oh, business . . . or modelling . . . or some shit, anyway.' She perked up. 'But don't worry, he's never here these days. He spends most of his time at his boyfriend's house.'

'Won't he want to meet me?'

'Nah, he doesn't care.'

I asked what she did for a living. 'Phone sex,' she said with a giggle and a toss of her head that I took as a secret sense of triumph. I laughed and thought to myself: a house with a gay Swedish model and a pregnant Maori phone sex worker? This was beginning to sound like a backroom pitch for a bad new sitcom: they're the original odd couple!

From the marble foyer Krystal led me down a low-lit hallway of thick white carpet and turned right into my bedroom. It was explained that George, the current tenant, was due to move out tomorrow, and that a new flatmate was needed immediately. The room was large and fully furnished with a bed and television. Everything I could see was to be mine. At one end the room connected to a bathroom and at the other, through a set of sliding glass doors, a huge semicircular balcony that swung out around the length of the unit and finished at the kitchen, facing the sea. Krystal slid open the glass doors and walked out onto the balcony, leading me across the warm tiles to the edge where we stopped for a moment to feel the night breeze and listen to the invisible ocean in the blackened east. I leant out and looked towards the ocean: on the beach, firestick twirlers left trails of crimson phosphorescence in their wake. To the southwest, Orchid Avenue cut a ravine of neon jitterbug through the darkened high rises.

Inside, the light was low. The living room was big and well-furnished. In one corner sat a large television in a wooden cabinet atop of which rested a glowing purple fish tank, the darting creatures luminous in the ultraviolet light. The kitchen opened out into the living room and contained every conceivable appliance. Through the window at the bungee jump park across the street I could see a giant 'V' of rainbow neon: between the parted branches of light a man attached to a huge elasticised harness was being propelled skywards, only to plunge earthwards seconds later.

I looked around. The apartment was spacious and modern, luxurious in fact, and I could barely credit my good fortune in having found such accommodation at the eleventh hour. Unbelievably, it was also cheap. Which is to say that it was the same as I had been accustomed to paying in Sydney, but there the only optional extras were mould, low-flying aeroplanes and a choice of two types of cockroach: European or Classic. The Gold Coast had finally made good. Yet something was missing. Aside from the fish, the unit was entirely without evidence of its inhabitants. There were no postcards on the fridge or posters on the wall, just some ghastly art prints of flowers and cavorting cockatoos, clearly hung the day the building had been finished. The furniture had been carefully coordinated and was so unremarkable that individual pieces dissolved in the mind's eye to become a single amorphous *idea* of furniture. Like a doctor's surgery or a display room in a department store, this was an archetype of home, of comfort. A sagging sunhat doubling as a lampshade struck the only note of unconventionality.

I said I would take it. It was agreed that I would come by the next morning with the bond and the first week's rent. Krystal and I walked back down the hall and made our goodbyes.

'Well, I hope everything works out cool,' she said, and the heavy door made a heart-starting crash as it slammed behind me.

That night I got drunk. Savagely, deliriously, staggeringly drunk. I had gone to dinner with my friend Amy, the only person I knew on the Gold Coast, and afterwards we had gone on a pub crawl with several of her friends. It was now the next morning, about ten-thirty, and I was walking aimlessly through the streets of Surfers with a hangover that was like some sort of *Fantastic Voyage* journey through Oliver Reed's liver. Checkout time at my hotel had been at ten and I had managed to get about three hours of sleep before being forced to rise and gather my things. The weather that day was unseasonably cold and windy and I had several hours to kill before my afternoon flight back to Sydney where I would collect my things and then return. With every agonising step my head flared into squalls of pain; pain bringing with it memories of the night before; memories my conscious mind had until now seen fit to repress.

Shuffling off to the bank, I withdrew the cash necessary for my bond and then made my way to the Moroccan. I buzzed at the security door. There was no answer. I continued to buzz, almost hysterically.

Finally, an irritated male voice answered and I explained who I was. The sliding security doors opened before me.

Ren (short for Renato), as it transpired, was not Norwegian, or Spanish, or some shit, but a Swedish boy of Chilean origin and exceptional beauty. Opening the door of my new apartment in nothing but his white silk boxers and a cotton samurai robe that fell about his naked torso in blue arabesques of fabric, he barely acknowledged my presence before turning to stomp down the hall on the balls of his feet in a shroud of Nordic indignation. I closed the door and followed him to the living room, padding down the corridor carpet that, for some reason, was sopping wet. Despite his agitation the movements of his well-proportioned body were graceful as he slid himself onto the floral sofa, resting his head at one end and flinging a tanned leg over the fattened arm rest at the other. I sat down cautiously on the couch at right angles to his own, careful to avoid treading on a giant red-wine spill on the carpet, sprinkled with a token drizzling of salt.

Perhaps because of his South American parentage, Ren had none of the dour, inhibited manners associated with the Scandinavian races and soon he was chatting with me in his direct, staccato manner.

'So! Waddya do, man? You're a journalist, right, yeah?' His large foot waggled in my face.

I told him I was writing a book about the Gold Coast.

'Hmmph! Nothing to write, man.' He arose in a swift movement and, with a slight tug at his silk boxers, headed towards the kitchen.

'Why do you say that?'

'Well, what the fuck is here? They got no buildings, no history. Nothin' but drunk bitches walkin' round Surfers goin', "Can I fuck you?"'

I began to laugh. Ren's imitation of an Aussie bogan chick through a thick mélange of accents was a riot. He changed the subject. 'Oh, man! I was out till five last night.' He faced me across the kitchen bench as he poured a large tumbler of water. 'And then when I came home I found my friend from Sweden asleep in my room! I said, "Who the fuck are you?" And he's like, "It's Stephen." So I said, "Great! Let's go out again."' He turned his back to me and began to rummage through the fridge. 'So we did. And then Krystal's kids woke me up at seven-thirty. Oh, man, it's always the same thing.' He pointed to his bedroom. It came off the living room and had slatted doors like a broom closet: it was filthy, strewn with clothes and detritus; the bed had no sheet. 'You can hear everything.'

'I'm sorry I woke you,' I said.

He paused. 'Nah, don't worry about it, man.' He stopped his rummaging and drank some more water. 'You know Krystal's got three kids, don't you?'

'Ah, no.'

'One lives with us. The other two are with their dad in Brisbane. All three are here every weekend. It's fuckin' bullshit.'

'I see,' I said, momentarily distracted as I became aware of a second presence on the balcony to my right. Turning to look, I watched as a dark-haired girl stumbled out of the sliding glass doors of what was soon to be my bedroom, a mobile phone to her ear and a hangover that, even through dirty plate glass, I could see was appalling. She had made it halfway across the balcony before she looked up and darted back into the bedroom. I turned back to Ren. 'How old are you?' I asked.

'Twenty-one,' he replied, hunching down in the couch opposite, his legs spread, drinking the water with one hand and fiddling with his crotch with the other.

'And Krystal says you're a model?'

'What? Nah.' His eyes opened wide. 'Stupid bitch! I study Japanese at Griffith University.'

Suddenly, out of the bedroom and into the living room emerged a second girl. She was tall, roughly nineteen, and with big boobs shoehorned into a pink top. Her dyed-blonde hair was wet, the black roots in the centre of her scalp cascading in symmetrical rivulets of barren tundra beneath the melting glacier of bleach. 'Hey you, bitch!' demanded Ren. 'What's with the red wine on the carpet?' I looked down.

'Fuck you,' she said. 'I didn't fuckin' spill it.'

'Sure,' he said sarcastically.

'I fuckin' didn't, you stupid fuckin' faggot!'

With that, Ren grabbed the girl and wrestled her to the floor, striding her chest with his naked thighs. With increasingly frenzied pumpings of her bosom and bursts of hysterical laughter, she attempted to remove herself from beneath Ren's haunches. Then the phone rang and Ren lifted himself up to answer it. The girl picked herself up and flopped down on the couch with a violent thud of her big back. 'Hi there! I'm Krystal.' It was apparently a popular name on the Gold Coast.

The girl with the dark hair emerged hesitantly from the bedroom. 'Hello,' she said shyly, 'I'm Sheena.'

I chatted with them. They were eighteen and worked at Shooters, a gigantic beer barn on Orchid Avenue decorated in a mock Western motif. They had called in sick last night to get drunk with George and Ren.

Ren got off the phone and began to run around the room, chasing the girls. I went outside to inspect the view from my balcony. Leaning over the edge I craned my neck to examine the grounds of the complex. Eight floors below, the pale blue pool composed of two irregular overlapping circles lay unused in the cold. To the left sat a green barbeque area surrounded by little pavilions of mock Bedouin tents in white plastic. Behind those, bordering the edge of the complex, stood a huge wall painted in an illusionistic mural of drifting clouds. Towering sentinel-like to the north, completing a triangle that contained the pool in its centre, were the other two buildings of the Moroccan. These rose much higher than my own to terminate at their thirtieth floors in an absurd confection of pseudo-oriental balustrades and shining translucent domes. I thought they were marvellous.

I went back inside. Sheena and Krystal had each cracked open a tin of bourbon and Coke. 'Want one?' asked Krystal, as the wind rattled the glass doors. I declined. Ren began to pour himself the remainder of the red wine. I looked at Krystal. 'Did you just dye your hair again?' The black roots were gone.

'Yep, just done it in the sink.'

Sheena turned to Ren. 'I wanna see two boys kiss Ren. Will you kiss a boy for me?'

'Nah, fuck off, you stupid bitch.'

Her mouth dropped open. 'Ren, you are so rude,' she said before dissolving into delighted giggles. With that Ren disappeared into his bedroom and returned to deposit several magazines with a loud slap into Sheena's lap. 'Here,' he said.

'Ohmigod, I don't wanna look at cocks,' said Sheena before quickly opening the first magazine, a publication entitled *Stroke* and featuring the explanatory banner, useful for the embarrassed housewife who had been intending to pick up *Home Beautiful*: 'Jerk off stuff for guys'.

Sheena read aloud from the magazine while Ren and Krystal played a game of slaps, seeing who would flinch first. I turned to watch Sheena's reading: 'That summer I rode my bike down to the beach near my home in San De-ij-ee-o. I was only sixteen and the fleet was in town . . .' before turning my attention back to Ren and Krystal who were delivering one another a series of increasingly powerful blows. Just then, Krystal cracked Ren to the side of the head and he, in response, delivered a powerful punch to her right breast. Krystal let out a scream and buckled in pain, clutching at her chest. Turning her back on Ren she wobbled towards the bedroom, her body racked with sobs. Ren jumped up and ran after her. 'I'm sorry, I'm sorry,' he said, pulling little faces of consolation and attempting to stroke her back. Disgustedly she held her face in one hand and pushed his groping hand away with the other as she disappeared into the bedroom. Ren turned to me holding his hand to his chin and pulling his lips wide to reveal two rows of perfect teeth set in an expression of exaggerated concern. He knew he'd gone too far.

Sheena seemed unconcerned: '"What are you doing here?" asked the sailor with the black hair . . .'

'Is she all right?' I asked. Ren turned to me and shook his head nervously.

Suddenly, Krystal came flying out of the bedroom and, with a savage swing of her fist, cracked Ren on the back of the head. She was laughing hysterically. Ren was so dumbfounded by the eloquence of her deception that he just turned and stared. Krystal put her hands on her hips and raised her freshly bleached head in triumph.

By this stage George, the housemate whose room I was taking, had also risen from the bedroom. As I paid him the bond and he wrote out my receipt, the security buzzer issued a powerful screech. Above the intercom a small blue video screen glowed slowly into life to reveal the image of a blue-blackened face lost in shadow.

'Oh, shit. Is it him?' asked Ren.

'I dunno,' said George, carefully inspecting the screen. 'But let's get the fuck out of here.'

'Oh, fuck!' said Ren as he leapt from the couch and into his room.

I was confused. 'Wait a second. Who's "him"?' But no one was listening; they were all too busy groping for their swimmers as they made a dash for the door. In seconds we had all piled out of the unit and crammed into the lift that would take us down to a steamy indoor pool ringed in mock North African pillars. Inside, the oxygen was low and the air smelt like chlorine. My head smarted. I turned to George. 'Why are you leaving the unit?' I asked.

'Oh, you know. Just some personal reasons,' he said with a Mediterranean flowering of his palms before slipping into the spa between his two young friends. The girls squealed and Ren took slugs from his red wine. I was tempted to get in but was now running dangerously late for my plane and something told me that there would be ample opportunities for similar encounters in the weeks to come. I made my goodbyes.

'See ya next week!' called Ren from the spa and the girls cheered as I walked into the cold. Outside, the palm trees stood bowed in ragged parades of supplication; the bitter wind clawed at my face. My hangover, however, had shifted now to a kind of pleasant stupefaction. If this morning's events were at all typical, then I could at least be sure that my stay on the Gold Coast would provide the diversion I was seeking. Newly invigorated, I made my way to the highway and the bus which would take me on the hour-long journey to the airport.

Three

★

Trouble in Paradise

I RETURNED TO the Gold Coast a week later. It was early evening and as my bus made the long trip from Coolangatta Airport the sun set behind the mountains, bringing to the surface a jiggling parade of coloured neon. It was the day before the commencement of the Indy car race and the streets of Surfers Paradise were in a frenzy.

The Gold Coast is a city of events: they chart the year in the same way that the monsoon dictates the movements of tribal people. The Indy is the biggest event on the Gold Coast calendar. The week before, Ren told me that he had arranged a full program of parties in which I was more than welcome to participate. As I hauled my bags from the bus stop and walked up Orchid Avenue through the drunken crowds, I couldn't help but be caught up in the communal anticipation.

At the dining-room table in my new apartment Krystal and a powerfully built Maori woman in an All Blacks jersey were sharing a pack of cigarettes. 'Heyyyy,' said Krystal. I returned her greeting and asked if Ren was home. She said he wasn't, that he was at his boyfriend's. 'Do you know anything about the wine stain on the carpet?' she asked.

I said that I had no idea who had done it, but I needn't have bothered – she had already made up her mind.

'Those two fuckin' bitches piss me off,' she said with an aggression that I found incongruous in such an apparently placid individual. 'I'm gonna make 'em pay for the fuckin' carpet cleaning.'

We sat around the table together. The large woman's name was Betty – one of those discordantly dainty, old-fashioned names so favoured by Islanders. We had only just completed our formal introductions when the phone rang. Betty answered and Krystal drifted off to watch the television. The phone conversation turned to a party that was coming up in the next few weeks. 'Tell her I wanna get fuckin' pissed that night,' called Krystal from the couch. Betty relayed the message.

I asked Krystal when she was due.

'Three months' time, January. But I want it to come in December so that I can party on New Year's Eve.'

With that she rocked up from the couch and headed for the kitchen, supporting her enormous belly with one hand. Betty put the phone down and we began to chat: about the flat, about the Gold Coast. The conversation ran dry and I stared out the window at the rainbow towers of the bungee jumping complex. The phone rang again. Krystal answered and spoke in hushed tones for some time as I watched the television. After she put it down she said, very seriously, to Betty, 'He reckons his mum told him he's got some sort of inherited condition with his hands and that the baby might have it.'

'Oh, that's all crap,' Betty said, very forcefully. 'His mother is a total hypochondriac. Believe me, she's always dying that one.'

After making some discreet enquiries I soon discovered that the man on the phone had been Kane, Krystal's ex-boyfriend and the father of her unborn child. From what I could gather Krystal now had little to do with him other than phone calls. There had been some trouble in their relationship, possibly violence, or the threat of it, and now the pair were due to resolve their differences at a court hearing some time in mid-December. Krystal explained that their hearing had been scheduled for the previous month but half an hour before they were due in court there had been an anthrax scare and the proceedings were cancelled. She was convinced that Kane had made the threat.

Betty was Krystal's best friend and, as it happened, Kane's half-sister (they shared the same father). Despite their family connection Betty was estranged from her stepbrother, never having met him until she was a teenager.

Said Betty, 'When all the shit went down between him and Krystal, I rang my mum and asked her about it. She said, "Forget about it, that one's a lost cause. Just get out of the way."' She looked across at Krystal who got up and shuffled to the couch to watch *Dr. Phil*. Betty went onto the balcony for a smoke. A couple on the TV was having problems deciding when they should have children. 'People who think about having kids never actually have them,' said Krystal, resignedly. She looked at me: 'Maybe I oughta start planning them!' She burst out laughing at her own joke before lighting up another cigarette.

The phone rang again; this time I answered. On the other end a hoarse woman introducing herself as Candy asked if she could speak to someone called Hinemoa. I called to Krystal and asked if she knew anyone by that name. 'That's me,' she said, waddling up from the couch to grab the phone. She spoke for a short while and then hung up, sitting down again.

'I don't understand,' I said, after some silence. 'What is your name?'

'My name's Hinemoa. Krystal's my phone sex name.'

'Oh . . . I'm sorry . . . I didn't realise.'

'Don't worry about it,' she reassured me. 'All my friends call me Krystal.' With that she turned her attention back to the television. An advertisement was playing; I noticed that she watched them with the same impassive reverence she paid the programs. This particular ad was for a brand of four-wheel-drive car; its reliability emphasised by the metaphor of the car as a dog, which, after returning from a hard day's drive in the country, shakes its chassis and covers its exasperated owners in a great sheet of sloppy mud. Krystal's jaw dropped open in astonishment. She turned to me with her pretty eyes wide. 'Oh, wow! Is that a new function?'

An awkward social situation was saved by the entry of her son from the bedroom. With his potbelly poking out from beneath his Wiggles pyjamas, his stumbling toddler waddle and his soft little fist rubbing his big, mammalian eyes, he was exceptionally cute. Scooping him up to her chest, Krystal began to soothe his befuddlement. He squashed his fat cheek against her shoulder and stared at me accusingly. 'This is Drakkar,' she announced.

'Hello, Drakkar,' I said. The boy closed his eyes hard and turned his face from me. 'Drakkar is an unusual name,' I said. 'Is it Maori?'

'No, it's a perfume his father used to wear: Drakkar Noir. I really liked it, and it reminded me of him.'

'Lucky it wasn't Old Spice,' I said, and allowed myself a little chuckle at my own witticism.

Krystal stared at me blankly.

'What are the other two boys called?' I asked.

'Tejahn and Isaac. Tejahn I got one day because I was watching *Rikki Lake* and decided that I liked it. And Isaac I've always liked; it's a Biblical name.' With some violence Drakkar pushed himself down off his mother and went for a walk to the kitchen, returning soon after with a biscuit in each hand. He stared at me, stuffing his face with the soggy cookies, alternating from right to left for maximum effect.

'Hello, Drakkar,' I said again. 'Are you enjoying those?'

He looked up at me and grinned, bits of mushy brown crumb caked across his little white baby teeth. 'Nah!' he exclaimed in a loud, cartoonish voice and marched out onto the balcony to throw bits of cookie through the railings. Betty said goodbye not long after, and I retired to my room to unpack my things. The floor had not been vacuumed and the bed was unmade; the slightly disconcerting suggestion that the room was still inhabited evidenced by a red bedcover that had been left open by the last occupant to reveal on its underside the words 'permanent stains' written in black texta. I cleaned the room, made the bed and unpacked my things. After reading for a while, I switched off the lights to listen to a chorus of drunken shouts, roaring cars and breaking glass that rose and fell from the streets of Surfers Paradise. The sound of the waves crashing on the shore mirrored the motion of the ghostly curtains in my room, rising and falling under the force of the cool sea breeze that rolled regularly and gently from the east, calming me.

I awoke the next morning bathed in the aquarium light of ancient conifers and listening to the distant braying of dinosaurs as they moved in herds through the forest in search of food. I opened my eyes just in time to see a group of stunt planes in a V-formation, their bellies turned like manta rays, fly past my window with a force that rattled the glass in its frames. From the street a roar of car engines filled the room. It was eight o'clock.

Unable to sleep, I stepped onto the balcony to look down on the northern end of our complex. Down on the street a series of racing cars were snaking their way along the black tarmac in a sluggish, multicoloured pageant of metal and fumes. Everywhere the roads bristled with people. I went into the kitchen to prepare some breakfast. Krystal was feeding Drakkar. Some empty tins of bourbon and Coke sat on the kitchen table. I shouted good morning over the squeal of tyres and engines and began to make some coffee.

Not long after, Ren emerged from his bedroom. Spying Drakkar by the table, he scooped the child up into one arm and flung him about the room. Drakkar was soon in hysterics and upon release clambered up to the fish tank to slap the water, punctuating the splashes with cries of 'Fush! Fush! Fush!' before throwing in a great handful of food that sat on the rippling surface in a thick slick of coloured flakes. Ren pulled him down and began to scoop out some of the food, explaining that three months ago the fish had numbered over two dozen. Now there were less than ten.

Krystal reappeared with two young boys – Tejahn and Isaac. Their father had just dropped them off from Brisbane. The boys smiled shyly; unlike their mother they were blond, and while we wrestled in the living room their hair flashed in the morning sun. Krystal explained over the noise of the engines that she was taking them to her mother's house and that she would be back in a couple of days. I pulled a plastic bag off Drakkar's head and wrenched from his fists an assortment of deadly chemicals he had pulled out from under the sink before presenting him to his mother. She took him by the hand and began to trail him out the door. Drakkar turned, tripping on his thongs, to wave goodbye.

Ren and I sat at the dining table and ate breakfast. It was just on nine-fifty when the phone rang. Ren answered. The cars had stopped now and the man on the other end of the line was so loud that I could hear him from across the kitchen.

'Listen, you fuckin' cunt,' came the angry voice, made oddly diminutive by the tinny receiver. 'Me and my mates are looking for you this weekend with baseball bats and if we see you we're gonna break every bone in your fuckin' body – and I'm gonna break your arms personally.'

'Ahhhh, okay,' said Ren in a state of shock that might have been mistaken for sarcasm.

'OKAY! O-KAAY?' screamed the little voice from the telephone. 'Waddya mean okay? I'm gonna fuckin' kill you, cunt!' And with that the phone went dead.

Ren hung up the receiver, his face white, his hand shaking. I thought he might be about to vomit. 'That was Kane,' he said, and his soft brown eyes shifted from side to side.

'Krystal's boyfriend?' I asked.

Ren nodded. 'Oh, shit. What do I do?' He looked at me imploringly.

'Why does he want to hurt you?' I asked.

'He thinks I'm fucking Krystal,' he said, his Swedish accent growing ever more legible: 'Hay thay-unks arm fah-kyen Krys-*taal*.'

I laughed; the idea of this prancing disco queen penetrating any woman let alone one as unlikely as Krystal was absurd. 'Why on earth would he think that?'

'Hays fah-kyen cray-zay.'

And with that Ren dialed the Surfers Paradise police station to tell them what had happened. The police were understandably disinterested and all the advice they could offer was for Ren to keep a tape recorder handy in case Kane called again. Ren was distraught. He told me about an incident a fortnight before my arrival when Kane had cornered him and George in a well-known Orchid Avenue nightclub. They had escaped through the fire exit only after Kane grew distracted while soliciting help from one of his friends who was working the door. 'He knows everybody,' wailed Ren. 'His gonna fuckin' kill me.'

'I don't understand. Why would he think that you were having an affair with Krystal?'

'He's a paranoid schizophrenic. George had to leave for the same reason. He's very dangerous. He has eight previous convictions and he's built like this.' Ren put his elbows level with his shoulders and brought his fists into chest. 'I have to go right now. He knows I'm here and might try to come up and kill me.' With that Ren began to phone his boyfriend, who lived in a nearby tower. I stood up and made to leave too. Ren said that he would come and find me later that evening.

Downstairs a pair of scowling security guards wearing matching T-shirts flanked the sliding glass doors. I had already had a run-in with these officious pricks the night before; the woman with her pedantic blonde ponytail hanging through the adjustable band of her baseball cap was a particular nuisance. The trouble began when I had gone to the shop but had forgotten to bring with me my four-day 'Indy pass'. As a resident of a building fronting the Indy track I had been issued with one of these tickets and a guest pass for a friend (the latter craftily pocketed by George before my arrival). Initially I had assumed that this was some sort of goodwill gesture on the part of the organisers; compensation for four days of having to shout to make myself heard and of compulsory 8 a.m. wake-up calls. So it came as a matter of some astonishment when I discovered that not only was I required to have this infernal pass on me in order to get in and out of my home, but so was anyone else I might want to invite to my apartment.

It wasn't so much the trumped-up bureaucratic pettiness, the pitying head shaking, that angered me, but the very idea that without a ticket to a car racing event in which I had only, at best, an anthropological interest, I was not going to be allowed *inside my own home*. It was almost beyond belief that, in an era when debates about international terrorism and the curbing of individual liberties were raging in the Australian parliament, here on the Gold Coast the entire centre of a major city could be handed over to a bunch of hall monitors on steroids to do with as they would simply because someone wanted to watch cars spin around a track. It seemed unlikely to be tolerated in any other Australian city. I gave the security guards an imperious scowl on exiting and made my way to the track.

The track ran in a loop from Staghorn Avenue – the northern end of the Moroccan complex – north along the ocean to Main Beach, the final suburb before the central Gold Coast tapers off into a splinter of bushland known as The Spit. The paths around the track were sandy and there was much dust in the air, a symptom of the drought. All around me people hung off the balconies of their high-rise units, screaming and madly waving. Leaning out from surrounding towers, dozens of people with the aid of megaphones screamed aimless, violent abuse at their neighbours. 'Fuck you, you fuckin' motherfuckers!' they cried, and the expletives echoed across the track. Commotions and uproar rippled all around. Men on the fifteenth storey of a hotel called the Imperial Surf began chanting at women in the tower opposite: 'Show us your tits!' To my great surprise the women complied, prompting one boy to mime exaggerated gestures of masturbation that, from his position behind the railings of his balcony, made him look like a monkey in the zoo.

As I watched this sexual drama played far above my head I was reminded of a high school disco at the school gymnasium where the boys stood on one side and the girls on the other and the only people dancing were the homosexuals of tomorrow. Nothing had changed since the discovery of fire: men still behaved like children and women were more than happy to indulge them. I'm certain they were all having fun but I felt so removed from these entertainments I might as well have arrived that morning from some distant star.

Up on the balconies, the men had ceased their pleas and abuse and began now to use other tactics to draw the attention they craved. Dropping their pants, they staged a mass mooning for the benefit of the audience. Next to me a group of six men in matching T-shirts (the slogan 'Daddy's Home' was emblazoned above an image of a nervous sheep cowering before the encroaching shadow of a man in an open doorway) laughed and raised their beers in obeisance. Beside me a concerned father tut-tutted the bad behaviour and leant down to place on his son's head a huge pair of industrial earmuffs before lifting him onto his shoulders and walking away into the smoke.

The crowd at this early stage was fairly sparse and consisted for the most part of moderately prosperous middle-aged men and their lanky, scowling progeny. Both generations wore pastel cotton T-shirts, board shorts or jeans and hideous reflective wraparound sunglasses of the sort sported by the Australian cricket team as they emerge from customs at Sydney airport, having recently laid waste to the Oakley counter at Karachi Airport.

Scattered among the crowd, handing out fliers, discount coupons or calendars advertising various local businesses, were a large number of girls in a variety of matching outfits. These were the 'Indy Girls' and, for the most, their uniform consisted of a cowboy hat, crop top and hot-pants stretched tightly across their haunches to reveal (much to the delight of the passing parade of leering men) a series of smiling genitals upholstered in a rainbow of electric blue, hot pink or black-and-white checks – there was more camel toe at the Indy than at a Saudi livestock auction. Others were decked in bikinis so brief they seemed less like constructed items of clothing than sparkling pieces of tin foil, which, by the sheer fortuitousness of nature, had come to rest against their bodies in strategic configurations after the last strong gust of wind. With varying degrees of grace these girls tripped their way along the paths in a more or less continuous circuit, stopping only to sell a calendar, pose for a picture or remove a high heel from the sand. Some did their jobs with more enthusiasm than others, however, and by the afternoon eyeliner was beginning to run in sweaty streaks down tired, reddened faces.

I watched these women carefully. It seemed that they had brought to their role as Indy Girls a peculiarly feminine sense of hierarchy. At the top of the tree, due to their (alleged) international fame, were the meter maids. They were originally created in 1965 by the now-defunct Surfers Paradise Progress Association to feed money into the newly installed parking meters to dissuade irritated tourists from abandoning Surfers Paradise for beaches with free parking. Recently they had been the focus of national attention after a well-publicised 'war' between two rival meter maid organisations – one 'sexy', the other 'family oriented'. Essentially the battle revolved around the allocation of Chamber of Commerce funds and the registration of different variations of the 'meter maid' title. Once the sequins had settled, the 'sexy' faction emerged as the victors and it was they who could be seen teetering around the Indy track.

The meter maids wore tiny golden bikinis, matching high heels, white cowboy hats with sparkling golden trim and, wrapped across their chests, a red sash of the sort donned by beauty queens, although here featuring an advertisement for an Internet site. As though encased in crystal these women strode through the crowd stately and aloof, stopping only to stand and grin in cheerful rigor mortis beside the dozens of men queuing to have a photo taken in their presence.

One step below the majesty of the meter maids were the hundreds of 'bar girls' representing various Gold Coast pubs and clubs. Busty and blonde, the bar girls often doubled as go-go dancers at the beer tents. Stretched tight across their breasts they wore T-shirts printed in the logos of assorted liquor brands, creating strange distortions of letters and of lions, cougars and bears, like medieval manuscript illumination. As the objects of the most overt male sexual attention these girls could be seen all over Surfers Paradise, cantering across roads in their platform go-go boots, lycra hotpants and diamante-encrusted cowboy hats. While they walked they flicked their hair coltishly and waved to one another in self-conscious displays of busyness calculated entirely to increase their alleged attractiveness.

Lowest in the pecking order were the girls selling the Indy Girl calendars. Like slutty girl guides with flabby tummies and pink hotpants, they approached me with hope in their eyes and a touch of schoolgirl self-consciousness that was endearing amid the licentious atmosphere.

'Would you like to buy a calendar?' asked one very young petitioner.

'Not really. But can I ask you if you enjoy working at the Indy?' The girl gave me a distinctly disgusted look until I explained that I was writing a book. 'Yeah, it's okay,' she said.

Her name was Stacey and she was only fifteen. She got the job selling calendars because her sister had done it the year before. 'Do you get good money?' I asked.

'Not really,' she said before adding hastily, 'but I don't care about the money. I'm doing it for the experience.'

'For the experience of being at the Indy?'

'No, for the modelling experience.'

'Oh, I see. Do you really want to be a model?'

She looked at me as if I was stupid. 'Yeah, it's the best job you can have.'

'Really?' I looked at Stacey with her bad skin, poor posture and crooked nose. 'Do you think you have what it takes to make it as a model?'

'Yeah, I'm real confident. Nothing scares me. When I say I can do something then I can. My mum's the same, and she used to model.'

'I see. But modelling is something you want, not something your mother wants, yes?'

'For sure.'

'Well, good luck, Stacey.'

'Wanna buy a calendar?'

'Stacey, I don't know what day of the week it is. What good is a calendar to me?' I turned and walked to the north, Stacey's eyes burning angry laser beams into my back.

Along the strait the crowd grew thick and the heat more intense. Everywhere men roamed in gangs, their team uniforms of red, black and white like those of officers in an obscure division of the Nazi party. I approached one of the pits and stared through the steel grille at the mechanics toiling with the cars. Flesh-coloured balaclavas masked their faces, giving them the appearance of burn victims or ghosts. Some wore mirrored sunglasses hooked over their exposed ears, obscuring their expressions completely. I looked down and they stared up with a baleful blankness. I moved away from the edge.

No race was being run so I wandered to an area where a burnout competition was being held. From amid vast plumes of black smoke cheers rose up from the crowd; ugly expressions of exclamation and triumph appeared and disappeared through the shifting, nauseating haze. In the distance I heard the squall of engines and headed back to the start line to watch the cars. I was surprised by their tiny size; so small they looked as though you would have to drop fifty cents in them before they would move: an impression enhanced by their array of candy colours.

A team of four, all with the red-and-white Target logo of their sponsor, was preparing to start. The cars began to rev with what seemed an almost musical quality – the low drone of bagpipes punctuated by revs and backfires, as though it was a performance of an avant-garde symphony rather than the acceleration and combustion of machinery. Then, as though released from an invisible rubber band, the cars sprang forth and shot down the strait. The noise was unfamiliar and intense; soon growing into a grim squeal so powerful that it became unbearable and I had to stuff my fingers deep into my ears. With nothing but a flimsy wire fence between myself and these jets on wheels I became suddenly frightened of their physical potential and moved behind a tree less they should career off the track and fly into my flimsy body, spearing me with shards of candy metal.

With the second lap I became braver and moved back down to the edge. As the cars raced past I pulled my fingers from my ears and felt the buzzing pleasure of the pain that would signal my deafness for the rest of the afternoon. I crossed the track on a covered temporary bridge that shook as the cars went under me and walked out into the sunshine. On a podium wedged between a VB caravan and a slushy machine go-go girls were dancing in the baking sun; hot and sweaty, they looked at me reproachfully as I stared.

I walked on. A man in a T-shirt that read 'No Fear: torture the weak' lovingly re-buttoned his little daughter's blue dress in the grass next to me. Everywhere one got the sense that this entire event could spin out of control. I headed further to the north. Past me wandered a stumbling drunk with two long white cigarettes doubling as earplugs sticking out at right angles from either side of his head. I kept walking: past the ice-cream sellers and the cold drink vans; past the flabby white men baking in the sun; past several brown, shrivelled women in bikini tops and sarongs and under rows of hairy legs in the grandstands. The track was long, longer than I had realised, and now I was tired and my ears were aching. I left the enclosure and walked around the cafés of Main Beach, the social hub of Gold Coast 'high society', watching the people who displayed themselves outside: wealthy car mechanics with their feet on the seats and desiccated women who shrieked and threw their heads back with a tinkle of gold.

I continued through the towers of Main Beach, back along the empty streets and onwards to home. The squealing of engines was all around me, reflected and refracted off the surrounding high rises until it became a single noise, like a siren, persistent and violent, lending the streets a certain apocalyptic disquiet.

That night, back in my apartment, the neighbouring towers lit up. On their balconies hundreds of men and women began a party that would continue until the morning. There was constant communication between the towers: some people passed spotlights across nearby buildings; some harassed unsuspecting occupants with the red beams of laser pointers that would alight suddenly upon a shirt or a face to create a small rush of panic. Flapping their way through the towers' gorges, tropical fruit bats the size of eagles caught the spotlights and cast giant black silhouettes against the white concrete. Men yelled and signalled to women across the chasms of grass and cement, begging for an invitation. Other men made precarious journeys from apartment to apartment, clinging to the outside of the balconies, twenty stories up. At the pool below women exposed themselves under the spotlights in response to the shouted requests of the men above, sending the audience into a frenzy of cheers and werewolf howls. And it was to these screams and the distant strains of a crowd singing along to The Monkees's 'I'm a Believer' that I began to drift off on the couch, alone and exhausted in my new apartment.

Four

★

Enter the Dragon

IN THEORY, a Scandinavian penthouse party sounds like fun. Actually, it sounds like an event Hugh Hefner might host, attended by women and men of inhuman beauty, their long pale limbs sprawled languidly on architect-designed blonde-wood furniture as they sip vodka distilled from rainwater, opening their finely sculpted mouths only to remove their Kosta Boda tumblers and announce: 'Now we are may-king the paw-no.'

After the fifty-third such party, however, I was to learn that, in reality, a Scandinavian penthouse party is a lot closer to being stuck in a youth hostel in Germany with a bunch of stinky backpackers, a compilation tape called *Euro Disco: Can't Stop the Beat '96!* and a bottle of warm Polish champagne. So when Ren walked in that evening and shook me awake to ask if I would care to attend just such an event, it was with my innocence intact that I immediately accepted.

The Scandinavian student scene on the Gold Coast is, on the face of it, an absurd phenomenon, yet there are a number of obvious factors conducive to their choice of study destination. Foremost among them is the almost unbelievable generosity of the Norwegian government. Norwegian students, like many others in western Europe, pay no fees for their university education. In addition to this they receive a generous stipend on which to live and, if they study overseas, are given a return ticket once a year between their host country and Norway. (The Swedes are on a loan scheme, accounting for their lesser numbers, but are given the opportunity for two return tickets.) This astonishing act of largesse means that Norwegian kids can essentially study anywhere they like; and if the university they attend just happens to be in some trashy resort town with a big beach, lots of alcohol and sex, well, then so be it. (For this reason, many still choose the more traditional destination of the south of Spain, but a growing number are heading to the Gold Coast – for reasons that should be obvious to anyone who has travelled to the Costa Del Sol.) An additional incentive to study in Australia is that the Norwegian currency offers a very high rate of exchange on the Australian dollar, granting Norwegian students a disposable income far beyond that of their Australian peers. Thus three or four students can pool their funds and quite easily afford a grand apartment in a luxury building or even a penthouse in an older model.

Consequently, at the beginning of every year hundreds of Scandinavian students pour into the Gold Coast looking like scowling blonde iceblocks only to return home in nine months as tanned, satiated alcoholics. In 2002 at the Gold Coast campus of Griffith University, almost 30 per cent of the foreign students were Scandinavian. Add to this those attending scores of private business and computer 'colleges', as well as a significant number of non-students – backpackers, friends and returned students who can often be found working in cafés and pubs – all concentrated within a couple of blocks of downtown Surfers. Lucky children of oil and fish, they pass away the hours lounging on the beach, drinking beer and vodka and screwing one another stupid.

In addition to the 'Scandos' are an assortment of other, mostly northern, Europeans who form a loose party circuit; and it was to a gathering hosted by a pair of Austrian girls that we had been invited tonight. The apartment where the party was to be held was on the twenty-first storey of a tower just one block from the Moroccan, so Ren, myself and Ren's boyfriend Julian set out through the streets of Surfers. It was the first time I had met Julian; tall and very handsome with dark hair and a hint of slanted eyes that spoke of his Scandinavian heritage, he was in fact half English, which accounted for his name. Julian was Norwegian (which was the language of choice between the couple) and although he didn't look it, was considerably older than Ren – due to turn thirty in a month. The pair had met while Ren was working behind the bar at the Gold Coast's only gay nightclub – neither had realised that the other was a Scandinavian student. The couple had markedly different personalities: Julian was as introverted as Ren was demonstrative and it came as some surprise (given the Scandinavian reputation for liberalism in these matters) when it was explained to me by Ren with a covert role of his eyes that Julian was 'out' to nobody and that their relationship was a total secret. I was never to refer to them as a couple.

Upstairs we were the first to arrive but soon the party began to fill with tall, trollish people among whom I tried to mingle. The Scandinavians, however, seemed intent on proving themselves worthy of their reputation as the most boring people in Europe, so I spent the next while talking to the Austrians. They had old-world manners and were easily shocked by dirty jokes but were far more receptive to strangers than their stern, indifferent classmates. And so I sat at a table amid a crowd of Austrians, drinking a beer and listening to Ren recount the saga of Kane and Krystal.

Enter the Dragon

It all began some time around the middle of 2002 when Ren and George, the housemate I had replaced, found the Moroccan apartment and decided immediately that they wanted to move in. Unfortunately they were unable to pay the hefty rent themselves and therefore needed one more person before they could sign the lease. They turned to the flatmate agency. Enter Krystal. After having spoken to her on the phone the boys decided that she seemed like a cheerful and inoffensive choice; more to the point, she was prepared to pay the large bond and could move in immediately. And so, although Krystal had never met them face-to-face, their new flatmate went around to the estate agent's office that day and added her (real) name to the lease. She moved in that afternoon. Unfortunately their new flatmate had failed to mention that a child would be living with them, let alone that another two would be visiting on weekends, and when they rang the estate agent to finalise a detail of the lease, the woman on the other end of the phone paused before asking confusedly, 'Now, who's Krystal?'

Being desperate, Ren and George said it didn't matter that she had a child or that she hadn't told them her real name; they had filled the room and secured their dream apartment: the one on the beach; the one with full resort features. And there it seemed to end, until the following week when Krystal moved in Kane, his nine-year-old son Hemi (the product of a previous relationship) and Kane's best friend. It was only temporary, she explained: Kane would be gone as soon as he could find a place of his own. This was little comfort to George and Ren but there seemed little anyone could do about it — her boyfriend was not the sort of guy who came equipped with a complaints department.

Kane, as Ren had earlier informed me, was a paranoid schizophrenic who had worked as a bouncer at many of the clubs on Orchid Avenue. Recently, however, he had lost much of his work because of a reputation for violence, and now he hauled scaffolding at construction sites, helping to build the grand kitsch palaces of the Gold Coast. But scaffolding was only for the interim because Kane had two increasingly profitable side-projects: drug dealing and prostitution.

With eight previous convictions for assault and drug trafficking, Kane was essentially a career criminal. He had done time on a couple of occasions, once for trying to sell a kilo of hash. But Kane's days of marijuana psychosis were behind him; now he favoured a drug called GHB (gamma hydroxy butyrate). More commonly known as GBH (grievous bodily harm), the drug is a naturally occurring metabolite of an amino acid found in every cell of the human body and manufactured artificially, for the most, to be sold as an illegal nightclub drug (although it has been used in legal experiments for sleeping disorders, tachycardia and as an anaesthetic). Making the drug is not difficult; boiling up sodium hydroxide and a common chemical found in cleaning fluid can make GBH. A quick scan of the Internet reveals several sites describing the process, complete with Martha Stewart-like handy hints for the amateur: 'Never use an aluminum pan to cook GBH!'

In the 1980s, before it was banned, GBH was much favoured by body builders and soon became a common ingredient in many 'dietary supplements', a fortunate side effect being the production of extra human growth hormone. Spreading from the gyms of the US and the UK, the drug soon reached the dance floors of the emergent rave scene where the long-lasting euphoric effects created by GBH led to the fallacious reputation of the drug as 'liquid ecstasy'. GBH is in fact a depressant and when mixed with another depressant, such as alcohol, it can lead to sleep, coma and even death.

During the late eighties and early nineties the combination of GBH and alcohol was responsible for a number of deaths and it soon garnered a bad reputation among clubbers. (Six months prior to my arrival on the Gold Coast a girl in England pulled out all her teeth during a GBH-induced hallucination and a month after I left a Sydney man died after mixing the drug with alcohol.) The reaction of GBH with alcohol has made it popular as a drink-spiking agent in clubs across the world (it was GBH that heir to the Max Factor fortune, Andrew Luster, used to anaesthetise women before raping them, a crime for which he was jailed for life). For a man like Kane, GBH had a number of attractive qualities. Yet Kane's drug intake was not limited by any brand fidelity. Frequently Ren would walk out in the morning to find him snorting a line of breakfast speed off the glass coffee table; a diet Kane would supplement as the day progressed until, by the time he got home, his head would shake and his eyes would roll; his mouth clamped tight in response to any greeting.

Most worrying of all, if only from the perspective of his mental health, was Kane's addiction to steroids (which he also dealt). Often he would brag to Ren that he was injecting 200 milligrams a day, and that 220 resulted in liver failure. Kane's arms, Ren said, were like watermelons. To emphasise the point he made a circle with his tanned hands that was almost a foot across. Kane, with his vast frame covered in gang and Maori tattoos, made a fearsome sight, even without his reputation, and he was well-known to most of the Gold Coast criminal fraternity. When Kane walked down Orchid Avenue, everyone said hi.

Kane's foray into the world of prostitution was a supplement to his career as a drug dealer. Approximately twice a week he would 'fuck couples for money'. What exactly this entailed Ren was never game to ask, and whether Kane was in fact bisexual was an intriguing and unanswered question. One thing was certain – Kane was very keen to get Ren into the business. 'You're a good-looking guy,' he would say. 'You should do it with me! Ya just root two couples a week and you can make two thousand bucks, easy. Then you live like a king until you do it the next week.' Ren declined these overtures with a suitably diplomatic degree of deference.

And so all four of them, Kane, Krystal and the two children, lived in the front room for the next five weeks (Kane's mysterious best friend slept on the couch). Surprisingly, it wasn't nearly as bad as one might imagine. In fact Kane was a fairly amiable housemate; he wasn't stingy with his drugs and would frequently offer Ren gifts of speed and cocaine. Ren would refuse these not so much out of any moral or physical aversion to chemical imbibing, but rather from the fear that to accept would be to place oneself in an awkward economic relationship with a man with whom it was advisable to have as little to do as possible. Besides, he couldn't see the point of taking speed at eight o'clock in the morning.

The days grew into weeks and it became increasingly apparent that what had been intended only as a temporary arrangement had grown to be permanent. The boys became nervous. Krystal had begun to regale them with stories of Kane's past, of the various acts of violence and irrationality he had committed, symptomatic of his mental illness and drug psychosis. In addition to his huge intake of drugs and steroids, Kane was on an extremely strong dose of medication for his condition; medication he took only irregularly. Her boyfriend, Krystal told her housemates, was 'a psycho' who had beaten to a pulp every friend he had ever had. Once he had been committed to a mental institution in Bundaberg, but had become so violent towards the staff that it was decided he should be transferred to a high-security ward in Brisbane. Unfortunately, before the transfer could be made, he literally escaped and disappeared back into the heady maelstrom of the Gold Coast. In New Zealand he was still wanted for his 'involvement' in a murder.

Enter the Dragon

As the weeks wore on Kane's behaviour grew increasingly violent and bizarre. His son Hemi was often the unfortunate target of his rage. Ren would wince, powerless, as Kane screamed and shouted in the small boy's face, sending him on his way with the occasional backhander to the cheek if he returned from the fridge with the wrong brand of bourbon. One afternoon Ren got home from university and heard Kane shouting in Krystal's bedroom: 'I know you're fucking him! I know you're fucking him!' Believing the pair was having one of their regular fights, Ren snuck past and stayed in the kitchen. After some time Kane emerged from the bedroom and greeted Ren with a typical display of fraternal joviality. Ren asked where Drakkar was and Kane explained that neither Krystal nor her son had arrived home. After some roundabout enquiries it was soon established that the bedroom had been empty and Kane had been screaming at phantoms.

And so it continued, every day growing more unbearable until, one morning, Kane snapped. Luckily, Ren had gone to university early – a rare occurrence. Midway through a lecture he received a call on his mobile phone. It was Krystal. 'Don't come home,' she warned. 'Kane's not happy.' As it transpired, Kane had decided that Ren and Krystal were having an affair and, in response, had gone to Krystal's workplace with the intention of killing her. After attempting to batter down the bolted doors, Kane marched into a neighbouring Chinese restaurant and demanded that the owners allow him access to a common service entry. When they refused Kane became violent and threatened to kill them, overturning chairs and tables, sending packets of chopsticks and a stack of finger bowls crashing to the floor. The police were called and Kane was arrested, but released soon after. Krystal took out a restraining order on him and threw all his stuff out that evening. But it was too late for Ren – since that day he had been on the run.

The table was suitably horrified. Perhaps unexpectedly I was more amused than concerned. It was difficult to take anything Ren said seriously; listening to him tell this story was like watching Lucille Ball mime her way through some fiasco for the benefit of an exasperated Ricky: 'Renato, you got some 'splaining to do!' Ren, however, grew increasingly solemn, swearing that he was glad to be leaving as soon as the university term was up in late November and praying aloud that he would manage to avoid Kane until then. Julian looked at me and shook his head. 'That guy's going to kill someone one day,' he said before turning to Ren with a covert look of tenderness. 'I only hope it's not you.'

Five

★

Nowhere to Run

ON THE COUCH in the position in which he had collapsed the previous evening Ren lay sleeping, a streak of wet drool running down his cheek and an occasional room-clearing emission spreading silently from his backside. Four days had passed, Indy had ended, and there had been no appearance from Kane. Even so the death threats had continued and Ren, now too scared to answer the phone, had left it to me to play the role of Fate's receptionist. The result was that after three days I had become acutely familiar with the sound of Kane's voice. Against myself, however, there was never any suggestion of violence. In fact, Kane was unfailingly polite, never asking more than to give Ren a message that he had phoned, accompanied on special occasions by a demented cackle in the manner of a B-movie serial killer who has just announced that he'll never be captured alive.

It was not only Ren who was being threatened. Krystal too was getting calls, warning her not to take out the domestic violence order that she had planned to file against him. At one point he had even resorted to saying that he was going to hang himself. 'Well, just get Hemi out of the room first,' she had retorted. I admired her determination and apparent fearlessness.

That morning I was due to make my first trip to Southport. During the early 1900s Southport had succeeded the more westerly Nerang to become the centre of the modern Gold Coast. It was once the original holiday destination for the fashionable citizens of Brisbane before they spread across the Broadwater to Main Beach and Surfers Paradise. Southport is also the site of the Southport Magistrate's Court, the local court for most of the Gold Coast region. In any city the local magistrate's court serves as a crossroads of humanity, a convenient microcosm of the society it serves – a Petri dish of the human condition. The Southport court seemed, therefore, like the perfect opportunity – a ready-made drama where I could spend my days in search of interesting cases and characters that might serve as a structure for this book ... or so I had assured my publisher.

In a life-imitates-art moment, Krystal was due to appear in court that afternoon to have the domestic violence order served against Kane. Initially I had asked to come along, and she had been enthusiastic, but when I realised Kane would be there I quickly changed my mind. We agreed instead to go to the court separately and meet that evening back at home.

The buses on the Gold Coast are yellow and cheerful, and the drivers wear a uniform covered in little smiling suns wearing sunglasses, as though protecting themselves from their own radiation. It was something to ponder as I stepped up to pay my fare. I settled down and put on my walkman. Across the aisle sat a thirty-something man in blue stubbies and a matching singlet, the dirty sole of one bare foot hanging over the edge of his seat. In defiance of the fact that I was listening to music he looked at me and shouted, 'You know in Canberra – at the taxation office – where do they get the information?'

I looked. He had an open, cherubic face and curly blond hair. He did not feel threatening. I turned off my tape. 'I don't know,' I said.

'Hmm. Do you know Kerry Young?'

'No.'

'He was a *Sale of the Century* champion. He knew almost everything.' He paused, locked in thought. 'Where do they keep all the things they've learnt? Where do they keep the information?'

I told him I was as confused as he.

'I was going to go fishing today,' he said, changing the subject. 'I'm on holidays from Victoria. But I have to get my rods out of storage.'

I said that was a good idea, as it looked a nice day for fishing. Outside the window the fake palm tree was passing against the clear blue sky. My new friend turned away and sat silent for a while. I put my headphones back on. Then he turned back and shouted, 'When you study, how do you remember all that?'

I got off the bus in Southport at the Australia Fair mall. The mall, connected by a covered bridge, stands on both sides of the main road running north to south through the suburb. I walked north. It seemed the court was conveniently located near a number of pawnshops and second-hand dealers, presumably so that drug addicts could sell their worldly possessions and then have only a short walk for their afternoon appearance.

Outside the court doors a group of people sat chatting and smoking. There was a pleasant social feeling, a sense of common fortune. Inside, the court building was modern and cool. I checked the list of the day's trials. Nothing of consequence had been scheduled so, with little other choice, I decided to visit the arrests court. All criminal cases must first go through the arrests court. Some are referred to trial but some small matters such as drink-driving are dealt with directly by the magistrate if the defendant wishes. It is a swift and mechanical justice, but not without a certain fascination, reminiscent of eighteenth-century records of Old Bailey transportation hearings.

I settled down in the crowded gallery beside relatives and friends and those awaiting hearings. A huge number of people were seen in the hours before lunch. A pig shooter who used a stolen hand gun to kill feral animals got off with a fine; an Aboriginal boy with a girlish face was ordered to be examined by a psychiatrist; a muted dullard in a brown tracksuit pleaded guilty to stealing a credit card with which he had purchased from a string of Kmarts hundreds of dollars worth of 'party goods', including streamers and paper plates; a reeking vagrant with a head like a sad cartoon character entered a guilty plea to the charge of being an 'habitual drunkard'; two boys were fined for stealing a barbeque; a man with a head pointed and shiny as a rifle bullet pleaded guilty to kicking down his ex-wife's front door; a schizophrenic heroin addict complained his home had been robbed and his bed soaked with urine; an angry car thief said that his wife was having their second baby, and had six others to different men; a woman in the dock who looked like Janis Joplin kissed the glass and her boyfriend waved in return; a fat man in the public gallery took off his shirt and sat naked and sweating. A recess for lunch was called.

I walked outside. On the TV in the foyer Jerry Springer was giving his final thought for the day with a tautological earnestness that was both absurd and oddly appropriate: 'Love is not a conscious exercise; we love who we love involuntarily . . .' I was conscious of the fact that somewhere in the building Krystal might be giving evidence against Kane. I was anxious not to bump into the pair.

I exited the court and headed back down the hill towards the Australia Fair mall: a vast, bleak and disorienting shopping centre, not so much soulless as a giant complex of the undead, like a haunted Mayan temple at midnight. I wandered through its chambers until I found the food court. Looking around I realised that a number of people who had just made an appearance before the magistrate were occupying many of the tables. I sat and watched the crowd. Dozens of middle-aged women in bikini tops and sarongs, their skin like desert mummies, preserved by hot wind, drifted from shop to shop.

I returned to the court and sat back down. Beside me a fuming solicitor in a sagging bottle-green jacket and navy pants, made shiny from wear, was arguing with a violent young man. 'Apparently twenty criminal charges were not important enough for you to deal with. Apparently you just thought you'd dump it all on me today when I have twenty other people to attend to!'

'I'll attend to your fucking face,' said the young man and motioned to hit the solicitor. His mother grabbed his arm. 'My son could never have done all the things they're accusing him of,' she said. 'They're saying they all happened on the same day – it's impossible.'

'Madam,' said the solicitor, 'it is called a crime spree. It is perfectly possible and it happens all the time, especially with little pricks like this.'

The day wound on. A man was given a fine for screaming at police who would not let him use the phone in the station. A drink-driver lost her licence and said she was worried she would be unable to pay the rent on the caravan where she lived with her three children. 'I moved down from the Northern Territory to make a new start for myself,' she said before bursting into tears. 'My husband was given a psychiatric discharge from the army.' She was but one of dozens of people that day, albeit the most affecting, who had felt the urge to make entirely unnecessary pleas to the court: details of their personal history or their own philosophical musings, as though they needed desperately to talk to someone, anyone who would listen. 'This is all in my past,' said one man. 'And now I will live with it for the rest of my life.' Even on the Gold Coast it seemed there was no escaping history.

I left the court at about four o'clock. On the television in the foyer an episode of the soap opera *Passions* was playing to an empty house. A woman dressed as a witch was wrestling with a crimson Satan, screaming with mantic intensity, 'I'm stronger than you! I'm stronger than you!'

My first day at the court could hardly have been termed a success. Pessimism, however, is not only cheap but unproductive. The first day of any enterprise, I reasoned, was always a wash-out. Things would get better.

The bus stop in Southport was outside the mall and under a dilapidated awning constructed at such a height and angle as to offer only a thin strip of shade running against the wall. The effect was to force shopping-weary pensioners to decide whether they were to sit and fry in the sun or stand and crumple in the shade. As I stood waiting a fight broke out between two young men. It was essentially a glorified hair-pulling contest that ended only after one boy had his T-shirt torn off. After some vicious recriminations and a frenzy of finger-pointing, the newly-naked boy sat down with his girlfriend opposite me. He began to explain to an admiring red-headed teenager that he had been beaten because his opponent practised a form of kung fu unknown to him. He replaced the black cap that had been knocked off his head in the excitement. The word HUSLER was embroidered on it in large white letters. His girlfriend leant behind him and began to squeeze a pimple on his back.

'Why does your cap say "HUSLER"?' I asked.

His girlfriend turned to explain. 'I went in and asked for "HUSTLER" and that's what they gimme two hours later.' She shook her head in resignation and I laughed as the pair walked away to catch their bus.

Back at home, Krystal, Julian and Ren were watching a psychic on TV. Julian had his hand on Ren's knee; the first time I had seen him act affectionately towards his boyfriend. Drakkar stood on the balcony tipping a glass of orange juice through the bars. Krystal said the court hearing had gone well, that the judge had sympathised and made a special mention of Kane's appalling record. He was now not allowed to come anywhere near her person, or else be arrested. Ren was pleased.

Krystal fished into her handbag and produced a credit card. She said she had found it that day; apparently the woman who had used the ATM before her had left it in the machine. 'I don't know what to do with it,' she said.

'Just call the bank and tell them you found it,' I said.

'Nah!' she said, mocking my naivety. 'I mean: I dunno how I can *use* it.' She paused. 'Do you reckon I should buy something over the phone with it?'

Julian looked at Ren and said something in Norwegian.

'But you can't just use somebody else's credit card,' I said.

'Why not?'

'Well, for starters, you might get arrested.'

She looked at me glumly. 'But I wanna buy some shoes and shit.'

It was strange, childish logic — both absurd and irrefutable. For a moment she sat in sullen meditation before adding, 'Besides, they won't know.'

'They will when they get the bill.'

'But people do it every day.'

'And people get arrested every day.'

With that she went quiet and put the card thoughtfully back into her handbag.

Soon she gathered up Drakkar to do some shopping. 'I'm taking the kids to Sea World for their birthday tomorrow,' she announced, heading towards the door. Her tone became wistful. 'I love going to Sea World but every time I've ever been I've never been able to go on any of the rides because I've always been pregnant.' I began to laugh and she giggled as she walked outside. 'Oh,' she said, popping her head back in, 'if a guy called Johnny buzzes the door and asks about who dented the car, just say you don't know anything about it.'

With Krystal gone, Julian began to speak in English. 'That woman,' he said tersely, 'is not a fit mother.'

His prissy, self-righteous tone immediately raised my hackles. Krystal, I began to argue, on the scale of neglectful or abusive mothers, hardly even registered a rating. Sure, she drank and smoked while pregnant but this was standard procedure among the phone-sex classes — it was when they started nodding off on street corners you had to start worrying. At least Krystal's kids were alive and apparently happy, unlike the three children of a woman who had the previous week committed suicide before facing trial for their murder — in an example of the kind of absurd symbolism that has ensured the redundancy of modern fiction, it was alleged she had incinerated them alive in the family car just outside Dreamworld. Julian and Ren, on the other hand, were citizens of two of the world's richest nations blessed with what were probably the two most comprehensive welfare safety nets on earth. Their complacency irritated me. Julian was, I reminded him, from a family that placed a high emphasis on education, a commodity scarcer than perhaps he realised. Krystal, uneducated, immature and moderately irresponsible in matters of health and safety was, nevertheless, a hard worker with a large extended family and far more competent than many single mothers I had met – she was never going to be Miss December in the Nursing Mothers' Association calendar, but she wasn't exactly Joan Crawford either.

The couple still had their reservations. Ren, who had grown especially fond of Drakkar, was greatly distressed by the child's new habit: a freshly hatched squawk of 'Fuck me! Fuck me!' I conceded that I found this disturbing too (I was also growing fond of Drakkar) and it probably meant Krystal had been taking him to her workplace. But, I reasoned, perhaps she hadn't any choice.

The night petered out. Ren left for Julian's unit and I had no one to talk to. I began to read and take notes. Krystal and Drakkar returned home with their shopping and I helped them carry their bags to the kitchen and went back to my room. After about an hour the security door buzzed. I walked into the living room and looked at the blue screen. Peering into the camera was a boy of eleven or twelve, his face distorted by proximity. 'Hey! Let us in!' he demanded. I knew instantly whose child he was. In a growing panic, I returned to my room, ignoring the violent petitions of the intercom and wondering whether I should stay and hope that they would simply go away, or leave before they forced their way upstairs. As it was, Krystal made up my mind for me. Before I had time to do anything else I heard the heavy clunk of the front door. A minute later there was a knock on my own. I opened it gingerly. Krystal was standing in the corridor, smiling gently. 'He's here now,' she announced as though I were a doctor about to receive my next patient. 'But don't worry because he won't do anything. I told him he can't bother you guys.'

With one hand I made shushing gestures and with the other closed the door in her face. I switched off the light, hoping that Kane would not realise anyone else was at home. In the corridor I could hear voices and the approach of an unfamiliar footfall. It seemed that

I had two options: I could stay in the bedroom and pretend I was fine – bluff my way out of any potential confrontation – or I could hide. There seemed little contest. I looked under my bed but it was too low. I thought about lying on the floor by the far side and artfully drawing a sheet over myself like a ninja I had seen once in a film. But as I began to struggle with my bedding it suddenly occurred to me that maybe I was not behaving in an entirely rational manner. I looked at my wardrobe. Sliding open the door as quietly as I could, I got into the closet and slid it back just far enough to see out with one eye.

The room outside was cast in shadows. My heart was beating in my ears. In the wardrobe sat my bag, some old clothes and the grotty red bedspread I had banished from my mattress. I got comfortable among the soft detritus and sat for some minutes, thinking about famous journal writers. I thought about the need to maintain the facade of unflappable calm, to cultivate an air of indifference to one's personal safety. I remembered Bruce Chatwin in *The Songlines* going so far as to claim he had slept on the desert floor in defiance of the snakes when he had in fact fretted for hours before deciding to sleep in his guide's truck. I thought about Ernest Hemingway, Norman Mailer, Hunter S. Thompson – tough guys, all. I wondered if any of these men had ever hidden in a cupboard, let alone seriously considered the possibility of throwing a bedspread marked with the words 'permanent stains' over their head in an effort to disguise themselves as a lump of clothes.

It took about ten minutes in the darkened cupboard before I began to feel rather silly. Perhaps – just perhaps – I was overreacting. What's more, my legs had fallen asleep and a plastic strap from my backpack had lodged itself up my arse. Quietly sliding back the door, I stepped out to listen carefully at the entrance to the corridor. I could hear no noise but the faint hum of the television emanating from Krystal's room. After another ten or fifteen minutes of pacing about, my curiosity became unbearable and I stepped out into the hallway to follow the noise of the television.

Creeping down the unlit passage, I craned my neck around the entrance of Krystal's corridor. There was an unfamiliar perfume in the air. At the far end of her bedroom I could see the TV playing cartoons in the dark, sending flashes of blue and white light across the room in a lurid strobe to animate the furniture, toys and clothes lying on the floor. The sound was very loud and the exclamations of the cartoon characters ferocious: 'Boing! Boing! Agggghhhhh!' I crept further down the corridor. Slowly, carefully, as though pressing my face against a strong wind, I put my head around the corner to where the bed was positioned. 'Hello?' I called. No answer came and I stood for a moment in the dark while the cartoons flashed on the TV and the light played across the empty bed. Then, from the bathroom I heard a voice. I edged my way towards the half-opened door. Inside, the room was pitch black – the globe had blown earlier that day. I listened intently. Echoing across the tiles I could hear a child splashing in the bath, singing disjointedly and speaking to himself with an unusual intensity. I realised it was Hemi. Walking quickly out of the room I phoned Ren at Julian's house and warned him not to come home. My Swedish friend was understandably distressed.

I returned to my bedroom and began to watch television and debate my choices. A video clip for the song 'Errol' by Australian Crawl began to play. It was filmed on the Gold Coast. The tone was celebratory and euphoric, not unlike what I had felt driving over the Southport Bridge for the first time. There were surfers and girls in bikinis, water parks and dolphins. It was the Gold Coast of the 1980s, the Gold Coast of my childhood, the Gold Coast of good times, before AIDS or the greenhouse effect, when malls with blue reflective glass, digital clocks and dolphin murals still looked like a glimpse of an exciting future. It was a time when big bands like Australian Crawl made film clips here (only semi-ironically) as a homage to the Australian Dream, surfing into a coast of skyscrapers before jumping into a jacuzzi to have champagne poured over their heads by blonde girls in gold bikinis and heavy blue eyeliner. The gap between fantasy and reality never seemed quite so ironic.

Some time later there was another buzz at the intercom. On the security screen a young woman was demanding to be let in, saying that she was a friend of Krystal's. I said I didn't know where Krystal was and hung up to disappear into my room, ignoring the repeated buzzing. After some time the noise stopped and I lay on my bed reading, in which position I must have fallen asleep, because I never heard Krystal return.

The next morning I saw Krystal before she left for work. I was angry and confronted her about Kane, saying that I was under the impression he was out of her life and would never again be returning to the apartment.

'I know it freaked you out,' she said apologetically, 'but it won't happen again. I told him he couldn't come up here any more.' I said that this was a good thing, but hadn't she taken out a restraining order against him only yesterday? 'Yeah,' she said by way of explanation, 'but it's just that I was craving oysters and I didn't have enough money to buy 'em. So I rang and asked him to take me out to dinner at the ANA seafood buffet.' She smiled a big, lopsided smile. 'Oh, God, I wanted oysters,' she said, bunching her hands together into greedy little fists, 'big, fat Pacific ones!'

Six

★

1-800 G-E-T O-U-T N-O-W

THERE WAS OUTRAGE in the air. The front-page splash of the *Gold Coast Bulletin* was a story about a survey revealing the Australian business community had little faith in the Gold Coast. The 'southern states' apparently viewed the city as a hive of scam artists and con men looking to do little more than make a fast buck and move on. It seemed symptomatic of an endemic insularity that the citizens of the Gold Coast needed a survey to tell them this. But at least the paper had a story. No such luck for me. For a little over a week I had been dutifully attending the public gallery of the Southport Magistrate's Court in the hope that I would stumble across a case sufficiently interesting to function as the central narrative for this book, but to no avail.

'There's nothing much on for ages,' said the rumpled court reporter for the *Gold Coast Bulletin*. And he wasn't lying. Many of the major cases had been postponed until the next year and, unbeknown to me, most homicides and many other serious crimes were routinely transferred to Brisbane. On some days there was no other action but the arrests court and now I had found myself reduced to sitting in on an endless round of drink-driving, petty theft and assault charges. It was banal, venal, sordid but, worst of all, boring. Was this what I had signed on for: people who stole credit cards and then bought paper plates at Kmart?

I walked out of court that day into the breezeless afternoon sun, dejected and faithless. Sitting on a planter box by the front door was a grossly obese woman in green track pants, her legs spread wide and a big black eye rising like a purple soufflé. Gathered in symmetrical bundles at her feet sat several plastic bags of shopping. Tight across her huge chest she wore an oversized novelty T-shirt emblazoned with the logo 'I used up all my sick days so instead I called in dead!' I looked more closely: her hair was matted and the plastic bags full of junk.

The landscape of Southport was now familiar. The mismatched dilapidation, the relentless heat, the shuffling citizens all leant the centre an air of the Third World: a hot, decrepit dump of a place that had grown and then simply stopped, like a thirsty geranium. It was a scene worthy of V. S. Naipaul in one of his more depressing descriptions of the crumbling colonial Caribbean. Yet over the last fortnight I had grown tolerant, if not fond, of Southport because, unlike Surfers Paradise, it had both the amenities and the rhythms of a home. In Southport were sights I never realised were missing from Surfers until I saw them there; simple, ordinary things: children in school uniforms; pensioners struggling with their shopping; a child with Down Syndrome; an old man with one leg; a religious zealot handing out pamphlets from a plastic push cart; women screaming at their children; homeless people asleep in the park; a smart new public library – even a lone Gothic teenager wandering through the crowd in slope-shouldered defiance of the relentless sun.

Unremarkable these things might have been, yet only now had the sense of alienation I felt in Surfers Paradise grown apparent. Unlike the centre of a normal city, Surfers had nothing that seemed to signal a world beyond: nothing of any practical use or service, no sense that people were tied to anything other than the absolute immediacy of their experience. Southport was dreary, but Surfers was like the horror movie town inhabited by ghosts where you wake up in the morning to find only tumbleweeds and bones.

I walked east towards the town centre. Standing on the corner of Scarborough Street I looked right towards Australia Fair and then left, into the distance. The road stretched into a featureless hazy eternity. I was hot, hungry and sweating profusely. For reasons unknown I decided to go for a walk. Crossing Scarborough Street I walked northwards, away from the mall, armed only with the vague plan of finding something to eat – I would rather have gone hungry than face the food court again. For several blocks I saw nothing remarkable save a few surviving Queenslander houses from the late nineteenth century: their lacy fretwork and latticed veils an elegant reminder that this was once a fashionable tourist resort. Further I walked, past a demented cluster of unrelated shops, of tattoo parlours and Smith Family outlets; the only promising place to eat, a Philippino restaurant, was shut. After half an hour I realised I was unlikely to find anything of interest, so I crossed the road and walked back towards the mall. I had almost reached the magistrate's court when I saw a sandwich board standing out the front of a shop selling New Age therapies and magic paraphernalia. 'Your fortunes told,' it read. 'Talk to Fiona, a qualified psychic.'

Along with tattoo parlours and Internet cafes, the Gold Coast has a particular superfluity of New Age gimmickry. On almost every block one can expect to see palmists, tarot readers, Indian psychics, Chinese astrologers, crystal therapists, numerologists, psychic healers or aromatherapy clinics – the supply and the variety was infinite. Many Gold Coast businesses combined psychic readings with apparently unrelated services: bookshops, cafés and even laundromats offered a sideline in extrasensory transcendence. On the Gold Coast you could have your nails buffed and your aura read before your varnish was dry. In a place where people have come to make a new life, everyone was trying to cheat fate. The wisdom of providence is not for those who build ninety-storey towers.

I entered the shop. Inside was the usual array of crystals, wands, tarot cards, pentagram rings and ugly velvet dresses. I asked the shop assistant behind the counter about the possibility of seeing Fiona. She pointed to a back storeroom. The half-closed door muffled some clandestine rustlings. 'She's available now,' said the assistant. 'Just head round to the reading room.'

The reading room was at the back of the shop in a yard connected to the street by a brick alley painted in the smile of a white leather Elvis melting slowly into the porous brick. The yard was strewn with pieces of broken bicycle equipment and festooned with various dangling New Age accoutrements: bamboo wind chimes, Native American dream catchers and a sun dial mandala hanging on the back fence. It was an unremarkable hippy backyard, but it was a welcome island of eccentricity in the banality of Southport.

Fiona arrived and ushered me into the tiny porch where she was to tell my fortune. She was a middle-aged woman with large, gapped teeth and short red hair. She wore a purple tie-dyed dress of medieval cut complete with baggy, cone-shaped sleeves and a skirt that flowed off into a rippling lace train, looking very much like an heirloom tablecloth that had been thrown into the wash with the coloureds. The combined effect was that of an ageing Pre-Raphaelite Ophelia who had sailed down the river on a bundle of weeds some time at the turn of the nineteenth century only to be revived seventy years later in the middle of Jefferson Airplane's set at Woodstock.

Fiona unlocked a cabinet and removed her equipment: a pack of cards, a bag of runes and a wooden wand with a big amethyst tied to its tip. 'We have to be careful,' she explained. 'We've had so many thefts back here.' The image of a frustrated junkie trying to unload a hot Chinese astrology map and a bag of runes at Captain Cash greatly amused me: 'Look, dude, if youse can just give us thirty bucks youse can have the astral wand for nothin'.'

Once seated, I was instructed to shuffle a deck of angel cards before removing three at random while my medium did a complicated jazz ballet routine with her forearms to call upon the Great Spirit of the Universe. She flipped over my selections. 'Oh, look at youuu!' She seemed very pleased. 'These angels,' she pointed to two of the scuffed, agreeable images on thick heavy card, 'are absolute love and care angels. This guy here is the most powerful love angel. It's clear that you are a deeply caring, humane, passionate and loving person.'

Clearly my angels of unnecessary sarcasm and malicious bitchiness were on some sort of heavenly hiatus.

'And this one here,' she said, pointing to the remaining card, 'is money. You'll never have problems.'

Well, one out of three 'aint bad.

The ordeal of the cards over, it was now time to consult the runes. After carefully basting the suede pouch with the amethyst wand, Fiona invited me to pluck from the dark hollow three of the smooth bone tiles. I presented them for inspection. Fiona took the tiles, arranging and rearranging them on the table before her, slipping them with a rhythmic clacking through her fingers. This meditation complete, there followed a series of excruciatingly inaccurate insights into both my past and contemporary life. So appalling were these sagacious pronouncements on the fate of my relatives, former love interests, love interests to-be and career aspirations that in response to many I simply nodded and agreed, commending her on her prodigious abilities of extrasensory perception, too embarrassed to contradict her.

'I'm seeing papers... you're a student.'

'No.'

'I mean a lawyer.'

I told her I was a writer.

'Yes, see! I told you I was seeing papers.' She paused and stretched her face into a smile. 'It's a gift. I can't explain it.'

Fiona specialised in statements that were general enough to be accurate, and these I pounced on to encourage her further in the vague hope that she may eventually get something right. She saw correctly, for instance, that I had some ambition to work in television, possibly in the United States. But this did not make a great impression; practically every young Australian writer with a modicum of ambition has vague hopes to one day live overseas and write a television show.

The awkwardness continued for some time: no, my deceased grandfather's name was not William; yes, I know a Felicity; no, she does not work in nursing. Fiona charged on, unperturbed. 'I'm seeing water. Do you live near the sea?'

'Why, yes! How ever did you know?'

'Get out of there.'

'What?'

'That apartment has some very bad vibrations. You must leave it at once. Go somewhere peaceful, somewhere by the river. You are not a person of the ocean.'

Having endured a series of such predictions (interrupted only by a ten-minute sales pitch in which she attempted to enlist my help in a charity farm-relief concert she was organising), I did not treat this warning with any particular gravity. And yet there was just the smallest suggestion of discomfort, some prickle of a raw nerve, in this prognostication as I sat here and thought about Kane and Krystal and the terrible problems Ren was now facing.

I paid Fiona her $30 and made to leave. She smiled her forced, gappy smile and cocked her head to one side, asking me if there was anything I would like to purchase from the shop. I said no and made my way back to the mall. At the bus stop I saw the cherubic man I had met that first day on the bus. He was still barefoot and wearing the same blue shorts and singlet. 'Did you end up going fishing?' I asked.

'Nah, I got kicked out of my hotel.'

'Oh, what happened?'

'Someone done a turd in the pool and they said it was me.'

I was beginning to think he wasn't on holidays.

I was sitting in the living room with Drakkar when Krystal pulled a letter and a video from her bag. It was fan mail of a sort from one of her Western Australian clients. Written in large childish script and signed 'Ice Man', the contents were a combination of sleaze and prurience common to the disturbed: 'On the tape I'm doing it with two girls. It was always a fantasy of mine but now that I'm married the very idea makes me SICK!!!'

'We get this shit all the time,' Krystal said, throwing the video onto the table. 'It's fuckin' disgusting.' She said the fan would be calling her tomorrow to discuss the contents of the video.

I took the opportunity to ask her about phone sex, her clients and working conditions. She said that she had been employed after answering an ad in the newspaper and that she had been working for a year now – one of the longest-serving employees. The owners, before starting the business, had run strip clubs on the Gold Coast. When I asked who they were she said she could not tell me; she still did not know their real names. It was a situation not uncommon in the sex industry.

At the call centre the girls sat in a large communal office but some special girls, Krystal being one, got their own room with a bed for long shifts. Most of her customers (Krystal called them her 'wankers') were regulars and in the best tradition of prostitution some didn't want phone sex but merely to talk about their problems. A number of men used phone sex as an aid to their sex life (couples would often ring); some relied on it totally. Surprisingly, given her docile exterior, Krystal was especially popular with men who wished to be spoken to roughly, and with great relish she would demonstrate the shouted commands favoured by her clients: '"Stick it up your ass, you stupid little faggot! Don't talk back to you mother!" We put 'em on speaker phone and piss ourselves laughing.'

Men rang from everywhere – the US, Europe and Japan – and the business was very profitable. Despite calls being charged by the minute, Krystal got a flat rate of $22 for every call and so she often encouraged men to hang up and call her again rather than chat for hours. Consequently she earned a surprisingly large income. When I asked why she did phone sex, she said it was for the money. I probed for elaboration, but she could think of no other fulfillment that the work gave her.

I asked her some more questions about her life. She said that she had left school at the end of year ten; she was fifteen at the time. Her first child had come at seventeen and she had been pregnant ever since. I did a quick calculation. 'How old are you?' I asked.

'Twenty-three,' she said, with the qualification that she would soon be twenty-four. It was the first time I had felt any genuine shock about Krystal's situation, not so much at the fact of her sheer youth but at the realisation that this woman who was about to have her fourth child was a full two years *younger* than myself.

I asked her how she met Kane. As it turned out, the pair had grown up together in a coastal town a couple of hours north of the Gold Coast. Both their extended families had been part of a Maori 'culture group' performing traditional Polynesian singing and dancing on the island resorts offshore – Kane's family in one troupe, Krystal's in the other. Together the families would take off in the evening boats to entertain the tourists, occasionally swapping shifts or loaning out members of the troupe. The families were close but Kane's status had always been ambiguous; only his father was Maori – his mother was a Polish Jew who, for reasons that were unclear, had been unable to care for him. Kane's heritage was a trifecta of displacement.

In early high school Krystal left the seemingly idyllic world of island dancing and moved to the Gold Coast with her mother. Kane stayed behind. It wasn't long after that she met Johnny, her first boyfriend, with whom she had Tejahn and Isaac in rapid succession. After being with Johnny for five-and-a-half years the relationship ended and Krystal, while pregnant with Drakkar, took the kids and moved in with her uncle in Tugun, a southern suburb just north of Coolangatta. Kane, as it turned out, was a friend of her uncle's, and when he moved to the Gold Coast around the same time he also moved into the house with Krystal and the kids. Within two weeks Kane and Krystal were officially 'together' and, after having Drakkar, the couple moved back to their childhood home near the islands. Kane had found a house.

Overnight Kane changed from a charming and sociable personality into a violent, paranoid monster. Nightly he would beat her, accusing her continually of imaginary sexual relationships. One night he split her mouth open and broke her cheekbone, accounting for her crooked smile. Krystal ran for help to the neighbours. Kane was arrested and later committed where he was diagnosed as a paranoid schizophrenic and bipolar. Krystal returned to the Gold Coast and the oldest boys went to live with their father. Kane rang her every day from the psych ward saying he was sorry. After he escaped, she immediately took him back, assured that he was on medication and had changed. It was to no avail. The beatings began again, both on her and the kids, and they broke up once more. Three months later she moved into the Moroccan and as soon as her pregnancy became obvious, invited him to move in with her, which is when Ren's problems began. The rest as they say, even on the Gold Coast, is history.

I asked her why she had taken Kane back the second time.

'I dunno,' she said glumly, and turned her attention to the television.

There were times when talking with Krystal was like trying to communicate with an autistic child.

That evening I had agreed to appear on radio. The topic of discussion was the life and death of Kurt Cobain; a forum prompted by the recent publication of his private journals. (When I had told Krystal that I needed the phone to myself in the evening so that I could talk on the radio she looked at me and said, 'Oh! Can you mention the phone sex line?' At first I assumed she was joking but, as I looked closer, I realised her expression was one of serious hope.) Afterwards, I thought the discussion had gone well. But myself and another panelist had made a few remarks in dubious taste and they never asked me back, so perhaps it hadn't.

That night I had a dream. Kurt Cobain was my brother and he had been threatening to kill himself for some time. It was late afternoon and raining. In the corner of a favourite room of a forgotten house where I had lived as a child, my mother and sister wailed uncontrollably. Kurt walked through the room on his way to a closed door across the passage. Beyond the door lay the inevitable. My sister and my mother, physically supporting one another in their hysteria, pleaded with me to help. Kurt walked past and I grabbed him by the sleeve of his T-shirt; I could feel its softness in my hands. I pulled his arm back and forced him to face me. His eyes were glazed, his expression demented. 'Please, please don't do this,' I said, with tears in my eyes. 'You don't know how you make people fall in love with you.' And with that, the distress of the dream became too great and I woke with a start in the dawn light. My breathing was heavy and my lips tasted of salt. I had been crying in my sleep and my face was wet with tears.

At the time, although it left a strong impression on me, this was nothing more than a bad dream (complete with mortifying overtones of teenage infatuation) and probably induced by a growing depression and anxiety that my decision to come to the Gold Coast had been a mistake. So it was with casual dismissal and a hope for a better tomorrow that I chose to think little more on the subject and return to sleep. And there in the forgotten night this episode may have remained, if only it hadn't become the first of many bad dreams I was to have in my apartment; dreams that I could not so easily dismiss and which, in time, might have given me cause to be less flippant about the predictions of a grinning middle-aged psychic in an ugly purple dress.

Seven

★

The Garden of Earthly Resort Features

DRAKKAR AND TEJAHN were not twins but their birthdays were in sufficient proximity to warrant a combined party. 'I wanna give 'em a really good birthday,' said Krystal. 'You know, hire a clown and shit. Just spoil 'em.' The next morning she went shopping, returning just before ten with the food: fifteen bursting bags of groceries that I helped carry from the basement. And so we began to prepare. There was meat and rice, salad and watermelon, hot chips and crisps, lollies and a box of pink fairy floss the size of a coffin. In order to avoid any further volunteer work I disappeared with my friend Greg who had come to visit for the weekend from Brisbane.

When we returned after midday the apartment was a hive of Maori mothers and their children. The New Zealander population of the Gold Coast (both Maori and white) is one of the city's most notable demographic features. In the eyes of New Zealanders the Gold Coast is a fabulously exotic destination and in the last ten years they have come here in their tens of thousands – New Zealanders constitute almost 50 per cent of all foreign immigrants to the coast. This migration, however, was not entirely appreciated by the locals, most of whom seemed to view the Kiwis as little better than social security parasites, ingrates and whingers. This was mostly unfair. Apart from the fact that the days of living on the beach on the dole are well and truly over, a number of wealthy New Zealanders had made the Gold Coast their home (the Gold Coast is full of weird chain stores you only find in Auckland). What's more, their image as loafing cheapskates was belied by the fact that seemingly every blue-collar or menial job in town was filled by a New Zealander: every waiter, cleaner, cop and construction worker, it seemed, was a Kiwi. Any group house on the coast was likely to accommodate at least one New Zealander and I had obviously hit a rich vein.

Soon Krystal announced that it was time to head down to the barbeque. One by one, each clutching a dish, like kitchen hands in a medieval banquet scene, we trailed out the door to the lift and stepped out into the sunshine. Everywhere at the barbeque children swarmed like one of the forgotten plagues of Egypt. There must have been close to fifty and when they all jumped in the pool they turned the water black with their flailing limbs. Remarkably they were all related in some way and played together in unusual harmony. Meanwhile, all across the garden, gangs of towering women with breasts like watermelons roamed; mothers draped in tropical fabric, stomping barefoot across the grass and through the palm trees, delicate oleander flowers plucked and placed behind their ears. Many of these women looked very much like Krystal, and a number were pregnant.

The scene was one of apparent harmony and yet I could not dismiss a certain gnawing reservation. Only one male relative was present, Krystal's maternal uncle – a huge man, very black with a curly mop of Einstein hair and no front teeth. Other than him it seemed all the fathers had decided to stay at home or, more likely, had only existed long enough to impregnate their girlfriends. And with that realisation, in a garden with so many buxom women lording over the meagre male population and the seemingly infinite hordes of children, the gathering now acquired a certain quality of grotesque fecundity, as though it was the set of a bad Russ Meyer movie: *Return to the Valley of the Self-Fertilising Women!* Filmed in Sex-a-scope!

Greg too had begun to notice and was now taking an inventory of the various women and their relative charms; signalling out for special attention one lithe teenager who looked nineteen but who I later found out was a good five years younger. Greg nudged me: 'The one in the spa totally looks like she murdered Captain Cook.' I looked at him. With his three-beer-leer and a bad reputation for this sort of thing I began to grow very concerned that he might be about to plunge us into the middle of a vengeful tribal payback that would end only in both our deaths.

Soon the clown arrived. Plonking down his big, black stereo, blasting out Britney Spears and the Spice Girls, he sent the children into a frenzy of dancing and screaming. Dutifully they held their excitement in check long enough to have their faces painted. With their cheeks and foreheads smeared in glitter and pigment (some with black noses and white whiskers, others with menacing filigrees of blue spider web) they seemed to resemble a tribe of vicious pygmies airlifted to civilisation as the unruly guests of an ethnographic museum. The signboard with the rules of the pool in prim black and white that sat by the water's edge began to look like a conscious irony as the children tore across the hot, scraping cement to plunge headfirst into the shallow waters or throw streamers and balloons at one another, clogging the pool filters.

In the middle of this bonsai riot, louder and more frenzied even than his cousins of ten or eleven years, was Drakkar. Although unable to swim, Drakkar had absolutely no fear of the water and would stand on the edge of the pool to plunge himself into the blue depths on the casual assumption that the nearest cousin would fish him out before he drowned. This system worked well until the cousin unlucky enough to be appointed Drakkar's temporary protector strolled blithely away from the water to fuel up on chips and Coke. With mounting horror I watched as the tiny boy climbed the steps of the spa, shuffled his way out onto the white concrete edging and gleefully flung himself into the water. Dropping my beer I dived in after him, bringing to the surface a slippery bundle of brown limbs that struggled obstinately in my arms. As his head broke the water he began to splutter and his red eyes squinted. He looked at me and grinned, then let out a cough that sent a big trickle of water down my chest. I went back to the barbeque after placing him in the care of one of the older boys.

Although the women were generous with their offers, the food at the barbeque was a convincing explanation for a worldwide shortage of Maori restaurants, so Greg and I discreetly ducked off across the road to the local Sushi Train.

Once back at the party I pulled out more beers and offered one to Krystal's mother who accepted enthusiastically. Mother and daughter bore only a modicum of resemblance. She was a stringy, energetic woman with a brutal crew cut and a flimsy tropical dress; when she spoke her blue rubber thongs drummed a frantic tattoo against the soles of her feet. After some chat I asked, diplomatically, whether the fact that Krystal had had her children at such a young age gave her any cause for concern.

'I've always just let my kids do what they want,' she said simply, and downed her beer. 'Besides, I like being with the grandkids. It's better to have them young. I had her at about the same age.'

'And what about Kane?'

She shot me a slighted look. 'Don't even mention that bastard's name to me.'

'But they've broken up, right?'

She snorted. 'Yeah, well . . . that's up to her now.'

We turned to watch the children in the pool. Standing on the edge of the spa Drakkar was staring into the depths with a look of intense concentration. In one swift movement he dropped his swimmers, grasped his penis, arched his back forward and, like a little imp on an Italian fountain, pissed straight into the water. A group of poolside middle-aged women in plastic sun visors and matching one-piece lime-green swimsuits dropped their copies of *New Weekly* to shake their heads and mutter disapproval. Greg and I fell into hysterics as some of the older children left the water in disgust, scolding their cousin; the younger ones staying in the steaming spa oblivious to, or uncaring of, the pollution.

After four hours the party had begun to die, the children to tire. The light had grown soft and gold as the encroaching shadows of the neighbouring buildings inched their way across the hot concrete. All around the blue pool statuesque Maori women wandered through the foliage in the creeping dusk, their coloured sarongs hitched in patterned papooses to accommodate the outsized babies whose fat, strong arms hung awkwardly over the bulges of blue, red and orange. I looked down at Drakkar; damp and cradled in my arms, his enormous wet eyelashes like big black spiders in the crevices of his soft brown face. He was so tired that he didn't hear them sing 'Happy Birthday' around a big pink square of cake, and his breath remained steady and oblivious to the fading cries of the children who ran all around us, smearing their cheeks in sticky handfuls of pink and white cream; some still sucking alternately on greasy blackened spare ribs that they held in their free hand. I didn't wish to leave this party, this Gauguin scene where I sat lazily, Drakkar's back pressing rhythmically against my arm, but the women were on the move: children gathered into herds, plates stacked. The day was at an end.

Krystal's mother stood up. 'Right, who's coming with me?' She shook her car keys at the assembled herd of idling youngsters. No one responded. 'Well I'm not going home on my own. One of youse is gonna keep me company.' With that, a selection of children was procured from the protesting mob and we waved goodbye as they made their way back to the car. Krystal lifted Drakkar from my arms and I looked across the pool to watch the visored women, who had followed the shifting patch of sun in their deck chairs, compare tattoos.

I looked around, drank my beer and realised that, for the first time since I had arrived, I felt happy to be on the Gold Coast. What I didn't know was that it would also be the last.

Eight

★

Lifestyles of the Rich and Childless

THE NORTHERN SUBURBS of the Gold Coast are like some horrible dystopian vision of the future in which all the young people have died of radiation poisoning and old men in walking frames and ill-fitting Panama hats roam the earth. Appearances, of course, can be deceptive. The number of families moving to the Gold Coast *en masse* belies the fallacy of the city as 'God's Waiting Room' (the median age of thirty-seven on the Gold Coast is only two years above that of Brisbane, although Queensland as a whole is ageing). However, there is still a significant retiree population in the city and while the southern suburbs actually have more elderly people, the baleful, numbing blankness of the northern suburbs lends the region an almost macabre quality – *The Twilight Years Zone*. North of Southport, along the ocean to Runaway Bay (and on), the city becomes a seemingly endless strip of malls, petrol stations and bunker-like houses, all with the inhibiting, faceless uniformity of retirement villages. These marina developments line their private canals with defensive shoulders behind huge, forbidding walls all painted in a variety of tedious pastels: row after row of drawn curtains, hot rooms, movement-sensitive floodlights and door combination locks. Whole streets in this area are entirely walled off; entire developments hermetically sealed behind wire and brick, the only method of communication to the outside being the silver intercom boxes that sit by the gates, glinting in the sun.

As an individual with only the remotest of egalitarian instincts I am often suspicious of many of the so-called values ascribed to the Australian national character – 'mateship' and 'fair go' are terms that see me crawling into the nearest dark pit for mortification. Yet even I could not deny the aversion I felt in the face of these ghastly compounds. Crime alone could not justify a 'gated community' in Australia: they were the sort of thing one expected to see in Jakarta, Johannesburg or some other Third-World hell-hole where lepers and children bang tin cups as the silver Mercedes roll through the boom gates. This was nothing but the architecture of fear and paranoia, the dark side to the hedonism of the Australian Dream, where the facade of good times crumbles away to reveal nothing more than a terrible void of miserly self-interest; a void in which values have been replaced with 'rights' – the *right* to a better lifestyle, the *right* to reward – and where the vision of paradise was selfish and adversarial. I felt suffocated just looking at them.

I was in a cab heading northwards to Hope Island, the site of a new gated community being constructed by developer Craig Gore. I had seen Craig on the TV news. He had just purchased a helicopter that had cost over a million dollars and then had the whole thing painted in a special kind of purple holographic paint designed to change colour in the sun. The paint job alone cost him almost $250 000. Craig's development was called Aurora, which was characteristic of the names for the most recent breed of resorts that, although designed to elicit some sort of exotic association, were now called Zen, Aqua, Pisces and Soy Latte. It was the same thing as Monte Carlo and St Tropez, but with a New Age twist, and without the charm.

Craig's development had piqued my interest because it was a new concept for Australia. Aurora was, in essence, a glorified retirement village, but rather than appealing to the traditional retirement home market it was designed for wealthy pre- or early retiree empty-nest baby boomers. Aurora was to be an 'adult community'; a major selling point was its status as Australia's first 'child-free' development. People under eighteen would not be allowed to live at Aurora and if grandchildren came to visit they would not be permitted outside the front door unless under strict adult supervision.

Craig was from a famous pedigree of Gold Coast developers. His late father was Mike Gore, one of the most notorious of the 1980s 'white shoe brigade', a group of developers and real estate agents so-called because they would frequently be seen walking about town shod in their white canvas boat shoes, as though they had just stepped off their yachts, which often they had. Today very few of the white shoe brigade are still in business on the Gold Coast – most went broke in the late eighties or early nineties, and it was Mike Gore who came to personify their rise and fall.

In the same way that Freddie Mercury's name was perennially preceded by the adjective 'flamboyant', Mike Gore was forever pursued by the moniker 'maverick'. Like Lang Hancock or Laurie Connell, Mike was one of those unlikely iconoclasts of the 1980s who, although undoubtedly motivated by a great deal of greed, was possessed of a certain charisma, a kind of demented enthusiasm, with which one could not help but be fascinated. Even though he ended up making his fortune as a used-car salesman, Gore was full of peculiar plans and dodgy schemes: in the 1960s he embarked on a doomed venture to import 'sacred soil' from Lourdes and sell it to Catholic priests. His greatest legacy, however, was the building of Sanctuary Cove, a hotel complex and Australia's first gated community. Created for withered society couples and the golf-mad Japanese, Sanctuary Cove became a convenient parable for the rise and fall of the 'greed is good' decade and a lasting symbol of the excesses of Gold Coast real estate speculation. Sanctuary Cove sits right next door to the site for Aurora.

In 1984, with much support (both financial and political) from his good friend Sir Joh Bjelke-Petersen (Mike was Sir Joh's backer in his 'Joh for PM' campaign) Mike began to build Sanctuary Cove. In January 1988 the complex was complete and Gore hired Frank Sinatra (by this stage little more than an icon, his voice clapped out and his enthusiasm long since dry) to open the complex for the then-record fee of US$1 000 000. Whitney Houston came too. Only a month after this event, however, Mike was forced to sell out his remaining 50 per cent share in Sanctuary Cove to a Japanese company and by 1991 he had decamped to Canada to escape bankruptcy. He died in Vancouver three years later.

Mike's relationship with the Gold Coast was ambiguous. In 1986 he found himself in a great deal of trouble with the local population when he published a double-page advertisement designed to stir interest in Sanctuary Cove in a number of major newspapers nationwide. It began: 'Whenever I fly my helicopter over Surfers Paradise I feel we owe God an apology. How could we have done this to the world's most perfect beach?' and it became a good deal less flattering from there. It was not, the locals thought, a fair assessment of their achievements and, in some ways, they were right to feel aggrieved because, truth be told, the Gold Coast was never 'the world's most perfect beach'. In fact, before building began in earnest during the 1950s, Surfers Paradise was, as one of the founding mothers of the city described it to me in conversation, little more than 'a horrible windy swamp' (echoing the sentiments of navigator John Bingle who described the area in much the same terms in the first recorded coastal observation of 1822).

The area known today as Surfers Paradise is naught but a splinter of sand bordered precariously on one side by the Nerang River and on the other by the ocean which (before it was stabilised with artificial dunes and the river subsumed into canal developments destroying much of its ecosystem) would regularly be cut off from the rest of the land by the encroaching ocean. Where Palazzo Versace and Sea World now stand was once a tidal marsh in constant flux, shifting the mouth of the river, joining and rejoining South Stradbroke Island to the north. It was man, not nature, who fashioned the Gold Coast into 'paradise'.

The notion of the Gold Coast as Paradise Lost, however, is persistent. Many times, usually from someone about to knock back a two-for-one tequila sunrise, I have heard the refrain, 'Before the development, mate, this place was paradise.' And not just on the Gold Coast. From Spain to Bali, people who have no real way of knowing what it was like before the development, people who are apparently enjoying themselves regardless, still feel the need to reiterate the notion that they are in a debased and corrupted paradise. This is because the Gold Coast is, on some level, a utopian enterprise, and inherent in every utopia is the notion that at some point in the past things were better – it is the 'memory' of this ideal past that gives us motivation to create a better future. Thus the Gold Coast functions as a parable for both the Fall of Man and the hope for his redemption: our expulsion was at our own hands and we are doomed to repeat our mistakes: even as we create so we must destroy, only confirming the uncomfortable suspicion that heaven and hell are just two sides of the same coin.

In the footsteps of his father, who once infamously claimed that Sanctuary Cove would keep out 'the cockroaches of society', Craig's Aurora development was, in its own way, a utopian community, albeit a smaller one, fortified within the borders of the city his father had denounced as a failure. The better time here, however, was the 1960s, the imagery of which was being ruthlessly exploited for the benefit of selling apartments in his 'adult community'. The television commercials for Aurora had an almost messianic quality, featuring slow-motion shots of hippies dancing and helicopters landing in Vietnam accompanied by slogans like: 'You changed the politics . . . You changed the music . . . Now it's time for a change.' Subsequently, people who had little or nothing to do with changing anything or, if they had, had now well and truly forgotten any ideals they may have once cherished, were being convinced that by moving into Aurora they were doing something good not only for their 'quality of life', but for their souls. It was evidently a very powerful advertising technique because Craig's apartments were selling like plaster dolphins.

We entered Hope Island and passed one of the billboards advertising Aurora; it featured a naked, cross-legged woman, her back turned to us in a yoga posture accompanied by the slogan 'Reject old thinking'. I spotted Craig's office in an elevated yurt-like structure in a strangely solitary suburban street in the middle of a giant swampy expanse that had, once upon a time, been sugar cane country. It was distinctly muggier here than at the beach, the distance warped by heat.

Upstairs, Craig was not to be found. His secretary said he was doing some surveillance from his helicopter and would be back soon. In the meantime I was presented with a series of news articles about Craig and a copy of the corporate magazine produced in conjunction with the development. The magazine was called *Highlights* and featured a heavy use of the term 'lifestyle' seasoned by generous pepperings of inappropriate exclamation marks, as though the author was continually shouting the good news; a technique which only threw into high relief an embarrassingly poor command of syntax: 'What was wanted is easy to understand if you look at what isn't wanted!'

Highlights was full of rhetoric placing the Aurora customer in direct opposition to the generation of their parents: 'The "baby boomers" simply don't want to become their parents ... rambling around a large old home built for a family that doesn't live there anymore or ending up in a retirement home, quietly fading to grey. They know there's more to life than that.' That baby boomers were the target market came as no surprise; such a direct appeal to selfishness would, I suspect, have been an acute embarrassment to their parents, a generation scarred by war and the Depression.

According to *Highlights*, Aurora's residents were not just happy but immortal; seemingly every page reminded us that, thanks to pilates and sunshine, baby boomers would be physically invulnerable in a way their parents were not. To this end Craig's resort was outfitted with specially patented 'Lifestyle Centres'. It was at these structures, presumably, where life intersected with style and the Good Life was born. No grey hair for them! These people wanted to *live*!

Highlights was full of imagery of this better life: a fifty-something woman engaged in a round of golf bursting forth with a volley of forced laughter; a beautiful prostrated deity laying face down on a massage table, a pink turban on her head; lobster halves in the shell. There were no postmen in Aurora and no garbage trucks: the mail was sent to a central pick-up point and the garbage was compacted and then frozen into cubes. These were the happy citizens of Hamelin after the departure of the Pied Piper, free to enjoy their decrepitude in peace.

News came that Craig was about to arrive. I went outside and watched the purple helicopter descend from the sky like a giant Christmas beetle. I am not easily impressed, but when someone arrives to meet you in a holographic purple helicopter only an incurable killjoy or someone who owns their own holographic purple helicopter could fail to experience the dimmest stirrings of awe. Craig obviously knew this; I could feel it as he shook my hand and said hello, never once looking at my face, removing his sunglasses only to turn his head to the sun.

Craig's head was square and acne-scarred, like a piece of rough-hewn basalt. He looked older than I knew him to be but he had an energy that was infectious and a pair of shiny eyes framed by soft, girlish lashes that lent him the look of a cheeky child. In his meeting room a troop of 'creatives' from a Brisbane advertising agency had arrived to discuss the cover for the Christmas edition of *Highlights*. Craig sat down and leant back in his chair, his legs spread like a schoolboy. He began to go about the process of gently intimidating his underlings. The consensus was split between the option of the naked yoga woman I had seen on the billboard with the addition of a Santa hat and a more innocuous soft-focus image of tinsel and glass baubles. Craig liked the yoga woman but was worried about offending his customers. 'I like this one too,' he said, holding up the image of the baubles. 'It's like a David Jones catalogue. It says, "Come on down! Your credit's good."'

Craig was funny. He told jokes in bad taste between stuffing his mouth with Promite sandwiches and, when he got really excited, throwing the phone to the ground. He reminded me of Rodney Dangerfield's character in *Caddyshack*: 'Hey! Everybody's gonna get laid!' But there was a slyness and a cunning to his good humour which he peppered with threats that had the creatives eyeing one another nervously.

After a while a photographer for the *Australian* arrived. He was ten minutes late and Craig had no intention of interrupting his meeting. Half an hour later his secretary buzzed the intercom. 'The photographer is still waiting.'

'Tell that cunt he can wait,' growled Craig, and everyone giggled nervously. Craig was happy with the impression he was making.

Fifteen minutes later, with me in tow, he strode out the front. 'G'day, mate!' It was all smiles and handshakes. The photographer wanted to picture Craig standing by the chopper, but the tycoon insisted we all get in and go for a ride. With Craig at the controls, we lifted up and over the construction site, a patchwork of pink and grey. Craig showed us the canal he had built; it was to be the last ever dug on the Gold Coast and he had only managed to get approval because of its alleged benefits as a storm channel, which was ironic because I had never before viewed the canals as anything more than glorified guttering. But now I was overcome by a most surprising sensation – I was actually in awe of his achievement. The canals might have been full of midgies and sharks; they might have killed all the fish, poisoned all the oysters and scattered the birds, but, up here in a liquid-purple helicopter, this giant trench (3 kilometres long, reaching all the way to the sea and deep enough for yachts, like something the Incas might have built) seemed to have all the quality of great art – it made me excited to be human.

After a short ride we returned to earth and deposited the exhilarated photographer. Craig told me to stay in the chopper and moments later we were taking off back over the development. We spoke through headphones.

'Don't you think it's a little bit paranoid to be creating gated communities on the Gold Coast?'

Craig was dismissive. 'I always hear this. But you southern people all live in your high-rise apartments with your security intercom and your concierge. What's the difference?'

I was going to point out that very few of us 'southern people' live in high-rise apartments, and that Hope Island, full of fading hippies trundling between their yachts and their burnt umber apartments was hardly Darlinghurst at 3 a.m. But his was a legitimate point: people who complain that their fabulous inner-city lifestyle is being ruined by the presence of prostitutes and the homeless are the same people who will be moving into Aurora in twenty-five years' time.

We flew over Sanctuary Cove, radiant like a green chessboard in the light. Craig began to point out the features: hotel, golf course, marina. 'Were you close to your father?' I asked.

'Yes . . . yes I was, actually.'

Craig landed the chopper and we were met by Mike, Craig's half brother and his employee, who sat waiting in a black Range Rover to take us to a display home that doubled as a sales office. The house sat in a field of mud. Piped New Age music played at the entrance with an incongruous disregard for its surroundings. Inside Craig greeted a sales assistant and led me to a mini-theatre. We sat down opposite one another across the aisle and Craig flung his leg over the back of the chair. 'I get tired of people saying, "You're a chip off the block" and "You're just like your old man."' There was some detectable bitterness in his tone. 'That was years ago. We've moved on. People should just get over it.'

He pulled his leg down, bent forward and began to eulogise the benefits of the most recent Gold Coast property boom. 'When I went to the banks in Sydney and said, "I've got land on the Gold Coast for only $28 a square metre", they just looked at me and laughed.

I couldn't believe it. I said, "But you can't get land anywhere near the coast for this price." And they just said, "Sorry, we're not touching the Gold Coast." I couldn't believe it! This land was so undervalued, probably the most undervalued in the country, but because it was the Gold Coast they wouldn't touch it.'

'So, do you think that the image of the 1980s white shoe brigade is still a problem?'

Craig became quite agitated, almost heated. The leg went back up. 'You see, this is the problem: cynical southerners talking about the white shoe brigade and all that. It's all gone! I remember my old man and Sir Joh counting the cranes on the horizon to see how well the economy was doing. Those days are over.'

'But, Craig, I'm not saying they aren't. I'm merely saying that, right or wrong, deserved or undeserved, this image persists. I mean, as soon as you say "Gold Coast real estate developer" anywhere in the country, people start to snigger. The image of people on the Gold Coast as irresponsible cowboys still exists, if only in people's minds.'

Craig looked a little puzzled. 'Really? You think that's it?' Was it possible that he didn't *know*? Here was Craig Gore, son of Mike, and yet he didn't even seem to realise that most people thought that 'Gold Coast real estate developer' was closer to a Barry Humphries character than an actual person.

Craig began to mutter to himself; the words tripped out in staggered disconnections. It was as if I was not present. He swung his legs up and down. He leant an arm behind his head and rocked backwards. He scratched his ear and looked up. 'Yeah, maybe you're right.' He shook a finger. 'Maybe I'm coming round to your way of thinking.'

Craig said he had a film he wanted to show me. He got up and lowered the lights. I sat in the darkened theatre while he fiddled with a projector. The film began to roll and he left me alone. The opening shot featured words like 'Location!' and 'Quality!' (complete with exclamation marks) floating across images of rolling clouds. A soundtrack of some nondescript folksy guitar strumming left me feeling inexplicably anxious. The clouds stopped and the film cut to slow-motion black-and-white images of Sydney. The film-makers had done their best to show the city looking as congested and as miserable as possible; cars shouldered one another in bitter, bovine resignation while the citizens, their faces set in grey death masks, shuffled between appointments in soul-crushing urban crypts of vertiginous height. Then the lyrics of the song began and the reason for my apprehension became clear: oh, God, it wasn't . . . oh, yes, it was: 'Cool Change' by the Little River Band.

Let me tell you a little about 'Cool Change'. 'Cool Change', for those unfamiliar with it, is one of those middle-of-the-road FM radio ballads from the late 1970s that cannot be appreciated by any thinking person, even on the level of kitsch. It is a horrible misshapen relic created by a gang of atrophied hippies who represent not merely everything that was wrong with the 'spirit of the sixties' and its subsequent co-option by the forces of Easy Listening and international capitalism, but everything that is wrong about pop music itself. This song is so bad that to call it so is not to merely understate the case but to miss the point that for it to be any worse would require an inversion of the laws of space and time. 'Cool Change' is the song that broke a million clock radios; it is the song Dr Mengele is listening to in hell. In 20 000 years there will be aliens on distant planets receiving drive-time broadcasts of 'Cool Change' to whom, in advance and on the behalf of the entire human race, I would like to apologise.

The guitar solo kicked in. As the octaves climbed so too did the screeching chorus in auditory compliment to the flocks of birds winging their way to warmer climes (or was it a cool, cool change?) and newfound childless freedom in Craig's yet-to-be-built resort. As the images became more idyllic the lyrics became impossibly maladroit: 'The albatross and the whales, they are my bra-thers! It's kind of a special feeling when you're staring out to sea like a luv-er!'

With the introduction of the dreaded alto sax solo the whole thing cranked up a notch and the song reached a kind of orgasm of maudlin sonic awfulness. Images of computer-generated buildings alternated with footage of middle-aged couples walking their dogs on sand flats, the cuffs of their calico pants turned skyward in celebration of their recent decision to spend the rest of their lives trapped forever within a Special K commercial. By the time Craig walked back in the door I was laughing openly, only to correct myself as I became aware of his presence. He looked at me hard. 'So, have your cynical Sydney views changed now you've seen my video?'

The film began again on a loop.

I became flustered. 'I don't think I'll ever lose my cynicism about anything, Craig,' I said, idiotically. 'Still,' I added, hoping that my obvious mirth at this ridiculous corporate flim-flam was not permanently damaging, 'I'm twenty-five, not forty-five.'

'Yes. That's right,' he said, and sat down in the opposite aisle, swinging a leg over the back of the chair to display his crotch. I decided to change the topic. 'What do you see as the defining characteristic of the Gold Coast?'

'Lifestyle,' he answered, giving the stock response of every Gold Coast resident. 'Anonymity in Sydney is easy. You can live this wonderful life, a cosmopolitan life. People don't come to Queensland for that. People choose to live here for a *better* life. They realise that beating their head up against the wall isn't getting them anywhere.'

'Cool Change' continued in the background: 'The albatross and the whales, they are my bra-thers!'

'But Craig, everyone I speak to says "lifestyle", as if the Gold Coast was a fun park. Is there no sense of it being a home?'

'Well, what do you mean? People live here, don't they? More people than anywhere else in Australia are moving here every day. They can't all be wrong, mate.'

'I'm not saying that they are, but let me give you an example: cities like Canberra or Newcastle are similar sizes to the Gold Coast – Canberra is even a third smaller – yet it has two football teams, a basketball team and assorted others. Newcastle similarly. Yet the Gold Coast has nothing – not one sporting team. Isn't that indicative of either a city with no identity or, at least, without one that is very definite?'

'You remind me of Charles Wooley [*60 Minutes* reporter],' said Craig impatiently and just a little bit triumphantly. 'Always cynical, always knocking.' He grinned. 'Does that offend you?'

'Just a little,' I admitted, although I suspect I was offended for different reasons. 'But none of this is a criticism of the Gold Coast. I just want to know what makes this city a home for people.'

'Hang on,' he said. 'I'll get Mike. He grew up here.'

Mike entered, squatted on his haunches and I repeated my question. 'Yeah, it's my home,' he said, 'but the problem is that this isn't really a single, unified community. It's fifteen cities in one. And then there's the fact that tourism is our main industry . . .' He trailed off.

I nodded; I was beginning to understand a fundamental problem of the Gold Coast: this was not a city of the blood. You chose to live in this place; this place does not choose you. What loyalty, what sense of identity or affection could a city of prepackaged dreams ever hope to engender in its citizens?

Craig took me through the rest of the building. We entered a display house kitted out to show off the kitchen, bathroom and living room. The airconditioning had not been switched on; the doors were closed and the heat was ferocious. Along one wall ran a group of model houses. These represented the full variety of available styles: 'Lifestyle Homes', two-bedroom apartments and the formidably titled 'Super Apartments'. Craig had a laser-like attention to detail: the vase was dirty; the models of the houses were dusty. Would Mike get on top of that straight away, please?

Craig began the sales pitch. I didn't listen very attentively, preferring instead to look at the models; Craig's hand alighted upon them with an unexpected gentleness as he spoke. The buildings were handsomely designed, architecturally superior to the average Gold Coast confection. I ran my hand along the roofs of the models; they were smooth, pleasingly so, but with a hint of textured plastic that reminded me of the toys I had constructed as a child. I found the level of miniature detail in these buildings marvellous; their delicacy excited me far more than the prospect of the real thing growing outside.

Everywhere on the Gold Coast one saw such miniatures, especially in Surfers Paradise where they frequently sprang up, seemingly spontaneously, in fly-by-night shopfronts created solely to house them. In these offices they sat in the centre of the room, like Grandma's china or a treasured Japanese doll, under little perspex boxes or, even more excitingly, domes, to stop the dust. They were perfect platonic worlds – some replete with little plastic trees or little plastic people, walking a plastic dog – created to sell the larger version across the street, the version that rose before your eyes to fifty, sixty, seventy and, now, even ninety stories. With so many of these models in the office of every real estate agent in town (and who knew how many had been produced in the past) one might have created a complete miniature city to house an entire Lilliputian race. Along the length of the Gold Coast I had seen these models stored away in cupboards or on desktops, some perhaps of buildings that had never been built, existing now, as they always had, only in dreams.

Craig pointed to the kitchen wall. 'See the pots, pans, the appliances? Everything comes with it, mate. There's no reason for you to do anything.' And it was true: curtains, rugs, barbeque – even the back scrubber hanging from the taps in the shower – came with the house. One did have a choice of exterior and interior colour schemes, but only from a specific range of swatches that sat glued to the wall. Craig's hand moved over the swatches: umber, burnt umber, sienna ... He was right, there was no need to do anything. Just choose.

We left the building and drove off in the leather-seated Range Rover, back to the helicopter. The Christmas beetle took off and soon we were heading towards Jupiter's Casino. We flew over Southport, above the lawns of the Southport School, a Neo-Gothic building on the shores of the Broadwater, the Gold Coast's most exclusive high school and Craig's *alma mater*. Craig began to boo and shake his fists in mock rage: 'You fuckin' bastards!'

I looked at him and he grinned. 'I was kicked out of my high school,' I said in a desperate attempt to create some sense of solidarity.

'Hmph! My old man had to build the fuckin' swimming pool.' He became momentarily withdrawn.

We crossed Surfers Paradise and then Broadbeach; below us elegant tendrils of land branched out like fern fronds into unfolding, interlocking fingers of red-roofed peninsulas, contrasting sharply against the blue and green canals of the labyrinthine marina developments. It was remarkable that something so ugly at ground level could be so beautiful from the air. Next we crossed Pacific Fair, a moated pink mall of Jurassic proportions that, or so Craig informed me with a fervour that might have seen Mozambique or Uruguay tremble before us in awed submission, was the largest in the southern hemisphere. (This oft-quoted statistic is entirely specious. According to the industry journal, *Shopping Centre News*, Fountain Gate in Melbourne is the largest mall in the country. Pacific Fair doesn't even make the top ten, rated at thirteenth.)

The L-shaped mass of Jupiter's casino was our marker as we turned westwards to the hinterland. 'I remember when this used to be all bush,' said Craig. 'Now they're building up the side of the fuckin' mountain. "Oh, they'll never get to the mountains", they used to say. And look at it now: there's no land left. There's just no land *left*!' He swung out his hand and beamed.

Craig had worn me out. His energy was incessant, and I could only admire his almost maniacal drive, but by the time he had begun an evening meeting with his construction manager my eyes were closing, heavy with the exhaustion of the previous evening's night on the town. I announced that I was leaving. Craig waved at me from behind the desk and continued his discussion. Outside, the empty expanse of mud sheltered by the thin purple line of the horizon and broken by the shadows of racing kangaroos felt barren and melancholy. As I waited for my cab it was with no small degree of anger that I realised I couldn't get 'Cool Change' out of my head: 'I know it might sound selfish, but let me breathe the air! Time for a change . . .' And so on.

The cab arrived and we drove through the dusk towards the highway. The driver was an elderly man who collected Gold Coast memorabilia – old pub signs, surfboards and the like. He had moved to the Gold Coast from Tasmania more than twenty years ago

(Tasmanians, like New Zealanders, were everywhere) and when I asked why he liked the place he said it felt like his home. It was refreshing to meet someone who regarded this city as more than a temporary refuge, a hideout in paradise – a 'lifestyle'.

Lifestyle. There was that word again. Where had it come from? Up until the 1980s people were still spelling it with a hyphen, so it could only have been in the last ten years that its meaning had found consensus. The word had actually come into the world as a psychiatric term; an Austrian psychologist had invented it in 1929, intending its use to denote the patterns of a person's character. Some time around the 1960s it had turned a hard left to take on its contemporary meaning: roughly, a mode of living. There seemed, however, no commonality to the various things and experiences that constituted the definition of 'lifestyle': from heroin addiction to enjoying café food, from homosexuality to an ocean view, from living in a child-free resort to binge drinking while pregnant – things that used to be called 'facilities', 'diversions', 'perversions', 'addictions', 'inadequacies' or 'culture' could now all take shelter under the same umbrella. Seemingly the only commonality 'lifestyle' offered was the ability to make everything equal, to reduce humanity to a series of 'choices', to expunge from the world something that seemed more urgent, more human – call it, perhaps, a moral dimension.

Again, from *Highlights*: 'Your day takes on a new meaning when you can indulge in such pleasures as massage from a qualified Masseuse, the relaxation of Aromatherapy or the healing power of Rei-ki.' It was a child's view of happiness, not far from 'When I grow up I'm going to eat Coco-Pops every day'; life as a series of experiences lived one after the other, experience as an end in itself; choice as a moral quality. 'You want freedom, independence, and the ability to get on with your life from a secure, and very comfortable base, which is built to your needs.'

In the city of the future, 'full resort features' were not merely a pleasant diversion for the leisured classes – they were a moral imperative.

As the taxi drove out of Hope Island we passed the billboard of the naked yoga woman exhorting us with a discernibly Orwellian tenor to 'Reject old thinking'. I'm not sure I knew what the old thinking was, but I wasn't so sure I preferred the new.

Nine

★

Schoolies: When Munchkins Attack

IN THE LEAD-UP to schoolies week an article appeared in the *Gold Coast Bulletin* announcing that mud-wrestling had been banned from the local council's activities program. It was but one of many controversies that had dogged the event.

In the last ten years schoolies week has become a Gold Coast institution; in the last three or four, with a little help from media mythologising, it has grown exponentially. Schoolies week is in fact a misnomer. The period is more accurately schoolies month as each participating state, Queensland, New South Wales, Victoria and South Australia, usually has a different date for their end of the school year. The upshot is that the party, swollen by numbers from the local population, continues in earnest for four weeks and beyond. The ever-increasing success of schoolies, however, has been met with a mixed reaction on the Gold Coast, with many local business people arguing that the reputation for violence and criminality it brings to the city outweighs any financial gains made during the month. Making schoolies 'official', however, by providing, for instance, cordoned sections, would be an expensive organisational nightmare, not to mention a serious liability risk. Thus, for now, schoolies remains an unofficial event.

Another problem with schoolies is the influx of non school-aged tourists and (alleged) organised gangs who have come to schoolies for the express purpose of wreaking havoc and winning sex from the throngs of horny teenagers. In the next four weeks I was to meet men who had come from as far afield as New Zealand to participate. As squalid and pitiable as this behaviour undeniably was, the issue seemed to me to have been blown out of proportion (after all, if I remember being seventeen correctly, then a cow of legal age was in with a chance). The hysteria over gatecrashers was imbued with a rather chauvinistic, proprietary air: the fathers of the Gold Coast had marshalled themselves on the collective doorstep of the city, shotguns at the ready. The fear of 'our' children being corrupted (as though half of them hadn't been already) seemed to me symptomatic of a wider concern; the Gold Coast was a vision of Eden, and the first casualty of the Fall had been innocence. Schoolies was every father's worst nightmare since Eve ate the apple.

In the first week of schoolies every balcony in our complex exploded with thousands of children, screaming by day and by night in celebration of their newfound freedom. By the third or fourth day our entire building reeked of the chemical acridity of cheap deodorant and the all-pervasive funk of mouldering hops. The stench clung to the floor's synthetic fibres in an olfactory death grip with all the unctuous fetidity of hyena mating season in the Okavango Delta. Communication came from all sides across the canyons. Some boys wrote their mobile phone numbers on the walls of their apartments in chalk, or on the windows in shaving cream. Others took advantage of new technology and sent their details by infra-red. Many merely shouted. Gathering in huddles on their balconies, crowds of boys begged girls on the opposite balcony to get their tits out. Every now and again one would comply, sending the entire population of a tower into a frenzy. Occasionally, some boys would exchange the favour, dropping their pants to waggle their penises.

Down on the streets, rangy girls, their arms streaked in downy striations of Lolita-gold, swung along the pavements in contemptuous struts, the pendulous sheets of their shining hair swinging in counter to the bouncing of their breasts. The boys with their rolling, affected walk contrived to a maturity that was unintentionally comic. All around town, bands of lean toughs roamed the streets, yellow-helmeted and shirtless, riding purple scooters, slapping people as they drove past or taking the occasional tumble, only to rise again and stroke their reddened elbows before speeding off. After two days the whole town resembled 'spring break' in an American teen soap opera, except nobody here appeared to be using words with more than two syllables, or seemed to regret getting drunk and having sex.

Although my depression had lifted the air had soured with uncertainty. A couple of evenings prior, Ren and I had watched a video, a horror movie called *The Ring*. In this film a vengeful spirit wreaks terrible revenge on humanity through the medium of a cursed video cassette. The victim, immediately after watching the footage, receives a phone call warning them they are to die in seven days. The film is deeply terrifying and together we sat in anxious silence watching as a doomed teenager began to play the tape. Then the phone rang – our phone. Ren and I jumped simultaneously and began to push one another towards the persistent object. The caller ID said it was a pay phone. We paused the film and discussed our options. The ringing stopped – then started again. Finally I picked up the receiver.

'Hello?'

Without waiting to find out who I might be, the threat began: 'You're fuckin' dead, cunt. I'm standing outside and I can see you. I know when you're home and I know when you're asleep.' The phone went dead. Panic spread across Ren's face. 'He uses the phone outside the building. He waits and he can see when someone's got the light on.'

I went to my bedroom window and peered down through a crack in the curtains. The payphone was empty and I could see no one answering to Kane's description on the street.

Neither of us left the house that night.

Yet there was worse, and here morbid thoughts had begun to take hold. Krystal had been missing for three days and no one, not even her mother, seemed to know where she was. Betty, a regular visitor to the unit, had been phoning continually, and Krystal's mother was panic-stricken; her daughter had missed her birthday. 'If you hear from her get her to call me straight away,' she said anxiously and, as I hung up the receiver, a balloon left over from the birthday party exploded and I jumped a full foot in the air.

I wasn't the only one getting jittery. To avoid the possibility of being attacked by Kane, Ren had been spending almost all his time at Julian's place. However, after a fight with Julian's housemate over the television schedule (Ren had demanded to watch the gay soap opera *Queer As Folk* which had offended the housemate doubly), Ren had been kicked out and forced to move back into the Moroccan full-time. I had some sympathy for the housemate's actions; Ren was a fairly high-maintenance friend. The day before in a drunken haze he had decided that one of the fish in our tank was 'hurting the other fish'. After scooping it out with a colander he picked the flipping silver creature up and threw it over the balcony. This act of mindless cruelty had annoyed me greatly and Ren had spent the rest of the afternoon trying to ingratiate himself, like a child who has offended a parent. There were only six fish left.

But that was yesterday and this was today and now we had little more to do than sit on the balcony drinking beer and watching the passing flow of children grow drunker and increasingly randy – over at the Chateau a group of girls were signalling to us, and then using the toilet with the blinds open.

Tired of being bombarded with terrible commercial hip-hop, I dragged out my stereo and turned up David Bowie's *Hunky Dory*; if they were going to invade my auditory and visual senses, I reasoned, then I might at least give them a lesson about who wrote the soundtrack to the apocalypse. And the apocalypse was on people's minds. Returning from the spa, Ren brought news of a growing consensus, fuelled by information provided by someone's cousin's best friend, that schoolies was, most definitely, to be the target of a terrorist bomb. As funny as this was I couldn't entirely dismiss their paranoia; the Bali bombing was fresh in everyone's memory and the Gold Coast had been badly affected by casualties. Meanwhile, in Sydney, the World Trade Organisation riots had exploded into violence and the looming possibility of war in Iraq was sending people everywhere onto the streets. Yet the notion of political protest in these palm-tree-lined avenues was something absurd, even vaguely perverse, like Yasser Arafat turning up to peace negotiations wearing nothing but a pair of crotchless leather trousers. Politics here was a distant memory of a world left behind.

'Hello. Who are you?' came a voice.

I looked up; two girls, their hair hanging in strands of drying spaghetti, were leaning over their balcony from the floor above. I introduced myself and asked if I could come up and have a chat. They agreed immediately.

Upstairs I found four girls and three boys. Although all were Gold Coast locals, none of them, of course, were from Surfers Paradise, so the novelty of being there felt to them like a holiday. They had saved a great deal of money to be here for the week, easily enough for a holiday to Bali or Fiji, but they considered the novelty of schoolies to be worth the sacrifice. I asked them whether they had been having fun. It seemed that they had: one of their friends had to have her stomach pumped the previous evening.

The girls were all schoolies but their boyfriends were considerably older; one was in his mid-twenties and balding. None of the boys had been to university and only one of the girls, Jenny, who wanted to do psychology or nursing, showed any ambition to do so.

I asked them whether they were proud to be from the Gold Coast. They looked at me, a little perplexed. I decided to be more specific. 'Do you get angry when people make fun of your home town?'

They looked confused again. 'Do they make fun of the Gold Coast?' asked Jasmine, displaying that peculiar brand of Gold Coast obliviousness. I nodded and she continued. 'Yeah, I suppose it bothers me . . . but we're not from the Gold Coast. We're from Ashmore.'

This failure to recognise a city called the Gold Coast, even among its own citizens, was to be a theme of my investigations.

I asked them to nominate the best and worst suburbs on the Gold Coast. Main Beach, Broadbeach, Sanctuary Cove and Runaway Bay were deemed the best; Ashmore, Nerang and Palm Beach the worst. Then they added Woodridge because it was the major Aboriginal area.

I asked whether there were many Aboriginal people on the Gold Coast.

'I'm Aboriginal!' declared Jenny, momentarily excited. 'Well, sort of.'

I asked her to explain.

'Well, my dad found out that he was Aboriginal the day my cousin died. That was *such* a funny day!'

'In what way funny? How did he die?'

'Someone poured petrol all over him and set him on fire.'

'What! How did it happen?'

'He was walking through a park in Brisbane and a guy just came up to him and did it. When they asked the guy why he'd done it, he just said that he wanted to watch him burn.' Her tone was free of horror. She would make a good nurse.

'Did he die that day?'

'No. He lived for a couple of weeks afterwards. He'd had his legs amputated and he'd been castrated and everything, and he was getting better, until he got a blood clot and died.'

'Were you upset?'

'Not really. I didn't know him too well and,' she added with a resigned flick of her hand, 'he'd tried to kill himself twice before.'

'So how did your dad find out he was Aboriginal?'

'His youngest brother told him the day my cousin died. Their grandma had died before dad was born and he moved to Mount Isa when he was young, so he didn't know much about his family.' She began to giggle. 'His brother also said he was a homosexual but that he had never had the experience.' All her friends joined her laughter. 'His wife told everyone that he makes his own G-strings and walks around the house in them.' The room collapsed in a chorus of mirth.

I sat and drank bourbon and Coke with the group for a short time longer. After a while my inherently puritan nature was dealt a blow when one of the girls disappeared into Jenny's room to have sex with her boyfriend. Worse, in a room full of kids for whom the novelty of drinking was still an end in itself, I suddenly felt very old. I thanked the girls for letting me hang out and they invited me to meet them later in front of the Hard Rock Café. I said I would see them there and made my way back downstairs to my apartment.

I ventured out onto the street with my notebook at about half-past ten. Down by the beach the scene was like Munchkin Land if Timothy Leary had sabotaged the lollipops. I barged my way down Orchid Avenue to Cavill Avenue; the crowd was shoulder-to-shoulder on both streets. At six foot three, I felt like the tallest person in the world, a striding Cyclops in a sea of staggering Argonauts. I stopped out the front of McDonald's, where Cavill Avenue meets the beach. 'How's the crowd tonight?' I asked a cheerfully cynical paramedic. It was his sixth schoolies.

'Honestly?'

'Please.'

'Fucked. This is the worst year I've ever seen. Last year we had four bashings in total. Last night we had eleven bashings and five hospitalisations.'

'So you're not looking forward to the next three weeks?'

He grinned and without any trace of sarcasm said, 'No, I love it!'

I continued on through the crowd and down the steps to the beach. Several thousand kids were crowded in front of two stages. One played top-forty techno and the other top-forty rock. The Living End, Blink 182, Good Charlotte — every band that had ever given punk a bad name was being vigorously appreciated by strong boys with supple arms and alcohol-clouded gazes. All around me on the night air wafted the combination of deodorant and alcohol sweat.

Over the stages hung billboards advertising an energy drink. Above a picture of two green tins was the slogan 'Pick up a couple this schoolies'. The suggestiveness was surprisingly blatant and the air was thick with sexual anticipation. Just then, I felt a hand on my back and I was pushed from behind. Staggering in the sand to regain my balance, I turned to see a boy weaving his way frantically through the crowd, staggering and lurching as a pack of twenty ran behind him, mirroring his every turn. As he stumbled his way towards the waves the mob behind him grew. At first there were just the original persecutors but, within seconds, the number had grown to dozens as spectators, eager to view the imminent bashing, joined the crowd.

A girl next to me was knocked over in the stampede. 'Help! Help!' she screamed as her legs buckled and her body disappeared under dozens of mostly male feet. Soon she had been rendered invisible by an avalanche of sweaty torsos. From beneath the mound of limbs a thin wrist appeared. Grasping at the flailing arm, her boyfriend lifted her from beneath the crush. After dusting herself off and straightening her skirt, with barely a word of complaint, the girl and her boyfriend turned to follow the others in pursuit of the boy.

And so the inevitable came as the boy tripped and fell. But now the crowd had grown to hundreds, moving behind the boy with the single-mindedness of a bee swarm. Before they could cover him he looked up through a clearing in the mob, his terrified face caught momentarily in the lights that shone from the stages. Within seconds he was shielding his head from a rain of kicks and punches as the crowd moved in and he was left with no option but to curl up and allow the human tide to wash over him. At the periphery of the melee some stood around and cheered: some for the fight, some at nothing in particular. My natural instincts to intervene were tempered by the realisation that to do so would be suicidal. I felt impotent and sick and remembered the stories I had heard in Third World countries about lynch mobs descending on the drivers of cars who had hit pedestrians.

It took only a minute for the police to arrive; there were about twenty. Grabbing at the boys, the cops restrained and arrested one token aggressor while the others ran off. The victim was dragged from the centre of the scrum, screaming all the while at his attackers and the police. 'YOU FUCKING FAGGOTS!' he shouted. 'I'LL FUCKING KILL YOU!' He was hysterical with fear, almost crying, and yet these pitiable attempts to revenge his wounded ego only made him seem ridiculous. One girl turned to me. 'I'm pretty dirty,' she said. 'My dad's one of those cops. Why have they gotta ruin everything?'

Now the police had formed a human wall around the boy who was trying to jump over them in an even more meaningless attempt at vengeance. One of the cops began to dance to the music; the others laughed and the crowd began to dissolve, walking back up the beach to join the others who were still jumping in time to the music, oblivious to the excitement behind them. I turned back and followed the dispersing mob. Climbing the sandy steps to the mall, I looked up to the south. From one of the far towers sparklers were being thrown from more than twenty stories, the blooming showers of sparks arcing downwards to leave sinuous tracings of blue and yellow incandescence.

'Who are you?' Two girls were standing in front of me, nudging one another excitedly as though they were at a school social, daring each other to ask me to dance. I said I was a journalist and that I was writing a book about the Gold Coast.

'Oh! Oh! Write our names down! Write our names down!'

Very carefully I had to spell out the names of Patricia X and Rachelle Y, seventeen years old, from Toowoomba.

'Are you enjoying schoolies?'

'Yeah. It's ace,' said Rachelle.

'Where did you get your alcohol?' I asked, pointing to the tinnies of Bundaberg and Coke in their hands.

'My parents bought it for us,' said Rachelle. 'I got a case of bourbon and Coke for my birthday.'

'That way we know our drinks are safe,' added Patricia, nodding.

'Is that something that worries you?'

'Yeah, heaps of girls get drugged and raped at schoolies,' said Patricia with more portentous nods.

The way she said it made it sound like an urban myth, schoolyard wildfire, but it did happen all the time.

'Well, have fun you two. Don't get raped.'

They giggled. 'We won't!' And off they wandered into the human sea.

It was then I remembered the girls from upstairs and the promise of our rendezvous at the Hard Rock Café. Realising that I had missed the deadline to meet them, I walked southward down the boulevard instead. The scene here was chaos, like a really big January sale at a department store where there are ten TVs for $20 and grandmothers use walking frames to break the legs of pregnant women. Here, if one boy was seen running then all others in sight would run after him, certain that he must have important information they didn't. If the cops were seen running, hundreds of children would trail them in a Pied-Piper fashion to the scene of a crime that, more often than not, was over before they got there. All around me detonated a disconcerting cacophony of beer bottles, dropped from the surrounding high rises. When a firecracker exploded among the crowd one girl called out, 'Finally! The terrorists are here!'

Down on the beach couples were having sex in open view of the crowds. Stretching out in both directions, the darkened mounds of humping limbs shifted back and forth, doing their best to look oblivious as they grunted into one another, like mating turtles in a nature documentary. I half expected to see a little gang of scuttling hatchlings scurry out from beneath hitched skirts and disappear into the crashing surf.

Back on Cavill Avenue I bought a kebab. Finding a quiet alcove I sat on the ground and began to eat. I felt drained and dismayed by all I had seen, like a Mormon who has been forced to attend a bucks party. There was nothing here for me; I could no more return to the spirit of seventeen than I could fake my way through Swedish. A man too old to be a schoolie sat beside me. We began to talk. He was from Sydney and had moved to the Gold Coast six months ago. The lifestyle, he said, was incomparable. I asked if he would ever leave. 'Nah, I wouldn't go back to Sydney for anything, mate.'

I took a bite of my kebab. A girl, not older than eighteen, walked over and pressed her stiletto heel into my foot. I jerked back in pain. 'Ohmigod!' she exclaimed. 'You're virtually begging for me to step on these feet!'

The man pointed up. 'See: that's what it's all about. Not like back in Sutherland where chicks put out and then cry rape and shit.'

Ten

The Fourth-largest City of the Future

JENNI PURDY WAS spending a lot of time explaining the technicalities of her receivership. I didn't really care. I wanted to hear something about Gold Coast 'society'; about the rich, about the people who seemed to be the other half of my Gold Coast folly. But I didn't have any specific questions, so I let Jenni talk a while. After all, she was paying for lunch.

'I nearly lost the pussies's house!' she said.

I paused. 'What's "the pussies's house"?'

'That's my house. You see, my husband and I have separate houses because he's allergic to cats. That's where I live with my pussies.' She grinned and I half expected Mr Humphries to appear and measure my inner thigh.

Jenni was the editor and publisher of *Gold Coast Magazine*, a publication covering 'society' and 'lifestyle' on the Coast. I had seen the magazine and thought that she might be a useful interview subject, so I called her office and made an appointment. The magazine was a glossy journal consisting mostly of advertisements for local businesses peppered with photos from opening nights. Jenni was an older woman dressed in a smart suit and oversized golden sunglasses with sparkling white diamantes encrusted around their rims – her reading glasses matched but they were silver. Her best friend Bianca was small and fragile and wore a dress with big pink flowers complemented with pearls, hot-pink nails, white shoes and a teetering pile of yellow lacquered hair, as though she had put her head in a fairy-floss machine. The girls ordered some more wine.

A decade ago Jenni had arrived on the Gold Coast from Sydney to open the new branch of a department store. One day, while on the floor during Christmas shopping, she met her current husband, a successful Gold Coast doctor. The store begged her to stay; but Jenni had other plans.

'Tell him, Jenni,' said Bianca.

'Oh, Bianca, I don't like to blow my own trumpet . . .' She closed her eyes and shook her head. 'I won an award, an honour in sales. But then the publishers of *Living in Paradise* put the title on the market, so I resigned and bought it.' Thus Jenni had begun her magazine.

Jenni was a great advocate for her adopted city. 'This place is the exact opposite of Canberra. There is virtually one small business for every ten people. And it's growing every day. We have everything except infrastructure.'

She was certainly right about the lack of infrastructure. No one had ever envisioned a city where the Gold Coast now stood and the consequence was that public utilities were under unprecedented strain. At capacity, the Gold Coast water supply could hardly cope with the summer population – the level was now at less than half and falling rapidly; even with water restrictions the supply would not last long. The highway, being a single strip from north to south and servicing the entire city, was in desperate need of a bypass. The boat traffic in the Broadwater had wrecked the ecosystem. The Gold Coast felt like a child suffering from gigantism, outgrowing every new suit of clothes within weeks.

Jenni wanted to talk business, about the new money that had flooded into the Gold Coast during the last ten years (Chinese, Japanese and Russian); of a mysterious murder by frogmen of a former KGB agent; of a woman who had once bought art for Aristotle Onassis; of the wars between the duty-free stores; of an award-winning hairdresser. Jenni was not happy with the current crop of Gold Coast 'society types', she told me. They were old hat, she argued, remnants of the eighties. 'We need a new professionalism here,' she said. 'These people are living in the sixties, the seventies, the eighties . . .'

'The fifties!' said Bianca, exasperatedly.

'I mean, *really*. We need a new breed. A new breed to establish this as the fourth-largest city of the future!'

The art gallery was miles away, in the industrial wasteland of western Southport. The street had looked closer on the map. Jenni had invited me to meet her there that night. I had been walking for some time and was beginning to wonder whether I was lost when I suddenly found the gallery in an unlikely alcove next door to a car yard. Outside, people were gathering in one of those oddly inexplicable rushes that seem to confirm the governings of the universe by the principles of chaos theory – how else could you explain the simultaneous arrival of eighty people exactly one hour after the official opening time?

Out the front I met Jenni and Bianca and, by sheer coincidence, my friends Rebecca and Sheryn – both women I had met on my first night out on the Gold Coast. Rebecca was attending because she had gone to high school with the artist, and Sheryn was friends with Rebecca. Anyone who was anyone knew everyone on the Gold Coast. Sheryn, a no-nonsense primary school teacher, was a woman of my own appetites, and together we made a beeline for the free booze and oysters. As we loaded our paper plates the gallery owner eyed us with a look of sour disdain that only plastic surgery can confer. 'I would chide you freeloaders,' she seemed to say, 'but I physically cannot open my mouth.'

The artist was the grand-daughter of a well-known Australian entertainment multimillionaire and there were a number of Gold Coast celebrities in attendance. After four rapid glasses of wine on an empty stomach, Sheryn and I began to get belligerent, standing off to one side of the gallery to make catty comments about the assembled crowd, many of whom, with their general air of desiccation, looked as though they were on leave from intensive military training in the Gobi Desert. Just as we were about to retreat outside for a smoke we realised we were standing at the centre of a large crowd which had begun to gather at the base of a small podium in anticipation of the speeches. With no discreet route of escape, we would be forced to sit it out.

The first speaker was the sister of a famous model and a Gold Coast celebrity in her own right. Her address was comparatively brief, but it was small compensation: the worst was yet to come. The artist ascended the podium, fumbling through sheaves of paper. By the third or fourth hour it was apparent that her correspondence course with the Fidel Castro Academy of Public Speaking had paid off handsomely. The tributes to her own hard work were plentiful and the thank yous so numerous anyone might have thought she had been smuggled out of a concentration camp. Sheryn and I could only stare at the floor and do our best to create an illusion of attentiveness between clandestine glances.

With the artist's first outbreak of tears some members of the audience began to make expressions of infantile sympathy: 'Awww.' Sheryn joined in, but exaggeratedly and with an obvious note of derision. I was doing my best to keep my laughter under control. 'I'd just like to thank my mum,' blubbed the artist, 'for taking us camping with Native Americans and doing sweat lodges and everything – you're the reason I'm here.' At this point the dam inside me grew close to breaking point and I began a repressed heaving so violent that it hurt my sinuses: sweat lodges! Native Americans! The artist continued. 'And now I want to thank me.' Everyone laughed, appreciatively. 'I think it was a brave decision on my part to forsake an easy life to become an artist. It's not the typical path, and that took strength.'

Sheryn leaned into my ear. 'Try becoming a primary school teacher in Helensvale, you stupid rich bitch.'

I could stand no more. A snot bubble bloomed out of my nose as I made a desperate attempt to incorporate my laughter into a complex routine of coughing, brow scratching and meaningful head nodding. The room was getting extremely hot and, under the pressure of the intense lights and the low oxygen levels, I had the sensation, probably more real than imagined, that everyone was staring at me. I was sweating like Rocky.

Pushing my way through the audience I ran out into the relative cool of the evening. A minute later Sheryn joined me, followed by the dispersing crowd. We collapsed into covert sniggers but when I saw Bianca wandering in our direction I regained my composure and introduced her to Sheryn. For a while we spoke about psychics until the conversation died.

'What the Gold Coast needs is some culture,' said Bianca as she took a slug of her drink. 'I remember being in the *best* seats of all the *best* operas and the *best* symphonies in Melbourne. And when the conductor would get up, turn around and bow, well, it was so exciting and so *beautiful*.'

I demurred, saying that with enough money any city could afford to import 'high culture'. What the Gold Coast needed was a sense of unity, an identity for its citizens. From there 'culture' would come.

'Well, we used to have a sense of identity,' said Bianca, with a wistful hint of the 1980s in her eyes. 'During the days of Skase and all the rest of them we had every top brand name. Orchid Avenue was a beautiful strip of the *best* international courtiers. Orchid Avenue and the Monte Carlo building were the places to be seen! But now ... it's all gone.'

'Well,' said Sheryn, with no small hint of irony, 'at least it was an identity of some sort.'

Moving inside, I began to inspect some of the art. It ranged from competently drafted nudes to the sort of landscapes I had last seen hanging on the wall at my local McDonald's. Its ambition hardly seemed to justify the claims the artist had made for her own bravery. Bonding over the mutual inspection of a sketch, I struck up a conversation with a guy a little older than myself by the name of Daniel. I brought up the topic of music, and it seemed we had similar tastes. I asked him about the lack of live music on the Gold Coast. He said it hadn't always been that way; he had once seen Nirvana at a venue where Palazzo Versace now stands. It was an unusual gig because they had been supporting the more obscure Violent Femmes and half the crowd had left by the time the headliners started. He said he valued the memory and I was briefly reminded of the dream I had about Kurt Cobain.

I told Daniel about my project and he was enthusiastic. As a child of the Gold Coast he had a lot of thoughts about the place but ambivalent feelings towards the city. In his late teenage years he had left and lived overseas for some time – the Gold Coast was too small and parochial for a young person with ambition – but he came back to raise a family. Like it or not, he reasoned, you couldn't escape your heritage.

Daniel knew a lot about Gold Coast folklore. He was intelligent and articulate and it was a shock to realise how few educated people I had met up until now.

'Have you heard of Miles Buisson?' he asked.

I said I hadn't.

'He was a young guy, a friend of mine who was murdered.'

Why was it that everywhere I went on the Gold Coast someone seemed to have a story of violence?

'A lot of people knew him. It was a defining moment on the Gold Coast when he was killed. I suppose he was a sort of Kurt Cobain figure . . . in a way.'

I *had* heard of Miles Buisson – on one of my aimless wanderings I had seen a plaque in a park in Broadbeach dedicated to his memory. The plaque said he had been 'tragically killed at the age of eighteen years'. Tonight, however, I failed to remember the connection.

Miles was a popular young surfer from Broadbeach who was murdered in January 1990 while sitting with his girlfriend on the beach at night. The pair had walked from Fisherman's Wharf (the same venue where Daniel had seen Nirvana) across the road and towards the ocean. As the pair sat in the dunes a man crept up behind them, bludgeoning Miles about the head with a log and then doing the same to his girlfriend before raping and throttling her. After a while Miles's girlfriend recovered consciousness and ran down the beach in a daze where she was discovered by a couple. The police were alerted and she was hospitalised – her face so badly broken that she required reconstructive surgery. Unfortunately it was too late for Miles.

Miles's death shocked the Gold Coast. It seemed to signal the end of the country town and the beginning of something new and unpleasant. An editorial in the *Gold Coast Bulletin* linked the murder to a growing permissiveness in society and the ever-present evil of film and television violence. Nevertheless you couldn't blame people for trying to make sense of what had happened. Discounting rape, the crime was utterly motiveless and its savagery unconscionable.

The killer was arrested about a fortnight later in Coffs Harbour. He was a homeless 24-year-old Englishman by the name of Colin Florey who had been drifting up and down the coast for a while. He offered no explanation for the crime and was jailed for life.

'A lot of people claim to have known Miles,' said Daniel. 'But they didn't. A lot of people turned up when the guy who killed him was being sentenced and screamed out the front of the court as he was led in . . .' He trailed off and I suspected he regretted telling me this story. The memories were probably less distant than he had realised; journalistic snooping can camouflage itself as a public service but what lesson can hope to be learnt from a story with no motive and no moral? 'Don't write more than a page about it,' he added. 'There's really nothing to say.'

Arriving home that evening, I was immediately confronted in the hall by a teetering pile of baby clothes. It was more than a metre long and a couple of feet tall: a vast array of cardigans, jumpsuits, dresses, booties and skullcaps festooned in an endless variety of embroidered rosettes, pink ribbons, marching ducklings, bursting hearts and frolicking bunnies. They were all brand new and most still had their price tags; they would have cost almost $1000.

I walked down the corridor. Krystal was sitting in the living room, smoking and drinking a cup of tea. It was the fourth day of her mysterious disappearance. I was relieved to see her but my mind foamed with suspicion. 'Your mother is looking for you,' I said.

'Yeah, I gotta call her.'

We sat in silence.

'Where have you been?' I asked, a hint of accusation in my voice.

She paused and rose from the table to wash her mug. 'Just at a mate's place.' She sat back down and put her feet on the coffee table.

'Where'd you get all those clothes?' I asked, gesturing down the corridor.

'Oh, you know . . . Target, Best & Less.'

Another silence.

'I didn't know you were having a girl,' I said.

'I dunno if I am.'

I laughed. 'Then why did you buy all those girl's clothes?'

'I dunno,' she said, shrugging her shoulders in a mixture of indifference and agitation. 'I wanna girl.'

Eleven

★

I Put a (Sexy) Spell on You

LEONARD WAS IN HIS mid-forties, short, slightly chubby and very pale with a moon face and a scraping of grey hair either side of a crisp left part. Tight over his sagging frame he wore a short-sleeved business shirt thin enough to reveal the darkened circles of his nipples. Perched on his nose were large 'aviator' sunglasses, the sort popular with policemen, made slightly unnerving by their yellow lenses through which I could see his eyes but not their colour. His eyebrows appeared slightly plucked at their edges and shot off at their crests into Menzies-like tufts of black which I think had been carefully combed.

Leonard was a shot in the dark. The magistrate's court had proven a disappointment and now I was on the hunt for interesting subjects. My journalist friend Amy had suggested Leonard who, as a self-professed 'witch' and 'Satanist' who made pornography on the Gold Coast and was one of the first people in Australia to have had a penis extension, certainly seemed to fit the criteria for an 'interesting' subject. Although

I didn't know it at the time, he was also to be my entrée into the world of Gold Coast pornography.

We ordered coffee. 'Is it true that you're a white witch?'

He raised an eyebrow and tossed back his head. 'White, black. There's no such thing. Only power.'

His voice was curious: even and unmodulated with a slight hiss somewhere between a vaudeville sissy and a late-night host of camp horror movies. Between sentences he had the unnerving habit of sniffing violently through only his right nostril so that his eye would twist to the side, like a stroke victim's, and one half of his upper lip would rise in a crazed snarl of pointed teeth.

'Do you perform ceremonies?'

'Oh, yes, sometimes, just to call upon the Great Spirit.' His tone became derisory. 'But most of these stupid hippies wouldn't know anything about the true nature of power. They're just a bunch of fairies prancing around with crystals...' He trailed off and stared over my shoulder. 'But I don't do it much these days. It's not good for my mental state, especially with the extremely high dosage of anti-depressive medication I'm on.' He looked back and sniffed.

I decided to change the subject. 'Is much porn produced on the Gold Coast?'

'Oh, yes! Most of the *artistic* production goes on here.'

For more than twenty years prior to his enterprising excursion into the world of pornography, and before he was fired, Leonard had been a journalist. According to his own testimony (and here there was a mention of secret black lists) he was unlikely ever to be employed again. In the interim between journalism and porn he had sold Amway and real estate, among other things.

'So, why porn?'

'Well, I've been a consumer of porn since the age of fourteen when

I first found Dad's stash, which is how most men start.' He paused. 'And the girls find Mum's vibrator.' Without warning he burst into an unpleasant, womanly laugh, only to stop suddenly and stare through his yellow lenses, issuing several powerful sniffs before falling silent.

'And what about your adult life?'

'Well, porn is an industry which I have always felt very drawn to. In fact it was always my secret but unrealised desire to work in porn. And so after I was fired from my last position I answered an ad for a job at a magazine that just said "must be broadminded". When I got there I discovered it was for a magazine called *Sally*, which had always been a favourite of mine as an adolescent. So naturally I was hired right away. I worked there for about a year.' He grasped the handle of his coffee cup between his thumb and forefinger, extending his pinky into the air, and took a sip of his coffee. 'But that place was run by idiots. Fools!' He slammed the cup into the saucer. 'And soon I was ousted by an ambitious editor who never much cared for me.' He arched his aquiline eyebrows over his yellow glasses and sniffed. 'Never be an unemployed professional over forty.'

'And so then you decided to start your own magazine?'

'Yes. You see, Brendan, it didn't take me long to realise that everyone in porn is an idiot. Porn is an industry almost wholly populated by fools and cretins. People of education and training don't do it. Once I realised this, I knew that the sky was the limit. So I phoned a photographer friend who I had met in France and approached him with the concept of starting a magazine.'

'What happened to it?'

'We produced one edition in two different versions – the Australian version and the real version, and then, unfortunately, we went under.' He trailed off and sniffed before adding briskly, 'But the new one is coming out before Christmas.'

'Why two versions?'

'Well, the Australian censorship laws are so puritanical and restrictive that we can't even show, for instance, a woman getting slapped on the butt.' He laughed and folded his hand outwards. 'I mean, which of us has not slapped a woman on the butt and said, "Giddy up, bitch"?' He drew his chubby chin back into his soft neck and peered at me over the bronze wire of his glasses. 'I mean women *want* to be tied up, they *want* to be dominated, they *want* to be humiliated and the politicians tell us that they can't. I think Hitler had it right when he said "Western politicians are all spineless worms."'

I felt affronted by Leonard's inclusion of me in his 'Giddy up, bitch' theory of the world. 'Perhaps some women do want these things you claim, Leonard, but aren't you just exploiting their insecurity and vulnerability?'

'You can be the dictator of an entire country and want more power and still feel inadequate.'

By this I assumed he meant that people fulfill their inadequacies in different ways – a point with which I would not argue – but he had failed to answer my question.

He continued: '"The only thing standing between an ordinary person and utter depravity is opportunity." Oscar Wilde said that and these women I employ love the idea men are watching and masturbating. It's all about self-esteem. Young women's self-esteem is based entirely on being sexually desirable.'

'These women': it was a telling phrase, and I wondered if Leonard considered the women who made porn for him separate from other women – women such as his wife and mother, for instance. 'Are you married?'

'Yes, and my wife watches enormous amounts of gay porn. When I'm not home she watches a guy get butt-fucked and pumps herself with a dildo. Good *luck* to her.' He pressed his thin lips tight together and sniffed. His mouth went into spasm.

'Do you have children?'

'Yes, three.'

'Do they know what you do for a living?'

'They do indeed. My daughter, who is ten, told her teacher just recently. And she was *fascinated*, as most young women are about pornography.' Leonard withdrew the comb from his pocket and began to comb his hair from left to right in considered, forceful strokes. I resisted the temptation to add that I was sure the teacher was probably about to share her fascination with the Department of Community Services.

'Is there any recourse of complaint for people who've been badly treated in porn?'

'None. Porn is full of liars, thieves, scum-suckers and sham artists. It's awash with organised crime and drug-fucked fools.'

'Aren't you worried about a potential threat to either yourself or your family at the hands of these people?'

'If some organised crime heavy came to lean on me,' he said portentously, touching the table with his fingertips, 'I'd shoot him dead. I'd kill him, and then I'd kill his whole family.' I began to laugh and Leonard's eyebrows shot up. 'I'm very serious,' he said. 'The government spent a lot of money turning me into a trained killer care of the Australian army.'

Lunatics like Leonard were tolerated on the Gold Coast, even celebrated, and, as repugnant and delusional as he undoubtedly was, I couldn't help but admire the fact that he could get away with it. The Gold Coast wasn't like any other city in the country: you came here because you wanted to be free of history, convention and expectation. 'We have doctors who have almost been struck off, lawyers who have been disbarred,' said Regina King, veteran gossip writer and social photographer for the *Gold Coast Bulletin*. 'People come here to reinvent themselves.' This elevation of crooks, shonks and outsiders to the status of stars (like a version of Warhol's factory with a better tan) endeared me to the Gold Coast. No other city in Australia – not even Perth – regarded the con artists and scam merchants of the 1980s with such pious nostalgia. If the only thing standing between an ordinary person and utter depravity was opportunity, then the Gold Coast was a mine of opportunity. This town was whatever you made it.

Krystal was unhappy. The psychic she had called knew nothing of her future and could speak only in vague generalisations. The phone came down with a slam. Her pregnancy, her financial situation, her love life – there was apparently no subject on which this woman could speak with authority. 'What an ignorant bitch,' she said exasperatedly.

The afternoon was late and the heat ferocious. From the pool area came the now subconscious auditory interference. Krystal looked down at the teenage throng. A gang of boys was jumping from a second-floor balcony across a dangerous expanse of concrete into the water. 'I didn't do any of this when I left school,' she said.

'Neither did I.'

'Actually, it was probably because I was pregnant with my first baby during schoolies.'

At first I thought this was a joke at her own expense but, as I turned and faced her, I saw it was merely a simple fact of her life and that she was neither bitter nor aware that it might have been any different.

Together we watched the television in silence until the phone rang. Krystal picked it up and began to talk quietly into the receiver.

Turning her back on me to muffle the conversation she began to issue a series of monosyllabic affirmations. 'Yeah, okay,' she said finally, and hung up. She busied herself at the kitchen bench, defrosting chicken nuggets for Drakkar.

'How's Kane?' I asked.

She scowled a little into the floor, like a child who has been sprung wagging school. 'Just . . . normal,' she retorted and continued to ply apart the frozen nuggets but not before I had seen, for the briefest moment, a certain flicker of her eyes and a souring of her mouth. It was an expression that lent her face a distinctly saurian cast and signalled, I was sure, a fierce but repressed anger which I knew instinctively to be directed at myself.

Twelve

★

The Kraken Wakes

AND SO THE TIME had come for the Scandos to hop in their long boats and row home. It was Ren's last day on the Gold Coast and I was sad to see him leave – if we love our friends for their faults then I loved him for a full range of endearing frailties. Having thus far eluded death at Kane's hands, his plan for the future, or so he claimed, was to move to Norway where he could be close to Julian and save money for the next year's term by working on a North Sea fishing boat. I replied that the day I saw a disco queen like Ren gutting fish for seventy hours a week was the day I would believe it. Ren's imminent absence, however, had left us in a tight spot: the lease was up, no one wanted the room and we were running out of time. 'Let's get some kinky Japanese sluts in here,' said Krystal encouragingly. The revelation that she was bisexual didn't exactly shock me, but I didn't particularly want to see the spare bedroom used as some sort of pimping service either.

'Do you mind if I do the interviews?' I asked.

Once again we were forced to turn to the dreaded flatmate

agency. Over the next week a succession of young hopefuls were paraded through the unit, but they were either too poor, too shady or too indifferent and soon we had grown desperate. There was one Kiwi couple who seemed promising: they had been sleeping in their hire car for a week and were desperate, willing even, to pay extra for the inconvenience of a second person. But at only twenty-one years of age neither had ever lived in rented accommodation and the real estate agent would not accept their references.

Krystal hatched a plan. Betty, she explained, had impeccable references and so, with her cooperation, it would be an easy matter of submitting her application to the real estate agent and then simply moving the Kiwis in under her name. Betty agreed and the Kiwis came over that afternoon. Their names were Jeremy and Lenore and they looked like something off the side of a Weet-Bix packet: huge, blonde and pink – the kind of people who would survive the Black Death. Ren was cleaning out his stuff when they arrived.

'Does anyone want some porn?' he asked.

'I'll have it!' said Jeremy enthusiastically.

Ren threw the magazines in his lap. 'Oh,' said Jeremy quietly, turning a brilliant shade of fuchsia, 'gay porn.'

Ren grinned, pleased with himself.

I asked them what they did for a living. They said they were semi-professional sportsmen, Jeremy in rugby, Lenore in hockey. They had been together six months after meeting at a rural university and Lenore had come to the Gold Coast to start work at a coaching clinic in January. I asked Jeremy why he had come. In response he literally jumped out of his seat with enthusiasm and flung his arms out wide by his head. 'My coach back in New Zealand has only been two places in the world: Christchurch and the Gold Coast! And he reckons the Gold Coast is the greatest place on earth!'

Armed with the assurances of this faultless counsel, they began moving their stuff in that afternoon.

For Ren's last night in town we started with dinner in Broadbeach. There were about twenty people in attendance, mostly Scandinavians and Austrians. Spirits were high; even Julian loosened up, telling us that he had discovered an enormous amount of gay porn on a computer belonging to his housemate, the same one who had screamed at Ren about not wanting to watch 'faggot shit' on the television. The prognosis was unanimous. Ren, meanwhile, told a hilarious story about how at the age of six his fundamentalist Protestant parents had presented him before their all-singing, all-dancing charismatic congregation to ask them to pray for his undescended testicle. In defiance of our helpless laughter the strategy worked, for within a week of the 'laying on of hands', and after many fervent exhortations to the deity on behalf of his genitals, the testicle divinely dropped. 'It was a miracle,' said Ren solemnly. 'The doctors said it would need an operation.'

Seated next to me was Alex, a jolly Austrian with an accent like a black-and-white Nazi. We had been drinking for some time and were halfway through our meal when he turned to me and said in a low voice, 'You know, last night I fucked a shkoolie.' I said Ren had told me. He laughed and leant in closer. 'You know, ve wideo-taped her, but she didn't know. And zen my housemate and I votched it zis mornink.' Ten minutes later he leant back in and said under his breath, 'I really liked it because she was a wirgin and it hurt her so much.'

What was this: simple sadism or the dark mysteries of machismo as celebrated in the novels of Norman Mailer and Martin Amis? Whatever it was, I found stirring within me vague and unfamiliar rumblings of chivalry. Should I call the police? Tell him off? Any grand gesture seemed doomed to failure; I might as well have slapped him with a leather glove. As it was I just drank some more and wondered how many other schoolies had lost their virginity under similar circumstances this summer.

After finishing dinner we made our way to a nightclub and, after some hours, finally arrived at Melbas, the favoured nightclub of the Scandinavian set. Since leaving the restaurant Ren and Julian had begun one of their regular spats, a fight which slowly escalated as the night wore on. In a final act of retribution, Julian jumped in a cab and deliberately left Ren in Broadbeach. By the time Ren came staggering through the door at Melbas, his contrition was pronounced. For some time the pair talked at the bar, an occasional surreptitious pawing punctuating their apologies. Then, without warning, Julian grabbed Ren and dragged him onto the dance floor, pulling him close and kissing him straight on the mouth. I looked around the room: forty sets of chiselled jaws dropped open to reveal 1280 perfect white teeth. The couple pulled apart. Julian looked at Ren and smiled, drawing him closer. As the couple drifted into the crowd arm in arm I found myself uncharacteristically touched by their happiness. Perhaps it was because theirs was the closest thing I had encountered by way of a normal loving relationship on the Gold Coast.

By this stage I was absolutely plastered, so when I spilt half a beer down the front of my jeans and felt the cold, yeasty brew seep into my crotch, I had only myself to blame. One of the great advantages of living in Surfers Paradise, however, is that if you happen to spill beer down your pants then it is only a short walk home for some clean ones, enabling you to continue drinking in comfort. Stumbling out onto the streets I arrived at the Moroccan in less than five minutes.

Not bothering to try and hide my damp patch, I rode the lift with a mildly horrified middle-aged woman, falling out on the eighth floor and leaving the elevator reeking. In the apartment I made for the kitchen and immediately began to pour myself a glass of water at the sink. As I drank

I looked down at the coffee table. A slight breeze from the open curtains was rolling several empty tins of bourbon and Coke along the glass tabletop, making an unpleasant metallic grating. I put down my water and looked across at the balcony. Outside, I could hear a muffled conversation. Silently, I made for the balcony door. Standing at an oblique angle I craned my neck to see a giant tattooed leg appearing and reappearing from behind the billowing curtain, a tin of bourbon and Coke clutched by a tanned hand resting on the knee. Almost immediately my skin broke into beadings of sweat; my heart lay suspended in my chest. I spun around and made for the corridor.

'G'day, mate!'

The voice came from behind me. I turned. It was Kane. I sobered up immediately. 'G'day, mate,' he repeated as he began to approach. 'How's it going?' He held out his hand. With that simple gesture all my hard work, all my efforts to avoid him were undone. Now he had seen my face. As though watching a slow-motion replay I took the hand, regarding it as one might a hand-sized spider, and said I was fine.

Ren had not been exaggerating. Kane was indeed enormous; grossly disproportionate in fact. His arms, sprouting from the sleeves of his over-sized tank top, looked like tattooed water wings, and when he put them to his side they stuck out at an odd angle to his body, as though he was continually midway through a star jump. His legs were slightly bowed, as if straining under the weight of his own torso, but his head was small and juvenile with big eyes and sensual lips. The combined effect was that of a small boy poking his face through a boardwalk cardboard 'strongman', grinning for a photo.

'How long you been living here, mate?'

I stared at the blue gothic script scrawled across his legs and arms. 'Oh, about two months.'

'You take that cunt George's room?'

'Yeah.' I nodded in uncomfortable silence. Absurdly I became suddenly self-conscious about the wet patch on my jeans. It felt like a really bad job interview, except here the unsuccessful applicant was to have his head twisted off.

Kane smiled and scratched his shoulder. 'Hey mate, don't worry about all that shit between me and Ronaldo,' he said genially, getting Ren's name wrong. 'He was making my old lady clean up after him and she's six months pregnant!' He turned his palms out and dropped his hands level with his waist, spreading his fingers wide in a gesture of disbelief and disgust. He leant closer to me. 'I mean, you can understand *that*, can't you mate?' With 'that' he leant deep into my face, cocking his head and blinking hard.

It was a non-question. I nodded and smiled some more. 'Yeah, um, sure.'

'I mean, don't think that I've got anything against *you*, mate!' He seemed very sincere and shook his hand reassuringly to indicate his neutrality. 'But that Ronaldo cunt, mate: I'm gonna fuckin' kill him!' His head bounced in concordance with his own statement. He laughed a little and his tone changed. 'You wanna have a drink with us, mate?' He gestured to his unseen guest on the balcony.

'No thanks, Kane,' I said, affecting my best oh-my-god-is-that-the-time manner. 'I've got some friends who are expecting me downstairs. I only came up to change my jeans.' And with that I disappeared into the bedroom to perform my intended task as quickly as possible.

Back downstairs I hurried my way back to Melbas in order to warn Ren. As I walked I phoned Krystal. 'Kane is in the house. Did you realise?' She was at a party in Brisbane. 'Yeah, don't worry, he's okay,' she said languidly. 'He's taking his medication and everything.'

'What? Who cares! What if Ren had gone up there?'

'Don't worry about it,' she said irritably. 'He'll be fine. I wouldn't have given him the key if he wasn't.'

For a short while we argued but after a few minutes I realised that I would gain no ground. Hanging up the phone, I sat on my own in the club. In a way, I suppose, Krystal had begun to fascinate me. Like an Indian mystic who has lived on nought but bugs and leaves for fifty years and whose corporeal presence is in constant danger of complete disintegration before one's very eyes, I simply refused to accept that someone could be so undernourished; that her soul could be so vacant and yet retain the apparent attributes of consciousness. Krystal's vacuousness was absolute. She had no hopes, no ambitions, no curiosity, few emotional reactions and, when she did express an opinion, had nothing to add but received wisdom. She lived not day to day but second to second, unable even to think far enough ahead to the evening's meal, which is why she relied on frozen prepackaged food. She had no concept of the future and no use for the past; a past that was without lessons – nothing more than a series of images, like someone else's slide show flashed across a white wall.

Initially I had mistaken her inertness for a kind of resignation to her limitations. Her impassivity had seemed to me almost plant-like, implying that she had subsumed ambition into a pleasant domestic self-sufficiency. But in the light of this recent betrayal I saw her now not as a plant but as a sea anemone: fixed and mindless, opportunistic and grasping. And I remembered now the way her hands had curled and her eyes, moist with excitement, had focused on her fingers to conjure with an almost erotic relish the oysters for which she yearned and for which she would have done anything: 'Big *fat* ones!'

Thirteen

★

All the Lonely People

WHENEVER BENNY SPOKE his chains jangled like the approach of a sleigh in a Russian novel. The ropes of gold around his neck were so many and varied that they sat upon his chest like a breastplate; from some hung golden crucifixes the size of small birds. Here in the foyer of the ANA Hotel (a lavish leftover from the 1980s stuffed full of chandeliers like parade floats, wood panelling and funeral flower arrangements) he looked both out of place and very much at home. Leonard the Satanist had recommended I meet Benny and now, seated in a deep leather chair wearing a pair of cut-off denim shorts and a pink Hawaiian shirt, he was only too pleased to talk. 'Stripping is a growth industry on the Gold Coast,' he said, and waved his hands to indicate growth. 'Here you have the hottest dancers in Australia. Girls come from all over just to be here.'

'And they're normal people too,' added Danger. 'Nurses, pre-school teachers, psychologists.' Danger was Benny's wife. Her real name was Danielle. She was blonde and pretty and her bosoms shot out the front of her chest in two gravity-defying mounds like hard-boiled eggs in hot-pink eggcups. The pair had met at a strip club where Danger had been working and between them they had five children from a number of different relationships. She was, Benny told me proudly, the winner of twenty-four State and national titles. Danger was the Queen Bee of Benny's strip empire.

Benny had big, wild Lebanese eyes that never seemed to blink. He grew up in the western Sydney suburb of Parramatta and became involved with organised crime at a young age. After a varied career he ended up doing time for importing cocaine. He had finished his four-year sentence only eight months earlier and was still on parole. 'I was known as the Mr Big of the Gold Coast, mate,' he said, his eyes misting with a hint of happier times. 'But . . . you know . . . life is consequences.' After his release from prison, Benny had become a licensed travel agent before starting Benny's Bad Girls, a strip agency with over seventy strippers on call twenty-four hours a day, making it, or so Benny said, the biggest agency on the coast. But Benny didn't want to stop there; he had plans. In his hand he held a blueprint for a series of Internet sites acting as an agent between brothels, sex shops and the customer. It was to be an international operation and it was going to earn him 'fifty million a year – guaranteed'. Benny held out the manila folder under my nose and flipped through the pages with great tenderness. At one point he became so excited he broke a coffee cup. 'I tell ya, mate, this is big,' he said, as a waiter picked up the shards of broken china.

Danger had arrived on the Gold Coast after being relocated in secret to escape two abusive relationships. One had been particularly bad – she had been in fear of her life on numerous occasions. 'I moved here because I thought it was very glamorous. When I was a little girl in Port Macquarie, the men would always say, "I'm going to the Gold

Coast; that's where the girls wear their shorts up their arse." I always wondered what this place was with the half-undressed women!' She laughed. 'So I had my boobs done and I've been stripping for eight years now.'

I asked Benny if he felt like a Gold Coast person.

'Oh, yeah, the day I came here I felt at home. And I've been here nineteen years now.' He paused. 'My parents moved around a lot, and because the Gold Coast is still growing you feel like you're growing with it. Sydney's a jungle. You can't beat the lifestyle here.'

After some more discussion about Benny's business plans – the CD-ROM, the boat cruise with a twenty-five girl show every half hour – he invited me to a nightclub party at which Danger was performing. The theme was bondage. I said I would love to come and it was arranged for me to phone someone called Francois who was organising the event. I thanked Benny and, as we walked outside, wished him luck in his business endeavours. Judging by the scale of his ambition, I could see that he would need it.

'Thanks, mate,' he said. 'Up here we've all got something we can get off one another. That's the story on the Gold Coast.'

For my first bondage party I decided I should look the part so I visited a fancy dress shop in Southport. It looked promising – in its window an advertisement proudly stated that it had supplied the costumes for *Big Brother*. A police uniform seemed suitable, I thought. I tried on the costume but the result was a distinct disappointment: the hat was white, the pants too short and the badge made of plastic. I looked like a sleazy ice-cream man. I decided to instead visit a sex shop I had seen on the highway in Miami. There I purchased a leather mask pointed at both ends, of the type worn by Eartha Kitt in her role as

Cat Woman, and, at a skateboard shop in town, a spiky leather belt and matching wristband. In my Guns N' Roses T-shirt and my studded accessories – the strap of my mask hanging in a rakish curl from the back of my tight jeans – I looked like a *Revolver*-era Lou Reed and felt tough and cool, part of something illicit and exclusive, as I walked through the heaving streets of Surfers Paradise.

The party was to be held at a strip club some blocks south of central Surfers – a grim neighbourhood reeking palpably of economic ruin. Along the highway stood a number of abandoned arcades: advertisements in their windows exhorting the benefits of Alpine holidays and cough medicine had turned blue from age. Shops once owned by Japanese, Korean and Chinese interests had been left to rot in the wake of the early nineties real estate collapse, their oriental glyphs slipping off at odd angles to reveal the yellowing stains of calcified glue. I found the club and announced to the woman at the entrance that I ought to be on the door list. She examined her sheet but could find no evidence to support my claim – evidently Francois had forgotten to add my name. I pleaded with her, but I needn't have bothered. She said she didn't care.

Climbing through a darkened stairwell I entered the nightclub and a curious scene immediately confronted me. At the base of the bar, dressed only in a pair of black briefs, a fat man lay grinning in anaesthetised ecstasy as two giggling women in short black dresses and perilous high heels tiptoed delicately across his torso, pressing their stilettos to his throat, chest and genitals. All the while they balanced in their right hands delicate martini glasses sprouting a plumage of paper umbrellas in emerald and vermilion. The girls laughed and took sips from their drinks, balancing with their free hand on the bar.

I looked around the room. The party was sparsely attended: little more than twenty people. The explanation was later proffered that the venue had changed at the eleventh hour and it had been too late to inform most attendees. I spied Benny and Danger. 'G'day, mate,' said Benny, and his big, crazy eyes spread wide. I sat down with them and Benny offered immediately to buy me a drink.

Danger turned to me and smiled hazily. 'How are you, darling?' She had the reassuringly maternal quality of a nurse or kindergarten teacher, a quality perfected no doubt over years of stripping. Nevertheless I enjoyed her company. Walking around the room were several women built like warders in a Russian women's prison, wearing knee- or thigh-high black boots and matching corsets of shiny vinyl or patent leather. A couple of them wore no tops at all, preferring instead to expose sagging, pointed breasts, glittering at their tips with various clanking baubles. Every hand gripped a soft, tasselled whip or riding crop. A few men wearing complementing vests and backless leather cowboy chaps sipped beer and strode through the empty room, trying to look busy. In a corner stood the woman who had served me at the sex shop: a monstrous female body builder with a shock of bright yellow hair, five feet tall and built like a cattle tick.

I began to chat with Danger. She was angry. Francois had assured her that a great deal more people had been due to arrive. For a professional stripper to perform in front of such a sparse crowd was a humiliation. Benny returned with the drinks. I asked him about organised crime on the Gold Coast. Benny said that times had changed. 'Bashings, stabbings and shootings are rarer these days,' he told me. 'People have become more professional – smarter. They've realised that that shit is counterproductive. Now the guy you have to worry about is the one who invites you to dinner.'

I looked up. The fat man, retired from his prone position at the bar, was walking about the room in his underpants, sipping a beer and exchanging pleasantries with the other party goers, red welts like scatter-shot speckled across his frame. On stage, one of the fat women had been handcuffed to a pole and was having her grotesquely outsized bottom gently flogged with a riding crop by a blond, rodent-like man. Soon he began hitting her harder, the flesh of her wobbling buttocks emphasised by the flickering of the silver strobe light, tracking the quaking of her rump and the fractured pitching of the man's arm to give the scene the appearance of an archaic pornographic movie. I think it was supposed to be terribly perverse, but by the time he began tying her to the pole in cling film I got a rather conspicuous case of the giggles: she looked like a great squidgy ball of scone dough or a leftover chicken sausage at the bottom of the fridge.

Leonard arrived. He was wearing a pair of well-ironed beige slacks and a white polo shirt; although dressed like an accountant going for an afternoon of golf, he still managed to look creepier than anyone else in the room. He began to take photographs of the girl cling-filmed to the pole. As he did so she cast an occasional glance over her shoulder – whether out of fear or anticipation I could not tell.

Thus far the party was proving a distinct let-down. I had come to be outraged, amused or, at the very least, made to feel naughty, but so far I felt about as bad as a teenager artfully concealing a stash of pornographic playing cards between the pages of a maths textbook. Perhaps it would get better when more people arrived. *If* more people arrived.

I began to chat with Danger again. She told me more about the abusive relationships she had left before finding a new life on the Gold Coast. She said her boyfriend had tried to hunt her down; that he had once smothered her with a pillow and then smashed all the bones in her face. 'He ripped my bottom lip off,' she said. 'My face is a different shape now than what it was.'

I looked closely. She was pretty – prettier than most strippers – but now I could detect a certain lopsidedness in her features. When I looked closer still, I could see the scars under her thick make-up.

Benny looked up at the fat girl in cling film. 'Imagine treating your woman like that,' he said disgustedly, before turning to me and asking whether I would like to come to a dinner. He explained it was a pre-production party for a porn film that was to be shot on the Gold Coast and that it would be a good opportunity for me to meet other people in the industry. I immediately accepted and we arranged a time for me to call him the next week. I went for a walk around the room before sitting down next to one of the chubby madams. 'She is so insecure about her body,' she said, pointing to the cling-filmed woman. This I thought probably took the cake for 'least difficult mental health diagnosis' for the evening.

I asked her what she did for a living. She said she was a bondage mistress by night and a social worker and psychologist at a mental institution by day. I adopted a tone of chummy irony. 'Are a lot of the people here in mental health care?'

'Yes, it's very common,' she replied, stony-faced. She pointed around the room. 'She's a nurse; she's another psych; and she's a case worker at a women's shelter.' As she spoke, one of the leather men (introduced to the crowd previously as 'the Colonel') walked past our table. He had a mobile phone clipped to the back of his buttock-less leather chaps and at the sight of this I began to laugh – he looked like an especially flamboyant electrician. 'What's so funny?' asked the mistress.

I explained, but she just looked at me confusedly. 'But everyone needs a mobile phone these days.'

To have a sense of irony *and* be a part of the sadomasochistic underground might have been hoping for too much. The po-faced earnestness of this event was the only funny thing about it. The fact that everyone was trussed up like a yard full of black vinyl turkeys seemed to have passed everyone by.

After my open mockery of the Colonel, talk between the mistress and myself grew sparse. Sitting to my left was a guy about my age. He had been there for some time, immobile, nursing a drink. I felt that by not speaking to him a certain social awkwardness had grown between us. I was on the verge of making an effort to converse when he looked at me, nodded mechanically and said hello. I returned his greeting and he offered me a smile, barren and brief.

'Why are you here?' I asked in my most jovial we're-all-in-this-together tone.

'I decided to drive here from Brisbane.'

'Why?'

'Because I had nothing better to do.'

His face registered no expression. He was not dressed for the occasion, wearing only jeans and a faded Brisbane Broncos T-shirt. He turned from me to stare at a performer on stage, electricity coursing through her body to excite a delicate cluster of plasma filigree in pink and violet, like a spinning electrical tumbleweed, sprouting from the centre of a glass sphere.

'I haven't slept in four days,' he added, unprompted.

As a one-time chronic insomniac I sympathised. 'Why haven't you been sleeping? Do you take speed?'

'No.'

'Are you depressed?'

'Yes.'

Before I could ask why the woman with the electricity had interrupted our conversation. She was calling for silence. With darkened lights and a pounding techno soundtrack, Danger burst onto the stage brandishing a whip and dressed in a leather corset and thigh-high stiletto leather boots with towering platform soles. She removed her corset and began to do handstands, spreading her legs into a fork. Leonard took photographs. I turned to Benny and asked if he would disapprove of Danger doing XXX shows; it was a topic we had spoken of earlier. He said he would, before adding: 'But this is nothing, mate; this is just like going to the beach.' At this point Danger sprayed her nipples with what appeared to be some sort of foam before lighting the substance with a candle. The tongues of flame slid across her body but she controlled their motion with a surprisingly dexterous manipulation of her breasts. After the flame died she repeated the trick on her winking labia, bending backwards to land on her hands and allow for a better view. Leonard flew into a frenzy of flash photography.

The foam between her legs having run its natural course, Danger stood up and dragged the insomniac on stage before chaining him to a pole and exposing his buttocks to the crowd. She looked out at the audience with a theatrical leer and spanked him with a riding crop. The insomniac, bent over on all fours, simply stared into the distance. Across the room the fat woman and her rodent man were now sitting at a table drinking from the same cocktail glass through two straws, like they were on the set of a *Happy Days* bondage special. I got the giggles again and the mistress shot me a censorious look.

After a bit more humiliation, Benny freed the insomniac with the handcuff keys and the boy returned to my table, his expression unchanged.

For a finale Danger dripped wax on her naked body and then, placing the candle in the middle of stage, stood above the tongue of flame before dropping into the splits to extinguish it with her vagina. Rising from her position to a smattering of applause, she walked to the back of the stage and disappeared with a wave behind the curtain. It was the most impressive strip routine I had ever seen, but nothing, not even the exhortations of the electrical woman, could induce me to stay longer. I looked around at the shining black bundles sitting about the room, sipping on drinks or staring glumly into space. I had come for *Weimar Berlin* and found instead the monthly meeting of a student union medieval recreationist society. So I felt a mixture of relief, curiosity and apprehension when I heard the insomniac beside me turn and say, 'Wanna get out of here?'

'Where do you want to go?' I asked.

'Anywhere.'

I looked around again. It couldn't be worse than this. It seemed there was little to lose.

The insomniac and I made for the door. I turned to wave goodbye to Benny and Danger. The girls were walking on the fat man again. He grinned and leant in to suck a stiletto heel.

The insomniac's car was parked behind the club. He opened the doors and together we got in, sitting side by side in silence. 'Um, what do you want to do?' I asked. He leant forward and fiddled with the car keys before releasing them with a soft tinkle to sit hard back against the seat. 'We could go for a drink,' I said, growing increasingly apprehensive about the wisdom of my decision. 'Or just go for a drive?'

'Yeah, okay,' he said, starting the car. We reversed out and headed north along the highway.

For a time we drove in silence until he put a tape in the stereo. It was *In Utero* by Nirvana. The song was 'Heart Shaped Box'. We had already passed through central Surfers and were now driving aimlessly to the north. Soon we would be in Southport. Kurt Cobain was now singing 'Rape Me': 'Rape me, do it and do it again; Come on and hate me, hate me my friend.'

One of the biggest sources of distress in my life has been a tendency to impulsiveness, and my decision to get in a car with a drunken man who had not slept in four days and whom I had met at an S&M party only twenty minutes earlier was starting to feel like one of my more ill-considered. I was keen to end this, now. 'I want to see Palazzo Versace,' I said. 'Do they have a bar there?'

'Yeah, okay,' he said, and turned the car towards Main Beach. I faltered before my next question. 'So, why are you depressed?'

He gave a little groan, more like an exhalation. 'Oh, I dunno . . . my dad, I have problems with my dad.' His voice still showed no real traces of emotion.

'Why?'

'My mum . . . has a lot of problems.'

I didn't see how this second statement connected to the first but I stayed quiet.

'I dunno . . . my dad . . . he's an abuser,' he said suddenly.

'Oh . . . well, that's awful. Have you spoken to someone about it?'

He ignored my question.

'Like, when I was a kid, I had a silkworm in a box – I fed it mulberry leaves from a tree that grew in the street. You know how you can do that?' He turned to me and kept driving. 'And then one day my dad just picks it up and fuckin' stamps on it. It had just begun to make a bit of a cocoon, too – you know the ones. Like, why the fuck did he do that?' He turned back to the road and gave the steering wheel a light blow. He was yelling now. 'I said, "Why the fuck did you do that?" And he couldn't fuckin' say why. Just 'cause he fuckin' could. I mean, what's the fuckin' difference: kill the silkworm or kill you? What's the fuckin' difference?' He turned to me and I shrank in my seat. 'I mean, what's the fuckin' difference . . .' He trailed off and together we sat in silence, Nirvana playing in the dark, my silent prayers for a speedy and preferably bloodless ending to this journey played on a loop inside my head.

In Main Beach we drove past a park and a Spanish Mission bathing pavilion from the 1930s – one of the only buildings on the Gold Coast older than forty years – then past the Sheraton Mirage, the most glamorous hotel of the 1980s. It sat hulking in the dark, its circular driveway fortress-like and inhospitable, a floodlit waterfall cascading down its gilded front. It looked like the most expensive hotel in Hanoi; a gift to the Gold Coast from Christopher Skase. 'Say what you like about Skase,' Bianca had said to me at lunch, 'but he did wonders for this city.' A number of others had voiced similar sentiments. That the 'wonders' of which they spoke consisted of this hotel and an ugly mall across the street seemed an indictment of the lack of vision I saw so often on the Gold Coast.

Parking a little north of Palazzo Versace, we wandered south to the entrance. The night was cloaked in a heavy sea mist; it was hot and wet and made us short of breath. Together we stood out the front at the edge of the circular driveway and looked through the doors, the valet standing in silhouette against the colossal yellow pillars in the foyer. Over the door hung a Medusa's head, the emblem of the Versace label; coloured lights trickled their way around the image in shifting rainbow rivulets like radioactive dye in the veins of a hospital patient. For some time I stood and watched the display, entranced.

'I'm going to walk down to the water,' I said finally. The insomniac nodded. I hesitated. 'Would you like to come?' He shook his head and I was greatly relieved.

I walked towards the water to a spot where the hotel connected to a shopping mall and looked out to the Broadwater, the mouth of the Nerang River. Because of the drought the river was extremely low, the sea flowing further and further upstream, bringing with it hundreds of highly aggressive bull whaler sharks that had begun to breed in the sheltered mansion-lined canals. Fishermen had been pulling the creatures out by the dozen, and some were very large. To my right the Palazzo glowed gold in the night and I remembered Miles Buisson and how the ground on which it now stood had been the last place he had been seen alive.

I turned and walked back to the front of the hotel, looking for the insomniac. He had disappeared. Through the haze, the Medusa's snake-wreathed head was growing agitated, flashing dozens of colours in a fan about its features like the threat of some angry desert lizard. I walked back up the footpath to where we had left the car; it was gone. Looking up and down the misted street I considered my options: I could walk home (which was quite a distance), I could call a cab, or I could go for a walk somewhere else. With little else to do, I settled on the third option.

I walked to the north, the occasional passing car the only noise to break the silence. The concrete footpath fell away to become sand and bush. I continued past dense trees and towards the lights of Sea World. I had no real idea where I was going but had formulated a vague plan to walk to a lighthouse that I knew to be at the end of The Spit.

Sea World seemed inordinately long as I passed it in the dark. At the end of its forbidding perimeter wall the road disappeared into black bush. For several hundred metres I walked towards it until I began to realise that this trek would be much further than I had anticipated, and all of it in absolute darkness through one of the last patches of wilderness on the coast. Conceding the ultimate futility of this excursion and my own terror in this isolated area, I turned back.

How weary I had grown of these fruitless meanderings. In other cities, when one went for a walk, one discovered interesting little byways, hidden sights and the irregular topographies that were the warp and weft in the fabric of a city. The Gold Coast, however, was as legible as a children's book; if it didn't look like an AV Jennings display village, then someone would soon make sure it did.

Arriving back at the entrance to Sea World I stopped at a roundabout to allow an approaching car to pass. Perhaps, I thought, I could hitch a lift to the lighthouse. But the car didn't pass me. Instead it swung around the roundabout and turned into a car park among the bush. I considered a number of possibilities but decided that this was most likely a late-night fishing spot – many of the cars that had passed me had rods hanging from the windows. I decided to follow.

In the distance through the thick grey gloom several cars moved slowly, their headlights floating through the mist in a glowing conference of deep-sea phosphorescence. The mist grew thicker as I walked and, worried that the drivers would not be able to see me, I moved to the very edge of the driveway and walked deeper into the car park. It seemed like a good night to get killed.

The parked cars were varied: Volvo sedans, sporty hatchbacks, beaten-up station wagons, sinister looking tradesmen's vans, an antique luxury saloon parked at an inconsiderate angle, even a plumbing van with a big plunger on the roof. I looked inside them as I passed. In one I made out the darkened shape of a seated man. I looked directly at him but he continued to stare rigidly through the windshield, like a crash-test dummy.

At the far end of the car park was a fenced-off hill, wild and ragged with native pines. In the distance I could hear the faint churning of the ocean. A sandy path led over the hill and disappeared into the mist. Two figures walked up the path in rapid succession, another came down and walked in my direction before stopping short and opening the door of his car. I made for the path.

Up the sandy hill the trees were thick on either side. The men ahead of me were disappearing through a broken wire fence and down an embankment into the trees. By this stage I had gathered that this was not a fishing spot; the silence of the men and the general air of wariness pointed to something covert and sinister. Steeling myself, I followed. The mist in the depression sat so heavily that it was impossible to see more than four or five metres in any direction. With great trepidation I ventured down the hill into a maze of paths. Among the trees and the mist men lingered alone on the corners of the paths, under the branches. Some nodded as I walked by, some strode past, ignoring me. The heat was noon-day in its intensity and my T-shirt stuck to me like cling film. My breath had the uncomfortable sensation of solidity.

I walked towards the ocean; a man stepped out from the mist, rubbing at the crotch of his jeans. I became afraid and doubled-back, finding an empty path and making my way through some low hanging branches to the dunes in the distance. In the dark, trees became men and men trees; bushes grew legs and walked. The silence was absolute. No one spoke. I decided that this adventure had gone on long enough. Walking back along the path and up the hill towards the fence, I came to a clearing where a group of men stood milling about in the fog. I looked closer. At the centre of the group one man was being knocked to and fro at both ends like an obscene push-me pull-you. I walked along the tree line, past the silent voyeurs. The man at the centre looked up, a baseball cap pulled low over his brow; under the shade of the brim his face was black and his mouth a black hole in the centre of that blackness. 'Fuck me. Fuck me,' he said, and reached up a hand as though he were drowning. I stumbled back up the path and disappeared under the fence.

In the relative security of the car park I sat down on one of the logs and caught my breath. The images of the night fought against one another in my mind, jammed like a switchboard of angry callers: the entrance to Sea World, the face of the Medusa, a fat woman in cling film, a squashed silk worm in a box . . . that black face, that imploring hand.

Beneath my fan dance of impenetrable irony lurks a core of deep superstition, a suspicion that the world is not altogether within my control. All my sharpest childhood memories seem to be of the dark: walking through the disused tiger cage at the zoo (it was cramped and airless and smelt of piss); an old anthropological film of frightened boys preparing to be circumcised that played inside the Papuan spirit house at the museum. I may not have come looking for the Heart of Darkness, but I had found it. There was no one to blame but myself – I had wanted to be shocked and where the vinyl turkeys had failed, suburban fathers in the sand dunes had succeeded. The likelihood of my becoming the emergency chat show guest seemed more and more improbable.

Remembering the fate of Miles Buisson, I decided this place was definitely haunted and, without any further deliberation, made my way back through the car park. As I walked towards the entrance I noticed on the opposite side of the road a small mobile home with bright multi-hued lights emanating from its interior. A steel rollerdoor was raised on one side to reveal a seated man in profile. He was watching television in apparent obliviousness to all the activity outside his door. Bizarrely, surrounding the television and the doorway of the caravan were dozens of coloured fairy lights flashing on and off in the dark, made huge and round by the surrounding vapour. It was then, with growing incredulity, that I realised the man, who was shirtless, was wearing bulging red pants, black gumboots and a red Santa hat (complete with white pom-pom) slanted at a rakish angle to one side of his head. Fascinated, I stared and wondered; then wonder turned to horror and I edged away from this macabre tableau to walk back briskly towards the road.

Suddenly out of the fog a tall figure appeared. I tried to avoid him but he veered towards me with a pigeon-toed gate and asked me the time. I told him it was after midnight. He stopped beside me and I looked closer. He was young, with chubby baby cheeks and honey-coloured hair: no more than twenty but at least six-foot five. His nervousness was palpable as he drew on his cigarette. I introduced myself and shook his hand. 'Are you here for schoolies?' I asked. He was, and he was heading back to his hotel in Main Beach where he was staying with friends. I invited him to talk as we headed towards the highway.

'No, wait,' he said. 'We can walk along the beach.'

Turning back we made our way along another path through the trees and came out onto the dunes. The fog was starting to lift. We began to walk in the direction of Surfers, along the ocean.

His name was David and he was from a small town in rural South Australia. He had driven to schoolies with a carload of friends. He said he had stumbled across this place on an evening walk.

I asked whether his friends knew that he was gay.

'No.'

'None of them?'

'Well, my ex-girlfriend does. She walked in on me while I was with a boy.' He giggled a little.

'Do you think you could tell them?'

'No, they wouldn't like it.'

'Perhaps they wouldn't mind as much as you think.' We were quiet for a bit. 'Have you had a boyfriend?'

'No, not really . . . I'm not very good looking.'

At first I thought he was being disingenuous, fishing for compliments. But then I remembered what it was like to be a teenager and to hate yourself: the forgotten days of staring into the mirror and seeing only a hideous creature too gormless and repulsive to ever be of interest to anyone, your every movement neutered by a self-consciousness so crippling that there were many mornings when you woke up wondering whether you might not be better off dead. Perhaps I was drawn to him because he reminded me a little of myself at the same age. 'That's ridiculous,' I said, before adding, quite sincerely, 'you're a very handsome boy and you're only eighteen. I don't think you'll have any problems.'

'You think so?'

I reassured him to the best of my abilities.

By now we had walked a distance away from the car park, and were just north of the Marina Mirage hotel. I suggested we sit down. For some time side by side in a dune we lay, staring at the skyscrapers running along the beach in the distance – a golden curtain hanging from a ruddy sky. It was the first time since my arrival that the Gold Coast had looked beautiful.

'I did sort of have a boyfriend once,' he said. 'But he began to stalk me.'

The story was a ghastly tale of teenage humiliation and small-town politics. With few opportunities to meet other gay men in his community David had turned to the Internet – the new forum for the isolated and lonely – where he had met a man from a neighbouring town. David had been seventeen at the time and the man twenty-two. He was the first man to show sexual interest in David and even though he had not been terribly good-looking (David was flattered enough by the attention to ignore the lack of physical attraction), they slept together on a couple of occasions, after which he told David he loved him. There followed a short period of furtive bliss. Then one day the police turned up at David's front door; they were investigating a sexual assault on a thirteen-year-old boy, and wanted to know whether David could tell them anything about it. Next, the boyfriend began to visit David's home, threatening to tell David's parents about his proclivities unless he offered him a false alibi. David managed to avoid the forced collusion and being outed but only after the boyfriend had been convicted of the assault. David was lonely, heartbroken and guilt-ridden, unable, he felt, to talk to either friends or family. It was his first suicide attempt.

David placed the back of his huge hand in my palm. I felt the weight of it and ran my thumb across the scars that traced a frantic scrawl through the flesh of his wrist. The other wrist matched. The scars were multitudinous, but they were not deep. Not deep enough to kill. 'Did you do it for attention or because you wanted to die?'

He shook his head. 'No, I wanted to die.'

I let go of his hand. 'So, how has schoolies been so far?'

'S'okay,' he shrugged. David had a universal teenage aversion to showing any kind of enthusiasm.

'Do you like the Gold Coast?'

His face brightened. 'It's the best place I've ever been.'

I asked if he had ever travelled. He said he hadn't but that he wanted to go to Estonia. I said that it seemed an unusual ambition.

'My mother is from there,' he explained.

I looked at him again; with his big sloping shoulders, his outsized limbs and blond hair I could see now that he might have been one of those Baltic giants who had sacked Rome.

'What do you want to do now that you've finished school?'

'I dunno.'

I pressed him further but David had few hopes for the future. He enjoyed computers but had given no thought to the possibility of making a career of his hobby. When I suggested that he study computer programming he said he had no ambitions for higher learning. It was his sense of having no control over his own destiny that disturbed me most.

We had been some hours on the beach and it was now almost three o'clock. I proposed we should head home. We wandered down to the damp sand nearer the water where it was easier to walk and headed past the hotel floodlights until we arrived at a clearing on the beachfront. David's hotel lay just beyond trees. We stood in silence, David staring at me, his brown eyes imploring. I pulled out my pen. 'Here's my number,' I said. David proffered his hand and I wrote it across the back.

'If you feel like talking or want to go for a beer or something, give me a ring.'

He looked at the number, then back at me, nodding and smiling shyly before turning to walk up the beach to the park. Down by the lapping waves the mist had lifted and so I walked along the sand towards home, to the golden curtain in the distance, leaving the darkness and the anguish behind me.

Fourteen

★

Clan of the Cave Bear

EARLY THE NEXT MORNING, Jeremy's heavy form crashed down on my bed and I awoke with a start. 'Brendan!' he whispered sharply, shaking my shoulder.

Jarred awake, memories of the previous night came flooding back. 'What?'

'Are you all right, mate?'

The sun shone brightly in the room. I was entirely conscious, but he continued to shake me back and forth as effortlessly as if I had been stuffed with foam rubber. In the last few weeks I had grown rather accustomed to these invasions of my person.

Jeremy was the loudest, the most frenetic and, in some respects, the most obnoxious individual I had ever met. I had, however, grown inordinately fond of both him and his girlfriend Lenore over the last few weeks. Jeremy was from Christchurch (although he would often pretend he was from Auckland, 'Because it's bugger') and Lenore was from Rotorua. Lenore was quiet and hardy and although her devotion to her boyfriend bordered on masochism, she was not above openly mocking him. The beach and the promise of work had lured them to the Gold Coast, but things were proving tougher than they expected; unless they could find employment immediately they would have to make their savings last until Lenore started her position with the coaching clinic. It had never occurred to them that jobs might be scarce on the Gold Coast.

Physically, Jeremy was a giant. In height he was comparable to myself but the proportions of his body were less classical than mythic. So shattering was his laugh that the neighbours once complained; so frequent and impolitic were his pronouncements on everything from pedophilia to immigration that he was guaranteed to offend any casual visitor to our apartment. Like Bamm-Bamm from *The Flinstones*, Jeremy was a monstrous child, the id incarnate, equipped with the kind of physique that allowed him to do damn near anything and get away with it. He was a qualified greenkeeper, but without employment he had only two major activities: going to the gym and bounding around the living room with his shirt off like an Irish wolfhound who has just devoured a bottle of ritalin. He said a doctor had once diagnosed him as manic-depressive but when I asked whether he often felt depressed he said he could not remember a single incident. The more accurate diagnosis, I thought, was closer to manic-manic.

Jeremy vacillated between two extremes: everything in his world was either 'the greatest' thing he had ever experienced or 'the gayest' (as in, '*Conan* was the greatest movie ever made', or, 'This milkshake is gay', or, 'Australia is the gayest country in the world'). He had a number of alternating obsessions: body building, food, the life of Arnold Schwarzenegger, martial arts (specifically nunchakus), anal pornography and chairs, the ergonomics of which he could discuss for hours and at great volume. As a professional greenkeeper, he also had a mania for grass and would explain at great length and with tender relish the different species that could be grown on lawns or golf courses throughout the world. When I told him I thought golf courses were a crime against man and the environment, he was genuinely hurt.

Compared to many people I am slight and frail, but compared to Jeremy I was a helpless foundling shivering on a hillside. When he discovered that I am exceptionally ticklish, for instance, he would regularly chase me around the room, tackle me to the ground and drill my ribs until my legs thrashed and I was forced to beg for mercy. Some of his gestures of affection, however, were more ambiguous. Frequently he would steal into my room and simply sit on my bed, watching me as I wrote notes or read a book, chatting occasionally but, for the most part, merely looking, as though I was a sleeping panda. Even more suggestively, he would sit beside me as I lay in bed and pat my hair or caress my bare feet with his fingertips before looking up to smile shyly and dance out of the room.

Odd as this behaviour seemed I did not think it was homosexual in nature (although I had not discounted the possibility) but rather a primitive form of communication. Living with Jeremy was like being a biologist in a community of mountain gorillas. To him I was a strange and foreign creature; he did not understand me – my clothes, my hair, the books I read, the food I ate – and thus, like the Amazon explorer who must stroke the palm of the curious Indian, it was the only way he knew to make his good intentions clear. Perhaps perversely, I found these odd little gestures comforting within the context of the increasingly apprehensive atmosphere of the apartment. What's more, Jeremy was an easy match for Kane and I felt certain that he would stand by me if push ever came to shove because, at heart, Jeremy was a creature without malice.

I rubbed my eyes and demanded he stop shaking me. 'I'm fine . . . what's the matter?'

'The cops came round to the house last night looking for Kane and when I didn't hear you come home I thought it was because he'd done something to you.'

'What were they after?'

'Shh, Kane's still here.'

With a single motion he sprang off my bed and, like a ballet dancer retiring after the final encore, fled through the curtains and onto the balcony. I rolled out of bed and began to dress. In the last ten days, Kane's presence in the house had become alarmingly ubiquitous and my attitude to his presence alarmingly resigned. Living with Kane was like waking up in the morning to discover that a very large and hungry polar bear had taken up residence in your bedroom; it was okay so long as you fed it a few fish and didn't make any sudden movements, but secretly you knew that one day you would run out of fish and the savage retribution of nature's justice would strike you down.

The first item of Kane's I recall appearing in our apartment was a portable black stereo. Krystal, who would use it to listen to soppy R&B love ballads (her life was rich in the textures of Jennifer Lopez's marital woes and the poignant romantic yearnings of Mariah Carey), told me she was 'borrowing it from a friend'. That was two days after we had signed the new lease with Jeremy and Lenore. The next day a boxing belt with Kane's name engraved on the metal buckle lay draped beside it on the desk in the living room. The night after, Kane came over with his son Hemi and began, not even surreptitiously, to move his things in. By the end of the evening the apartment lay strewn in detritus. There were garbage bags full of clothes, hip-hop CDs in broken cases, a television, a video of the film *Spiderman*, a tool box, a pair of dirty work boots . . .

And there were strange things too, bits of junk a bag lady might have kept and loved: a broken 1970s electric typewriter, bright orange and still in its original plastic briefcase; a tea towel with 'Adelaide' printed on it; a shopping trolley full of cracked electrical appliances; old mismatched shoes. The woman's sunhat doubling as a lampshade had been left by Kane after his last stay in the unit.

Krystal, who had become Hine or Hinemoa since Kane moved in, was keen to point out that this was to be a temporary arrangement; Kane was merely using the apartment as a stopgap between finding new accommodation. In some ways I wanted to believe her, if only because I still wanted to like her.

I walked into the kitchen. Kane was stomping about, eating his breakfast sloppily and watching an infomercial at a deafening volume. My days of hiding in the closet seemed very long ago. On the couch where he had slept sat a man I had dubbed the Gimp. The Gimp's real name might have been Bernie or Barney or Bogan – I knew it began with a 'B' – but I couldn't be sure because he had never bothered to introduce himself during the ten days he had been sleeping in my living room. In fact, the Gimp never said anything – just sat and stared at the TV, breaking his monkish silence only to issue a deep, simian laugh in response to one of Kane's numerous witticisms. Occasionally, without explanation, he would turn and look at me from across the room and then turn back to the television with the same blank expression; an expression that seemed to suggest he was seeing something beyond both the television and myself.

'G'day, mate!' said Kane as I entered the room.

'Good morning, Kane.' I threw him a fish.

Kane busied himself, eating my cereal and screaming insults at the television. Jeremy sat down beside him and began to make conversation. Oddly, Jeremy got along well with Kane; mostly, I suspect, because Kane was a little intimidated by him. 'So, have you found a place yet, bro?' he asked. Kane shook his head and said, 'But put it this way: my real estate agent's really happy that I've moved out of my place in Miami.'

Jeremy and I looked at one another. A glowing endorsement for an exercise machine filled the silence. Suddenly Kane said something almost inaudible, something that sounded like: 'Yeah, I know, I know.'

'What was that, bro?' asked Jeremy cheerfully.

'Oh, I was just sayin' that we should go play squash some time soon, bro. You know,' he added with more than a touch of hauteur, 'I was a national champion. But I had to retire after a ball hit me in the eye and almost blinded me.'

'Geez, that's no good, bro!' Jeremy replied. I just sat and watched the pair. Jeremy hadn't seen what I had – Kane had been talking to an empty chair.

With that Kane put down his cereal bowl and stood up, clamping his straw hat onto his head and pulling the cord tight into his chin. He looked like Vincent Van Gogh with steroid rage. A few moments later he marched out the door to work.

I sidled up to Hinemoa who had been fixing Drakkar his breakfast. 'So, has Kane found an apartment of his own yet?' I asked.

She shook her head.

'What's he doing then?'

She shrugged and stared angrily down the corridor, an anger that might have been directed at either my questions or at Kane. 'He's got no idea *what* he's doing.'

Fifteen

★

Porn to Run

THE DINNER WAS a chance for the cast and crew of the porno to get to know each other. Seeing as a number of them would be inside one another in two days' time, it seemed only polite. After the disaster of the bondage evening I was keen to be entertained by the porno crowd. At least, I reckoned, they couldn't be any more boring than the bondage geeks.

Benny picked me up wearing a red Mambo Hawaiian shirt, split low at the chest, the collar rising up to his neck to terminate in two big red fans to frame his glinting reliquary of clanking golden charms. He was again very friendly and instructed the three girls in the back to squish up in case I wanted to push my seat back (Benny always referred to his strippers as girls, unless he was talking about 'his' woman). I turned to say hello. Danger I recognised while the other two were introduced as Summer and Roxy. All three were wearing vacuum-packed vinyl dresses in assorted colours with lacing at the sides to expose great hoops of tanned flesh. Their necks and hands were studded and draped in reams of gold while, at the tips of their fingers, like the graceful fins of swaying tropical fish, fake fingernails extended into deadly varnished prongs of Barbie pink. On their tiny feet they wore massive platform shoes of varying height: some in clear plastic like little fish tanks, others in white vinyl, giving them the appearance of having a jet ski on either foot. Their hair was equally extravagant. Summer had blonde extensions like nylon carpet that had begun to fray at her waist while Roxy had a bob so white it was almost silver – as precise and as unreal as porcelain.

'Are you girls doing a show later?' I asked.

They looked at me, puzzled. 'No, just going to dinner.'

Actually, I had started to wonder why Roxy and Summer were coming at all. Benny intuited my suspicions. 'The producers would like to meet some other girls, you know. Who might be interested . . .'

Interested in what he did not say.

We drove south. The girls were in a good mood, chatting and laughing, and as the car drove over bumps their gold jewellery tapped audibly against the plastic of their dresses. Summer began to bemoan the state of her skin, an epidermis mottled by the unmistakable patina of the Gold Coast. 'I look thirty-five, not twenty-five,' she griped.

'Nooooo,' said the other two on cue. 'You look beautiful. *I* look old.'

As we drove through Mermaid Benny received a phone call. He grumbled and cursed before hanging up. The fourth girl we were supposed to be taking to dinner, Tanya, had been involved in a domestic fracas of some sort and would be unable to make it but asked if we could meet her nonetheless.

We drove into Burleigh and circled the dim, deserted streets in search of Tanya. Soon we saw her standing by a lamppost with her mother. The girl was very tall, wearing tiny denim hotpants laced up at the front and a soft white blouse that blew open in the evening breeze to reveal the tops of her breasts. Her mother wore a tight, brown 1970s T-shirt that read 'Iditarod Alaska: where men are men, and kayakers are king!' Both had obviously left the house in a hurry as neither was wearing shoes.

'What happened?' asked Danger.

'The fuckin' bastard was beating up mum so I got in the middle and got myself this.' She leant down towards the window and drew her hand across a curtain of blonde fringe – one side of her head stuck out several centimetres from her face like an actor in theatrical putty; it seemed to swell before my eyes. She stood back from the car; her movements were frantic and disjointed. She was clearly distressed. From the girls in the back there was much commiseration but, when Tanya and her mum asked for a lift to a hotel, Benny said we didn't have time.

Benny seemed to gauge some of my silent disapproval at having left the women on the street. As we drove he turned to me, bewildered, to explain that looking after the private lives of his strippers was a full-time job in itself. Only the week before, another of his girls, after a series of distressed phone calls to Summer, had killed herself in her apartment. Were people in the sex industry, I wondered, any more fucked-up than the rest of the world? Or was the rest of the world just better at hiding it? One thing was certain: although everyone here seemed very keen to emphasise the normality and the stability of their lifestyle, their actions rarely seemed commensurate with their rhetoric.

The dinner was to be held in an isolated restaurant just off the highway at the base of a mountain in Burleigh Heads. To reach the front door we were forced to climb a steep flight of wooden stairs, lending the building a distinctly Transylvanian air. Oddly, the entire structure seemed to be lit in green neon. Inside, the dining room was empty. After a bit of standing around we were accosted by one of the staff and ushered up a tall spiral staircase leading to a circular bar that overlooked the highway. Standing around the bar a group of fifteen or so was mingling, the green neon turning the shadows on their faces red, giving them the appearance of figures in a nightclub scene by Toulouse-Lautrec. Benny introduced me to Bill, the producer. Bill was in his late forties with intense blue eyes. He too was wearing gold chains and a Hawaiian shirt, this one in blue.

'Please to meet ya, mate.' Bill was effusive, but seemed a little unnerved by my presence. I got a drink and stood to one side, eavesdropping on Roxy, Summer and Danger as the latter pair discussed their breast implants: price, value, payment plans, scar tissue, rejection, the multiplicity of procedures. Never had I realised that such a world existed. Summer had just paid her implants off. 'I'm so happy now,' she said. 'After I made the final payment I thought, "Why didn't I just do this five years ago?"' Roxy nodded meaningfully. She was only twenty and had small breasts. The general consensus was that implants were needed, and desperately!

As we headed back down to the restaurant in a centrifugal procession of gold chains and purple vinyl, Benny pointed out for me the three women and two men who were to be the stars of the show. In a curious inversion of the laws of pornography the men in this production were better looking than the women. Twinkle was a stripper who had done porn before – she looked like the popular girl in high school who had been knocked-up at fifteen. The producers had apparently already reached an agreement with Roxy because she had consented to appear in the film. Fresh off the boat from Newcastle, Roxy was not beautiful but she had a certain attractiveness, most of which lay in the fact of her raw youth; a youth that, if Summer was any gauge, would soon turn to the proverbial autumn. The remaining female star appeared to be in her late thirties and, with a face that looked like it should be slaughtering cows in a rural abattoir, was, it can only be said, extraordinarily ugly. The men, however, were both tall and handsome: one looked like the character of the construction worker from the Village People, thickly built with rugged features and black hair; the other, unusually for pornography, was blessed with a flaming red thatch. What they had in looks, however, they lacked in personality, because both were scowling, uncommunicative bores who did little more than sit around looking nervous, squinting into their beers. Perhaps the knowledge that everyone in the room would soon be staring at their erections was enough to kill any normal conversation.

Taking our places at a single long table the affair began to take on a great sense of occasion. Seated between the chief cameraman (who had a full-time job with the ABC) and the abattoir worker, who didn't speak, I soon realised that the ritual fascination of pornography held a powerful psychological sway over all those involved. All around the table sat elderly hangers-on — Bill's producer and financier mates. These were tough, aggressive men who had made their fortunes in car detailing and construction; they owned mansions and ugly speed boats, cars with helicopter engines and season tickets to everything, and yet here they were, happy to fix coffee for a day or hold a boom microphone if only to be given the chance to look at three plain women and two men with bigger dicks than theirs have sex in highly contrived circumstances. I found it utterly incomprehensible. I turned to the cameraman and asked why he had wanted to be involved in porn.

'This was an industry I always felt destined to be in,' he replied.

Destined, no less.

I thought back to my interview with Leonard, to his explanation for his entry into the world of pornography, cloaked as it had been in talk of ambition and vocation, when it had, in reality, been nothing more than a humiliating necessity. My vague hope that these people would be less self-deceiving than the bondage turkeys was fading quickly.

As the typical Gold Coast cuisine continued to arrive in ever-increasing increments of ghastliness, the restaurant began to take on a distinctly sinister atmosphere. Huge and freezingly cold, I looked around the room and realised we were the only patrons. Sitting under the high ceiling at our big, long table in the strange green light with the blast of airconditioning making me wish I had brought a jumper, I began to wonder when the doors would lock, the waitresses turn to vampires, the food to crawling vermin and our bodies be consumed by ravenous porn queens of the undead. Just as I was struggling through a conversation with a man who repaired vintage cars, my phone rang. It was David. I went outside onto a green-lit balcony to speak.

'Can I see you?' he asked. He sounded distressed.

'Sure, but aren't you with your friends?'

'I've had a big fight with them. Can you come?'

With some small trepidation I agreed to meet him at a pub in Surfers in an hour or so. Back at the table Danger began telling some of her favourite stories, the best of which was the time she had whisked a stocking off the leg of another performer only to have the nylon become stuck between her teeth. 'It took two people to pull it out!' she exclaimed, and the crowd broke down with laughter. 'They all said that I should have made it a permanent part of the show.' Danger's sense of irony was a rare commodity among this bunch.

As dinner wore on it became increasingly apparent that it didn't take much to get Danger drunk and, after three glasses of wine, she began to slur her way into an argument with Benny. For some time they had been fighting over her desire to do XXX lesbian shows with

Summer. 'Noooo, but listen, right,' she reasoned, 'if I'm doing it to her then I'm the one in power.'

'That's right,' said Summer. 'If she's got the dildo then I'm the submissive one and she's the dominant one. She doesn't even have to take her clothes off.' Benny just shook his head and picked at his meal while Danger sat silent and sullen, slumped in her chair, sipping white wine and staring sadly into the distance.

Soon the party moved to the bar at the far end of the room. I pulled Bill aside and asked if it was all right for me to attend the filming. He said it was fine, on the condition that no real names were used because what he was doing was illegal. He gave me the address of where it was to take place and walked back to sit down. Twinkle straddled his lap and jumped up and down on his crotch. Bill laughed like a nerd. I decided to leave early.

I told Benny I was going.

'Hey, you want some money for a cab?' he asked.

I said I was fine and, against my better judgment, was genuinely touched by his offer.

I waited for my cab in night air that was hot and wet after the frigidity of the restaurant. The driver was silent as we drove north to Surfers. Just outside of Burleigh I spotted a hitchhiker: it was one of the oddities of the Gold Coast that you would see them sometimes dotted along the highway, reminding you that, in some respects, this was still a country town. I asked the driver to pull over and pick him up. After some argument he did so and the kid got in the back of the cab. We began to talk. He was sixteen and going to Surfers for the schoolies parties. After that, the conversation dried up and when we arrived in Surfers he got out of the cab and disappeared into the crowd without a word.

I struggled down Orchid Avenue, darting through the thronging crowd to arrive eventually at the bar where I had agreed to meet

David. I ordered a beer, sat down and waited. Soon I spotted a large mop of shaggy hair lumbering between the cavorting revellers. He sat beside me and grinned shyly. There was a long and awkward silence.

'What's the matter?' I asked.

'I had a fight with my friends.'

'What about?'

David explained that he had become inspired after our first meeting to tell his friends and travelling companions that he was gay. I groaned internally. Had I really precipitated this?

He said he done it that evening at the hotel but the problem had not been that they had cast him out or mocked him, but that they had simply not believed him. 'They thought I was joking,' he said mournfully, and I started to laugh. He looked at me glumly and said that in a fit of pique he had told them all to fuck off and that he was going to stay on the Gold Coast permanently. After the effect of my last piece of advice I was hesitant to voice my opinion once more, but I said that it would probably be in his best interests to reconcile with his friends.

Words were difficult to extract from David but it was soon apparent that he didn't really want to talk about his friends. He wanted to tell me about his life back home and how miserable he was and how he didn't want to return; how he wanted to stay on the Gold Coast forever.

David's life was like a gay version of a Bruce Springsteen song. His father was an alcoholic who had terrorised and beaten the family. His two older brothers had run away at the first opportunity to find jobs in remote parts of the country. A couple of months prior to David's trip to the Gold Coast his father left the family and moved to the outskirts of town. As far as David knew he was still there, alone, drinking himself to death, but he couldn't be sure because he hadn't spoken to him since, and had no intention of doing so. After his father left, his mother had a nervous breakdown. David described how he came home one day and found she had set the kitchen on fire. She said it had been an accident but he didn't believe her.

David was a child of the ritalin generation. During early high school he had been diagnosed with some sort of disorder and then prescribed the drug for a number of years. All the kids at school were on the stuff. They would trade their pills at lunchtime, crush them up and snort them off the desk before class. It had given them a taste for cheap amphetamines and the favourite weekend activity of most kids his age was to take crystal meth and then go drag-racing. But David didn't go drag-racing because he didn't have many friends; he had never been popular and the few friends he did have he saw as unthinking and callous and part of a larger conspiracy against him. David, I suspect, had a bit of a persecution complex, but nothing beyond what might be expected from an immature young man with a justifiable anger in the face of a world in which all expectations of happiness and the promises of stability and success had been seemingly denied him.

I thought back to my day at Aurora. By any reasonable standards of what constituted a 'lifestyle', David was a spectacular failure. I suppose he ought to have been renovating an apartment, shopping for antiques, checking out great new restaurants or wondering whether his superannuation was giving him the best return on his investment. But he wasn't. Instead he was about to return to his dead-end town and a familiar cycle of fear, shame and isolation. A 'lifestyle choice' for David was an oppressive misnomer: he was poor, he was young, he was gay and he had no say in any of it. He was not *Will and Grace*; he was not your charmingly flamboyant faggot friend who could help you pick out china patterns and impress your inner-city coffee klatch with his rapier wit and knowledge of movie trivia. He had big feet, sad eyes, poor conversation skills and, unlike the happy golfers in *Highlights,* was full of a tender human need: the desperate desire to be loved. And no lifestyle, not even one with pilates and burnt umber guttering, was ever any guarantee against loneliness.

Sixteen

★

Swing Party Down-under!

TWO DAYS LATER I awoke to the sounds of Kane and the Gimp laughing. They were listening to a CD of Guido Hatzis, a 'champion kick boxer' of indeterminate ethnic origin played by a radio comedian who specialised in prank phone calls of absurdly unreasonable requests accompanied by threats of violent retribution for noncompliance. It was very loud and Kane was laughing so frantically he sounded almost crazed. 'I wonder if they realise that Guido Hatzis is a parody of people like them?' I asked aloud.

'Listen to this bit!' Kane shrieked from the living room. 'It's the bit where he threatens to kick him in the fucking head!'

The night before I had attended a second bondage party. Benny had assured me that this one would be better and if by that he had meant there would be more people, then he was right. If, however, he had meant that it would have more atmosphere than, say, a Dungeons and Dragons convention at the Brisbane Airport Hilton, then he was wrong. But despite the general lack of entertainment or shock value, the night had been fruitful in other ways.

The party had been held in the basement of the Gold Coast Arts Centre, a cinema, theatre and gallery complex on the western side of the Nerang River and the city's only concession to 'high culture'. The fact that it was the venue for the party was no contradiction on the Gold Coast. I had arrived a little after nine and greeted Benny and Danger, the latter dancing atop a chair dressed as a schoolgirl. In the centre of the room the fat man was once more being trodden underfoot. I fetched myself a drink and sat down to take notes. Soon I was staring both horrified and fascinated at a man wearing nothing but a construction helmet, a pair of work boots and a tool belt that hung floppily over his dangling genitalia, glimpses of which could be viewed from behind as he strode through the crowd with a forceful purposelessness.

A voice announced itself in my ear. 'We've decided that no matter how sorry we feel for him, we're not going to talk to him.'

I looked up to see a very pretty thirty-something woman dressed in devil's horns, clutching a pitchfork in one hand and a can of rum and Coke in the other. 'We reckon that if you showed the smallest interest you'd never get rid of him,' she said as she sat down beside me. 'He's here on his own. Can you believe it?' She gesticulated her disgust with the pitchfork. 'I don't know if I should give him points for outrageousness or just feel sorry for him, which, frankly, is my instinct.' I laughed and she held out her hand, introducing herself as Rachelle. I introduced myself and explained my project. She grabbed me by the shoulder and waved the pitchfork behind me. 'Have you seen that tragic fat chick over there?' I turned; a rotund woman in black vinyl and a bobbed blonde wig was standing behind us. 'She said she would perform any fetish. Anything! I told her that my first fetish would be for her to lose thirty kilos immediately.'

I laughed with gratitude — a sense of humour was like crystal waters to my desert thirst.

'I am totally disappointed,' she continued. 'This is lame beyond belief. I was really hoping I'd get grossed out but so far the only thing that's offensive is the fact that people here actually paid seventy bucks to come.' I asked her what she did when not watching fat men get walked on in bars.

'I'm a koala handler at a wildlife park.'

Sure, why not? No one on the Gold Coast ever had a normal job. Everyone was an astrologer or a stripper or a New Age healer or got dressed up as Harry Potter and pranced about a movie set with an owl on their arm, grinning at tourists. No one was ever just an accountant, unless they were wanted for questioning by the National Crime Authority. 'Look at that couple,' she said, pointing to a pair of pre-retiree swingers jiggling by our table: she in a blue satin Playboy bunny outfit, he in a pair of clinging black underpants and bow tie. 'They look like a ballroom dancing couple from the local RSL who just took their clothes off.'

Together Rachelle and I sat and chatted until a stripper appeared on stage to do an old-fashioned burlesque routine, complete with saucy hip swings and glove peeling. 'She's a mate of ours,' explained Rachelle. 'She got us free tickets because she's doing her PhD in striptease at Griffith.'

The stripper was good. I hope she got a first.

Rachelle introduced me to her boyfriend Phil. He was skinny with an infectious hyper-caffeinated manner and a tendency to talk too close to your face. Together we sat and laughed at everyone else in the room and encouraged Rachelle to walk on the fat man. To our disappointment, she declined.

The next show consisted of a fat tranny with Bali braids being groped by three dweeby gay boys in nylon shirts and black satin pants. 'Erotic, erotic, put your hands all over my body,' sang Madonna in what I gather could only have been some sort of intentional irony. The show ended with one of the boys having his nipples tweaked as they all froze into dramatic human statues of the sort favoured by twelve-year-old girls at the finale of high school lunchtime choreography performances. Everyone clapped politely except Rachelle, who booed audibly over the crowd, some of whom began to give her distinctly unwelcoming looks.

By the time Rachelle and Phil finished their tinnies of rum and Coke all three of us decided we had had enough. The pair offered to give me a lift to Surfers, which I eagerly accepted. Before dropping me off they gave me their number and I promised to remain in touch.

I looked around my bedroom in the morning sunlight. Guido Hatzis was still playing in the living room: 'Maayyyyt, you better be prepared 'cause I am gonna come round and give you a karate chop to the shrote!' I was fairly confident that the filming of the porno would not be starting for a couple of hours yet and so it was to the sound of Kane's laughter and Guido's threats reverberating from the living room that I drifted once again into unconsciousness.

Several hours later I woke up in a panic with the realisation that I had overslept and was now running dangerously late. I hurried into my clothes and ran out into the living room to grab my bag. Sitting at the dining table was Hemi, staring out to sea.

'Hemi. What are you doing here? Where's your dad?'

'I dunno. I woke up and Mum and Dad were gone.' He was calling Hine Mum now.

'How long have they been gone?'

'I dunno. Three hours . . . I think.'

I sat down beside him – this wasn't the first time they had done this. 'Shouldn't you be at school?'

'Yeah, but I felt too tired today.' His tone changed. 'I wanna go to the beach.' He looked out to sea again.

'Hemi, I would take you but I have to go right now.'

'That's okay. I'm sure they'll be back soon,' he said brightly. 'You know,' he continued, unprompted, 'our old house was a hotel as well. I used to go and play with my friend Peter all the time. He had a Game Cube. Do you know what a Game Cube is? They're the best. I have a Sega but I only have one game – Skate Pro. It's pretty shit. On weekends the hotel had a barbeque and we used to go with all the guests . . . It was so great.'

For some minutes I sat with Hemi until, reluctantly, I made to leave. As I opened the front door Kane walked out of the lift. 'Hemi's waiting for you,' I said, perhaps a little too accusingly because, for a moment, I thought I saw some of my anger reflected in his eyes.

I arrived at the mansion in Broadbeach just in time for the filming of the Big Scene. Walking through a vast and wildly beautiful front garden of towering grey eucalypts and untended ferns I arrived at the front door where stood Benny and Trish, a hairdresser whom I had met at the dinner party and who lived in the house. They led me inside and I grabbed a beer out of the esky. If I tried to create a house in which to shoot a pornographic film I couldn't have done better than this one: a tri-storey sixties kitsch extravaganza of slate walls, wood-panelled ceilings, mock-marble floor tiles and zebra-patterned rugs. It looked like the kind of place the dad from the *Brady Bunch* might have brought marines to on the weekend. 'How does Trish afford to live in a house like this?' I whispered to Benny as I walked inside.

'Oh, she doesn't own it, mate.'

'Who does then?'

Benny's big eyes wandered. 'Oh, we know the guy who owns it,' he said.

'Who is he?'

'He's a good mate.'

Something in his tone told me it was in my best interests to stop asking questions.

I walked to the back of the vast living room. Beyond an acreage of glass opened a vista of tangled garden encroaching upon a leaf-dappled swimming pool beyond which, over an embankment, flowed a wide, sparkling canal. Against the glass doors sat a bar of orange leather surrounded by white vinyl couches, a fridge covered in tiger-striped purple shag-pile carpet, a freestanding white leather clock in the shape of Elvis Presley and a sad little plastic Christmas tree smattered with a few arbitrary dribbles of tinsel. 'So this is the set?' I asked Benny.

'Nah, mate, this is Trish's furniture. The set's upstairs.'

Climbing a floating staircase decked in shag-pile carpet (the shade of which might have been called Tequila Reflux on the Dulux colour chart), I entered the room where the Big Scene was about to be shot. At the far end of this gigantic space sat two tiger-print couches and a clutch of dissolute black-velvet beanbags sagging with the memory of their previous occupants. Immediately to my right was a massive television playing hardcore porn. The rear of the room was entirely glassed and more sliding doors led onto a huge deck overlooking the canal.

'Mate, we used to have the biggest parties here,' said Benny nostalgically. 'Three, four hundred people. Girls everywhere: girls doing shows, people snorting coke all over the place, people watching from boats on the canal. I tell you, mate, it was fuckin' wild.'

'When was this?'

'Ah, before I was busted, mate.'

The equipment surrounding the set was quite professional: one large camera ran on a track across the room flanked by two smaller hand-helds operated by a young guy in rugby shorts and an older

Smurf-like man with dark rings in his armpits. For such a small production the crew was multitudinous: cameramen, sound men, lighting men, hangers-on and talent. Looming over the bare patch of carpet were big black floodlights, fans for cooling the actors and dozens of cables running in thick, plaited vines of rainbow plastic up the lighting towers and across the floor to the editing suite. Bill stood behind the suite with the director (another crew member who worked for the ABC). He greeted me warmly and introduced me to the cast and crew, explaining that I might ask them questions.

In the middle of the lighting towers Construction Worker luxuriated naked in a beanbag while Abattoir Woman sucked his cock. This was the pre-show warm-up (known as 'fluffing' in the industry). Red and Twinkle soon joined the pair – Twinkle embarking upon the Herculean task of transforming Red's flaccid member into an effective instrument of intercourse. For some time we sat and waited, our eyes fixed nervously on Red's penis. The task was beginning to seem impossible (Twinkle had been persevering valiantly in the bathroom for the previous half hour) and soon the director was calling for quiet regardless of Red's erectile capacity, or lack thereof. I disappeared behind the control suite and waved a silent hello to Danger who smiled and waved in return.

And so the action began. The girls swapped partners and began to perform oral sex on the two men, both of whom remained resolutely flaccid. After several minutes a palpable tension spread across the set. The director stared worriedly at the screens like an anxious scientist watching a troubled space mission. It seemed to be some time before Construction managed to get it up sufficiently for some penetration. Grunting his way into Twinkle it wasn't long before the director called 'Cut', by which time Construction seemed keen to finish the job. Bill was nervous. 'If you waste any of that juice you're in trouble,' he said laughing, yet fully aware that something as petty as one stray ejaculation could ruin his entire day's shooting. Twinkle and Construction continued for a short time until Bill said loudly, 'Twinkle! Stop it!' and everyone laughed appreciatively, except myself who sat and stared in silence. Construction stood up, put on his pants and began to tighten his belt, his semi-erection like a hungry tortoise sticking impudently from the front of his open trousers. 'Are there any sandwiches?' he asked.

Indeed there were sandwiches. And cake and tea, so we all trudged downstairs to help ourselves. Sitting in a wood-panelled study the talk turned to porno war stories: the funniest things that had happened, the most bizarre requests. It was like hanging out with a bunch of retired boxers.

Someone mentioned a private swingers' party on the Gold Coast held monthly by a well-known local business identity. Abattoir piped up. 'I swing every weekend. I'm a serious swinger.' People giggled nervously. Her volume increased and her tone became oddly portentous. 'Recently I got to fulfill one of my major fantasies which was to be served as food at a dinner party.' The room grew quiet, the nodding more forced. Everyone was keen to be seen as 'supportive' of her 'lifestyle'. 'They put lollies all over me and inside me and then covered me with whipped cream and Cottee's Ice Magic and then I was served to the people at the dinner party. They ate it all off and then they took turns fucking me, all twelve of them.' The crowd went silent; whether it was out of respect for the story or the almost unbearable thought that it involved this battered old nymphomaniac was hard to tell. The room broke up again into chattering parties. In one corner I heard Construction say, 'As soon as you start thinking about it, it goes.' Red just sat quietly and scowled.

In a quiet moment I pulled Bill aside and began to ask questions. 'They're not using condoms. Aren't we living in the AIDS era?'

'Well, they've gotta have their papers, mate. They get a full STD check – not just AIDS, the works. They have to get pathology reports the day before we shoot. And then they have to have papers saying that they're clean. Without that,' he said with a dramatic school teacher-like folding of his arms, 'they don't get to work.'

'But that's nonsense,' I said. 'There's a three-month window on an AIDS test. They could have gotten it at any time in that period.' Bill rocked his head gently and rolled his eyes upwards. 'That's true, but what's the likelihood, mate?'

'Not that bad for people who make pornos.'

Bill shrugged and made a win some, lose some gesture that contrived to indifference. (About eighteen months after this conversation the Hollywood porn industry was shut down and plunged into crisis after a major male star infected his eighteen-year-old co-star with HIV. He too had been 'cleared' by tests which were, by their very nature, out of date. A further forty-eight people were listed as at risk of infection.)

'How much is the talent being paid?'

'Five thousand bucks flat for four days' shooting.'

'That's not too bad. What's the budget all up?'

'Sixty thousand dollars.'

I expressed surprise.

'If you don't spend the money, you don't get the talent, mate,' explained Bill, but our conversation was interrupted as Twinkle, outside in the garden, pressed her naked breasts against the window and ran her wet tongue across the glass.

'Twinkle!' shouted Bill in exaggerated anger and there was much mirth from everyone in the room.

In single file we marched back upstairs. The scene with Roxy was about to be filmed: posing as a next-door neighbour she was to burst through the screen door and 'discover' the making of the film (the plot centered around a 'film within a film' device, but *Fellini's 8½* it wasn't). She would then join in using a black dildo that lay like a Keystone Cop's truncheon on one of the couches. There was a brief rehearsal with Bill. He was very insistent that Roxy should call Twinkle a 'dirty bitch'. It was also very important she understand that the eroticism of this scene hinged on the fact that she did not need her husband's permission to participate in the porno. Bill's face had gone red and he was smiling fixedly; he was excited and, apparently, nervous. The actors returned to their positions while Roxy, in preparation for her Big Scene, stood off to one side, hitched her skirt and lubricated her vagina with all the studied nonchalance of a weight-lifter chalking his hands. The task completed, she walked out onto the balcony.

'Action!'

Roxy walked along the balcony and parted the flyscreen door to stare in amazement at her next-door neighbours. They hid their shame with shaggy pillows. Red's face split into an idiotic grin, unable to hide what must have been genuine humiliation at his total lack of libidinal responsiveness.

'What are ya doin'?' said Roxy in her best Newcastlese. 'You're filmin' a bloody porno, aren't you?' She began to struggle, her capacity for ad lib stretched to the limit. 'You dirty bitch. Why didn't you tell me?'

'Well, you can come and join us if you'd like,' said Twinkle.

'Awww, I dunno. Me husband wouldn't much like it . . .' Roxy thought a while about her husband. 'Oh, what the fuck!' And with that she dropped her skirt, picked up the enormous dildo and inserted the appliance to much applause from the appreciative swingers. A cut was called. Several members of the crew fell into a concerned discussion about Red's penis. A variety of sexual acts was performed upon the flaccid member, but it was all to no avail – Red's cock had all the rigidity of a Paddle-Pop in January. The sex went ahead regardless. There were multiple couplings, occasionally brought to a halt because carpet fluff was attaching itself to sweaty backs. Twinkle straddled Construction in a great number of gymnastic postures, all the while screaming, moaning and slashing at the air with frenzied flailings of her hot-pink nails – it was what I imagine feeding pterodactyls might have looked like. Abattoir, meanwhile, pulled and sucked at Red's penis; it stretched and thinned like white taffy. I became tired and went to sit in a beanbag before thinking the better of it, choosing instead to sit on a couch in front of the TV and twist my head to watch the reptilian writhings on the downy pink carpet. Outside the window the palm trees buckled in the hot wind; at over thirty degrees and with the added heat of the lights, I was ready to melt. Towering over the actors the industrial fan spun: mechanical dronings corresponding to the motion of the fucking on the floor.

The reader may at this point be wondering why I had decided to participate at all in this deadening afternoon saturnalia. My motivation, like that for just about everything I do, was that I thought it would be funny. I am not a consumer of pornography (the imaginative leap required to translate tiny dots of primary colour into erotic experience is beyond my capacity) but I had usually imagined something along the lines of a racier *Carry On* film: all French maids and well-hung plumbers. I thought they could have managed at least one mustachioed pool attendant. As it was, I might as well have been watching five people mowing the lawn or taking an aerobics class.

After some time Construction issued a volcanic emission and an end to proceedings was called. Twinkle wiped semen off her face exaggeratedly and everyone laughed. The actors rose from the floor. The girls had carpet burns on their backsides. Red and Abattoir shook hands, as though she hadn't just had his penis in her mouth. Obviously she saw her body as something separate from herself, and I wondered if she was happy in her own skin.

There was one more scene to be filmed, out in the pool. Red stood naked beside Bill, chatting and masturbating, as though two separate bodies were performing these functions. Twinkle interrupted them, throwing her arms around Bill's neck and jumping up and down like a child. 'I wanna do some more,' she screeched in a baby voice. Out by the pool the cameramen set up the lights. Across the canal sat a huge mock Tudor house: its architectural incongruity and the blankness of its reflective bronze windows looked absurd, almost menacing, in the heat. The crew shooed away some boys who sat in boats on the canal. Abattoir lay in a pool li-lo while Red, Twinkle and Construction, standing in the water, rubbed her body with massage oil (this scene was filmed out of chronology, thus Roxy had yet to 'arrive'). The cameras began rolling. Red looked at Construction and began to improvise. 'She's a very beautiful woman, isn't she?'

'She certainly is,' said Construction, his hand moving in a spiralling burnish across her pale, rippling flesh.

When I looked around, the only person holding back their laughter was me.

The scene ended. The light was failing. The women jumped out of the pool and went inside to shower while the boys swam lazily through the skin of leaves. Red was from Johannesburg and I spoke to him a little about South Africa before asking him why he had done the porno. 'We needed the money and my girlfriend agreed,' he said.

'You're facing prosecution, disease and public humiliation for five thousand bucks. Was it really just for the money?'

'Well, I guess I thought it would be fun, too.'

The men were not interesting conversationalists so I left and walked down the embankment to the canal. The light was softer now, the glitter of the canal less metallic. I stood on my toes and looked over the neighbours' fence. I jumped back. A huge lizard, probably over a metre long and perhaps some variety of water monitor, sat on the stone fence. My phone rang, startling me for a second time. The lizard stood stock-still. I answered; it was David. I asked him how he was doing. He was silent. I stood and watched the runabouts on the canal, waiting for an answer. The silence became awkward; David's breath was heavy. 'David, do you want to talk to me?'

'I love you,' he said.

'Oh . . .' I tried to recall what people said in films when this sort of thing happened to them. 'Um, look, David . . . you don't love me. You just think you love me.'

'I love you and I want to stay on the Gold Coast and be with you.'

'Ah, look David, you need to go back home and sort out your life. You should study. Besides, I won't even be here too much longer.'

'You're the only person who's ever been nice to me.'

'Well, I don't think that's entirely true, but it doesn't change the fact that this is, um, impossible and . . .'

'You're the nicest person I've ever met.'

'David, you're making me out to be something I'm not.'

'I don't want to go home, I want to see you again. I don't wanna see my mum or anyone . . . just you. Can't I please, please see you again?'

'David, you're making me feel like Woody Allen. I really think you should drive back home with your friends.'

And so it continued: David insisting that he didn't want to go back, me insisting that he ought. As I spoke I remembered the feeling of those embossed scrawls running across his wrists. How could I in good conscience send this kid back to his miserable home and what he saw as a hopeless future? The alternative, however – encouraging him in this hopeless crush – could only make things worse.

I decided to be firm. 'I'll give you my email address, okay? Any problems, just write to me. But you have to leave with your friends this afternoon.' I gave him my address, said goodbye and, before he could plead any further, hung up. I walked back to the house and sat by the pool in a deck chair. Bill handed me a beer, but I felt sick when I drank it. The combination of an afternoon of pornographic pilates and the knowledge I had left David to an uncertain fate left me feeling wretched.

Construction stood next to me, running a towel across his genitals which bobbed and wobbled by my nose. 'You had such a vacant look on your face upstairs.'

'To tell you the truth, I was getting very bored.'

He snorted. 'You weren't the only one, mate.'

Abattoir walked out, drying her hair. Her husband, a journalist with a minor Gold Coast newspaper, had come to pick her up. He was balding, overweight and sniggered at things that weren't funny. The pair discussed their plans for the evening. They were meeting another couple shortly. They had chatted with them over the Internet but had yet to see their faces. They laughed: the lies people could tell over the Internet! Anyway, they were in a hurry: a sitter was needed for the kids. She shook hands with everybody and then disappeared out the door to meet yet more strangers and have yet more sex. The woman was like a human bonobo monkey.

Twinkle reappeared from her shower. Bill and Construction had been discussing her in her absence. They had both agreed she was indeed 'a great character'.

Perhaps it was a transfer of the anxiety I felt for David, but Bill's pathetic infatuation with Twinkle had really begun to anger me. I have never been particularly against sleaziness *per se* (it is a quality maligned usually only by those who have never been on its receiving end) but the integrity of sleaziness relies wholly in its shamelessness. Sleaziness with guilt is like decaffeinated coffee or non-alcoholic beer – repugnant in its self-deception. And guilt was all over Bill's face. Everything from his PE teacher leer to the way he had tried to hide his erection during filming told me that he had a perfectly lovely wife living in the northern suburbs of Sydney who wore pants-suits and picked the kids up from school in a Range Rover. Twinkle, on the other hand, had been to the dark side of the moon and back. This chick had been to parties where the aim of the evening was to be bleeding from at least one orifice by the end of the night. As I watched Bill grinning his way through a conversation with Construction, I wondered whether he realised how utterly out of his depth he was.

'G'day – you bastards havin' a beer, are ya?' Like all great method actresses, Twinkle was always in character. Her relentless phoniness, obviously rooted in a desperate desire to please, made my skin crawl.

I made motions to leave and Bill offered to give me a lift. Benny and Danger had left earlier with their children who had arrived at the front door in their school uniforms. I got in the car behind Bill and one of the other producers. As we drove into Surfers I asked Bill why he had decided to make porn. 'Look, mate, the only reason I make porn is because I saw a gap in the market. It could have been jam or car parts or anything. I didn't make it because I thought it would be erotic . . . as you've seen today!' He laughed but I grew weary of these protestations of innocence. 'In fact, it's probably the most unerotic thing in the world!' He grinned his awkward grin, shook his head and continued on as he gripped the steering wheel tightly. 'I mean . . . that was *horrible*.' Bill turned to me, his face contorted with distress and another emotion that looked very much like regret.

*

By the time we arrived back at my apartment it was about six-thirty. As I got out of the car Bill promised I could see the finished product when it was completed. I thanked him and promised to call. Upstairs, I was annoyed to find Kane at the dining table playing some sort of board game with the Gimp. Hine was sitting in the living room watching a game show, her head cocked to one side, her eyes unblinking. Lenore was in her bedroom while Jeremy sat in the living room, chatting occasionally to the two men over the noise of the television. The game seemed to be chess, but featured the addition of wizards, warlocks and Monopoly-style lucky-dip cards. It was the sort of amusement I associated with socially awkward teenagers, not a 32-year-old man. Thudding gangster rap, relentlessly repetitive and abhorrently violent, blasted from the stereo. I sat and tried to drink a cup of tea. When Kane won the game he stood up, leant over the table and began to scream into the Gimp's face: 'Huh! There, I told you so! Who's the man?' The Gimp just grumbled.

For the next few hours I disappeared, a prisoner in my bedroom, waiting for the Gimp to leave and for Kane to gravitate towards Hine's room. By nine o'clock the Gimp departed to another couch across town and the room was free — one of the few advantages of living with Hine and Kane was that they went to bed early. I took the opportunity to watch some television with Lenore and Jeremy. They seemed withdrawn and for some time Jeremy just sat in silence. After about half an hour he turned to check there was nobody else in the room and leant into my ear. 'Kane told me he's moving in.' Lenore looked at me and nodded intently. 'Kane wants to kick you out and move Hemi and Drakkar into your room.'

There was little I could add. The plan that had been in motion since I had arrived was now a self-fulfilling prophecy. But I was not going to be so easily bullied. I resented Kane's conspiracy, and now that he was no longer the monster under the bed he seemed a great deal less frightening. I saw no reason why I should have to give up my resort features simply because this guy wanted them. The sting of pride had begun to infect me.

The three of us continued sitting in the living room. It wasn't long before the now-familiar ritual of the couple's evening fight began. Kane's voice echoed down the corridor: 'It's bad enough that you were fucking him for the first year while we were going out but now I'm providing for those kids that aren't even mine. And I gotta see that fuckin' arsehole here at Christmas *and* give you three thousand fuckin' bucks. I'm just gonna end it. That's it. And I'm gonna smash that cunt Johnny. I swear I'm gonna fuckin' smash him!'

Seventeen

Don't Hit Mummy

AND SO IT continued for four more days: Kane threatening Hine, Hine complaining to us, the ever-present fear that Kane would snap. Then, on the fourth morning, the buzzing of the intercom woke me. On the blue screen was a policeman; he said he wanted to speak to Hinemoa. I called for her in her room. 'Who is it?' she asked. I told her. 'Just tell him I'm not here,' she said forcefully. But it was too late. The policeman had already made his way up the lift and was now demanding the door be opened. Hine complied, casually. I moved away and did my best to eavesdrop. After he left she closed the door and called for Drakkar.

'What happened?' I asked.

She said she was being made to attend a new restraining order hearing. It was news to me and seemed irrelevant now that Kane was living with her. I decided to take the opportunity to corner her on the subject of Kane. 'Hine, Kane has to go. There are too many people here with both him and Hemi. Jeremy and Lenore think the same.'

She let out a big sigh and stared at the floor. 'Yeah, I know. I need to talk to him 'cause it's not fair on you guys.' This was the first time I had heard her acknowledge that her invitation to Kane had been an imposition on us. Gathering up Drakkar, she disappeared out the door.

I walked into the living room; a new computer, stealthily, magically, had moved onto the desk. Jeremy and Lenore were slowly waking up; they were still in holiday mode. I sat in the kitchen and chatted with Lenore while she made Jeremy a breakfast of four fried eggs and a bowl of cereal the size of an asteroid crater. Just then, Jeremy came flying out from the bathroom squealing like a schoolgirl: 'That's the biggest cockroach I have ever seen!'

I entered the bathroom and looked around. A standard tropical cockroach was scuttling across the shower recess. I began to laugh.

'This country is totally GAY!' screamed Jeremy, stamping down the hall to devour his breakfast.

In a matter of moments he was done. 'Oh!' he cried at me. 'Do you like Little Richard?' Lenore looked at me sideways. 'It's his favourite album,' she said. Running into his bedroom, Jeremy soon emerged to the thumping strains of 'Lucille'. 'Looooo-ceeeel!' he screamed, pumping his spherical, pneumatic backside in time to the music and swinging about his head in an unnerving helicopter motion his favourite set of nunchakus.

I backed out onto the balcony. Down at the pool row upon row of beautiful girls lay face down and topless like racks of freshly shucked abalone on large white plastic deck chairs. Their hair moved in liquid sheets across their shining backs as they wriggled with self-conscious modesty on sun-neglected breasts, causing their skin to sheen and flare in the sun. 'Let's go to the pool,' said Jeremy.

It was by then well into December and, although a number of teenagers were still hanging around, schoolies was officially over. The grass around the barbeque area kicked up countless condoms, rubbed into the dirt, and the pool filters were choked with plastic bags. The girls in the deck chairs, however, took no notice; they hardly went into the water anyway. Lenore and myself commandeered some deck chairs while Jeremy dived into the pool.

'So, is this what it's like back in New Zealand?' I asked, thumbing in the direction of the unit. 'Does everyone just get knocked up and fight with their boyfriends?' She looked at me and nodded. 'Yep. Every time I go back during uni holidays I say, "So, what are you guys up to?" They just say, "Oh, had another baby."' She sniggered. 'I know a million people like Kane and Hine.'

Lenore was in the middle of telling me about some of her Maori ex-boyfriends in Rotorua when Jeremy hauled himself out of the water. 'That city stinks!' he exclaimed. 'It's full of stinking sulfur, hot mud and dumb mutts like Hinemoa!'

'Shut up, Jeremy,' said Lenore.

'Did you know Lenore's school was voted the worst in New Zealand?' Lenore nodded at me. 'And I went to the best!' he said, thumbing his chest. 'They tried to expel me so many times, but my mum did so much fundraising they didn't dare!' Jeremy pointed to his girlfriend. 'Did you know she has never seen *Star Wars*?'

'Oh, shut up Jeremy.'

'Freak! Freeaak of nature!'

The talk turned once again to Kane and Hinemoa. They told me about things I had missed. Lenore said she had seen Kane threaten to hit Hine on the head with a hammer and Jeremy said that Kane had shoved her up against a wall by her throat. Most disturbing of all was an incident a couple of nights prior. Hine had just arrived back home with Drakkar. 'Baby's giving me hell,' she announced, before leaning on the kitchen bench for support. Seeing this from where he stood at the opposite end of the room, Hemi took a run up and, with all his might, punched Hine right in the middle of her wriggling stomach. She let out a shout and a moan and Kane flew into a rage. Grabbing Hemi by the arm, he twisted the boy back and struck him across the face repeatedly. Hemi broke into tears and Kane dragged him off to the bedroom. Whether he beat him further in the room Jeremy could not say. When Kane reappeared he announced to the couple with great authority: 'He's got ADD. If he annoys you, don't worry about just hittin' him.' Despite the beating, Kane hadn't bothered to check if Hine was all right.

After a brief game in which he tried to drown me in the pool, Jeremy told me more about Kane. Without a car, Jeremy had been unable to find greenkeeping work and so, out of desperation, had accepted Kane's offer to come and build scaffolding at construction sites. Even though the work was irregular Jeremy had developed a pleasant working relationship with Kane and had become a nominal friend and confidant. In recent weeks Kane had made the usual claims of Hinemoa's unfaithfulness, including in his vast list of potential suspects the mysterious Johnny (the father of Tejahn and Isaac); her female cousin Gina; a next-door neighbour at the Moroccan; Betty; a male cousin by the name of David; and the manager of a local nightclub where she had once worked as a hostess for Japanese businessman. It was a fabulous weft of lies, paranoid delusion and sordid truth, but I had given up trying to tell fact from fiction. I couldn't have cared less whether she had done it all or more, I just wondered why she felt the need to involve all those around her in her domestic disharmony.

Jeremy dived into the pool. 'I wouldn't worry about Kane,' said Lenore. 'Jeremy's pretty psycho himself. I've seen him get in the middle of brawls between fifteen people and bash them all.' She laughed and settled back into her chair. 'You know, he once gave a girl twenty stitches when he threw a beer bottle at her head.' I was aghast.

Jeremy arrived back from the pool. 'Jeremy,' I said, 'did you really throw a beer bottle at a girl?'

'Yep.'

'Why?'

'She called my mum a fat bitch!' he exclaimed, as though I was stupid.

'Why did she do that?'

'Oh,' he said casually, as if he had forgotten some incidental detail, 'I called *her* a fat bitch.'

Lenore giggled.

The afternoon blurred into the evening. Hine came home unusually early. Drakkar stomped about the room before climbing aboard my chest like an infant possum. 'What happened at court this morning?' I asked.

She slumped into a chair and explained the conditions of the restraining order had been modified so that they would be allowed to speak and 'a few other things'. This casual reference to 'a few other things' worried me deeply. I took her aside. 'Now, you are going to make him leave, aren't you? Because otherwise, we'll all leave.'

'Yeah, yeah,' she said irritably.

I turned. 'By the way, Hine, whose computer is this?'

Her eyes went big and her cheeks dimpled. 'That's *mine*,' she said, and giggled manically at some private joke.

Night-time: a huge storm. The rain fell heavy, even and straight. Some hours earlier Kane had arrived home from work with Hemi. In the living room the boy sat at the computer. He had spent all evening bashing at the keyboard and screaming incoherently at Drakkar, at the television, and at no one in particular. A margarine commercial flashed on the screen. A toothy, sun-streaked mother laid out a platter of grease-scraped delicacies for her appreciative children. 'Look, Mum – that's you!' screamed Hemi. 'And that's Dad!' The margarine father bit into a scone, grinning in wordless appreciation at his radiant spouse. At the sight of this Hemi made several senseless howling noises before jumping on the couch and thrashing an innocent pillow. Lenore boiled visibly.

Poor Hemi. I have always had a great fondness for children and the hardest part of this entire affair was to watch, powerless, as this kid became the next cog in a cycle of insanity and violence. In a world where people were smuggling babies out of China, it seemed enough to turn priests into atheists that someone like Kane could have a child simply because he had a functioning reproductive system. Hemi was in fact only one of Kane's children – he had seven, all born to different mothers, including one Kane had met while in a relationship with her daughter. Hemi was ten years old with lovely, pleading eyes. His left front tooth had come down but his right was still a baby, giving him a certain cartoonish goofiness. He was very skinny, a reminder that his father had once been a 90-pound weakling, and also a reminder that within Kane's little head atop his mountainous body sat, perhaps, the remnants of a now forgotten person.

As much as I felt for Hemi, however, I could understand Lenore's frustration. He was completely uncontrollable: his wildness, however, had less to do with a highly dubious diagnosis of attention deficit disorder, I suspect, than with a lifetime of abuse and neglect. Kane now had custody of the boy only because his mother was in prison. If the kid came good out of this it was going to make water-into-wine look like a Tuesday night magic show at the Coolangatta Bowls Club.

Hemi sat back down in front of the computer. I began to watch him. It was soon apparent that he had no idea what he was doing. A window appeared asking him to 'find file'. He typed in 'Kane'. Another text box appeared explaining that 'the document Kane.exe' could not be found. I leant over and offered to help him. 'There's no file called Kane, Hemi. Why don't you make one for yourself with your own name?'

'Because it's my dad's name,' he said oddly, quietly, and almost angrily.

'Here, I'll show you what to do,' I said.

'Grab a chair!' he exclaimed excitedly. 'Don't just stand there. You'll get tired!' He leapt up and fetched me a seat. We sat down. Hemi was grinning ecstatically, his thin little hands curled over the keyboard in the posture of an amateur magician conjuring a rabbit out of a hat. We came to the instruction 'create file name'. I told him to name the file 'Hemi'. He ummed and ahhed and began to scan the keyboard, his long skinny fingers running delicate tracings across the keys. After some prolonged examination he looked up at me with his pleading eyes and asked, 'Which one's the "heh"?' It was only after I'd pointed out the third letter in his name that it became apparent he could spell none other than his father's.

My phone rang and I had to answer. Hemi's interest in the computer soon waned. The hours wore on, the thunder died and the unit fell quiet until the only sound was that of the invisible waves crashing on the beach. For some time I stood on the balcony and watched a violent eddy of toilet paper and plastic bags, left by the schoolies, which swirled up from the centre of the Moroccan complex and then tumbled down the empty avenues in fibrous tumbleweeds. It was the only evidence that an army of children had just held the Gold Coast to ransom for a month. Then Kane's voice began to ring down the corridor. 'What do you fuckin' mean? *I* pay the fuckin' rent here! I'm not gonna give that cunt the fuckin' satisfaction! And I know you're fucking him!'

Who knew who he was referring to.

And so it continued for some time as Jeremy, Lenore and myself sat on the couch joined in a silent prayer that their fight would not become physical. For some minutes we listened, gesturing only with our eyes. It was hard to make out what was being said in the room; the shouts had become a muffled stream of static until they made no more sense than the waves on the shore. Then I heard Drakkar crying and Kane yelling in a mock baby voice, 'Oh, what's da matter? Are you cwy-ing? What's da matter, little baby? Don't hit mummy? Awhhh, don't hit mummy . . .'

Eighteen

★

Flip Out on Level Eight

THE NEXT MORNING I walked out onto the balcony and looked down at the gardens below. The previous evening's storm had been so violent it had blown all the deckchairs into the pool. The mock Bedouin tent over the spa had been torn down and now lay draped across the surrounding shrubbery, glinting brightly in the morning heat. I walked inside. In the living room I found Hine sitting on the sofa, her address book open on the coffee table and her mobile phone in her hand. 'I'm just gonna move all his fuckin' stuff out,' she said, and my heart skipped for joy, a joy that soon turned to frustration as her phone ran out of credit. 'Here, let me help you,' I said, presenting her with mine. Together, like a pair of schoolgirls making prank calls at a slumber party, we sat and dialled relative after relative until, finally, we reached a woman known to Hine as Aunty Judy. 'Aunty Judy'll do it,' she said vengefully. 'She fuckin' hates the prick.'

'Hey, Aunty. I got a bunch of stuff here: a TV, a stereo, a computer. You want it?' A pause. 'Yeah, um, it's just hangin' round the house.' A further pause. 'Yeah, okay, see you in an hour then.' She pressed the little red button on the telephone with great satisfaction. 'Aunty Judy'll be here real soon. I'll show that fuckin' psycho.' With that she burst into peels of delighted laughter. Rising from the couch I turned to Hine. 'What happens when Kane gets home?' I asked.

'Don't worry,' she said. 'I'm just gonna call him and tell him he can't ever come back here. If he tries to get in just don't let him up when he buzzes at the door.'

Although Kane had no key, this sounded like a plan in need of some finetuning but I didn't have time to make further arrangements – I was returning that day to the Southport Magistrate's Court. Despite the disappointment the court had proven to be, I had decided to go back that day because the man I had read about during my first week on the Gold Coast, the one who had allegedly tied up and tortured his housemate, was due to go on trial. It was a bizarre case and I had not yet dismissed the possibility that it might serve as a narrative for this book. Upon arriving at the court I became utterly despondent, therefore, when I discovered that the trial had been adjourned until March – almost three months away. In frustration I attended instead the case of a man who had been picked up by the police in a car park late at night and then arrested for assault. The accused was black, Fijian perhaps, and his face scarred by burns. The police said he had resisted arrest and spat on them as they tried to search him. The man claimed he had been beaten by the police with a flashlight in a public toilet block and called various racist names in the process. I sat in on the case for a couple of hours but soon my mind began to wander and I found myself staring out the window at the surrounding rooftops.

At lunchtime I sat in the mall and ate, wondering whether to return to the trial. It wasn't that I was uninterested in the case, but I had a feeling I shouldn't go back. Perhaps it was the disappointment of not being able to see the torture case, or perhaps it was some sort of premonitory sense that something else was about to happen, something far more interesting, that made me decide to abandon the court and return home.

Sitting at one of the benches outside Australia Fair was 'HUSLER'. He still wore the same hat and the same dirty T-shirt. He was regaling the old lady next to him with tales of his martial arts prowess. I was going to talk to him but felt too anxious and withdrawn. What's more, I was dying to see our apartment without Kane's stuff in it.

At home, the flat was uncommonly calm. Unusually, Hine's bedroom door was locked. The balcony doors were closed and the curtains drawn – frontline defence in Lenore and Jeremy's ongoing war against insects. In the living room, Kane's stuff was gone. The only other person at home was Lenore who was sitting in her room reading. She said she had slept most of the day, her efforts to find a job having proved futile. (She had quit one bar job after a man threw a flaming Sambuca in her face, scarring her chest badly.) I told her what had happened that morning and together we sat and talked in the afternoon heat, the air turning syrupy. We considered our best plan of action should Kane turn up. It was agreed that if we ignored him he would soon lose patience and return to his flat in Miami (his earlier claim that his lease there was finished had since proved a lie). There were many mutual celebrations of our good fortune.

At about half-past four there was a buzz at the security intercom. Lenore and I stood side-by-side to inspect the blue screen. It was the car park security video. Kane could be seen leaning from his car window, demanding to be let in. We returned to our respective bedrooms and continued our reading, the buzzing from the living room becoming increasingly frenzied. After several minutes the silence returned. I wandered into the kitchen and began to fix myself a cup of tea. Waiting for the kettle to boil, I watched as the steam rose from the spout to drip rain from the base of the high cupboards. I had always enjoyed this spectacle and the concomitant speculation of exactly how many cups of tea it would take before the wood rotted completely and the groceries spilled onto the counter. Lost in my contemplation I was unprepared, therefore, when the front door opened and Kane walked in – I knew it was Kane because I could hear him heaping abuse on Hemi. As casually as I could, I leant out from the kitchen and looked down the corridor. The door slammed shut and I could see Kane, toolbox in one hand, pushing Hemi in the back along the hall. My mind raced. How could this have happened? Could it be that I was so stupid as to forget to lock the door?

Hemi ran down the corridor and into the living room. Kane came charging behind him, his oversized tank top flapping.

'G'day, mate! Didn't you hear me?'

My heart raced; my mouth dried. 'No, sorry mate. I just walked in.' I continued to make the tea.

Kane looked at me for some time, holding his tool box.

I busied myself. 'How's your day been?' I asked.

His gaze broke. 'Oh, fuckin' nightmare, mate. It was thiry-three degrees in Nerang and I had to carry this fuckin' aluminium scaffolding. It fuckin' burnt me, mate.' He put his toolbox down on the desk where his computer and stereo had sat until that morning and turned his back to me to peel off his tank top, much in the manner of a forties screen siren dropping the strap of her nightgown before disappearing into her boudoir. It was a disarmingly sensual motion and I was reminded that he used to be a dancer. He spun around to face me, continuing his complaints for some time, telling me of the heavy loads he had borne that day upon his tired shoulders, grimacing and exclaiming all the while. I sympathised throughout. Kane turned back to his toolbox and began to root through the contents. I poured the hot water into my cup. Abruptly he stopped and looked up. Standing with his legs apart, he dropped his arms to his side and began to swivel from his hips, his head and spine on a single axis, like a He-Man figurine. He turned to face me. 'Do you know where my computer is, mate?'

I picked the tea bag out of the mug and pressed it together, squeezing the last of the tannin liquid into the cup, burning the tips of my fingers in my haste. 'No, I'm sorry Kane,' I said, shaking my head. 'I didn't even notice it was gone.' I threw the tea bag in the garbage.

His plastic body continued to pivot. His eyes scanned the room. 'Where's all my stuff, mate?'

'Geez, I dunno, Kane,' I said, peering in exaggerated sympathy at the desk. 'I just got home.' My fear grew in increments with the seconds.

Hemi switched on the television and began to watch a game show at geriatric volume.

'Where's Hine, mate?'

'I dunno, Kane,' I said, adding milk and sugar with casual gestures.

'Have you seen her today?'

'Nah, not at all. When I got up she was already gone.'

'Yeah?' He cocked his head, ambiguously.

With that he walked back down the corridor and I escaped to my room, leaving my door open so as not to appear conspiratorial.

Soon a profane wailing echoed through the unit. Kane came charging back down the corridor, stomped into my bedroom and interrupted me at my desk. 'Do you know what she's gone and done, mate?' He flung his hands out to his sides, his palms up-turned as he craned his neck forward. 'She's gone and locked all my stuff in the fucking room! And do you know why she's done it?'

I was torn: did my fear outweigh the annoyance at the assumption I cared about the answer to any of these questions?

'No,' I said.

'Because she wants money out of me, mate.' His tone became one of reconciled disgust. 'Because she wants money out of me.' With one hand he swatted at an invisible fly and stormed out of my room. Jeremy had just arrived home, his familiar, irrepressible jollity radiating from the living room. I walked out to see him and stood holding my tea.

'If I can't get in that room I'm gonna have to sleep on the couch, mate!' cried Kane. 'On the couch! It's a fucking disgrace.' He paced from one end of the living room to the other. 'Just wait 'till I see that crazy bitch.'

Half an hour passed. Jeremy, Lenore and I sat on one couch, Kane and Hemi on the other. Together we watched *M*A*S*H* – I felt the need to stay close to Jeremy. Throughout the program Kane voiced complaints interspersed with long periods of silence.

At the end of the show Kane turned to me, his arms crossed and his ludicrous watermelon legs spread wide: 'So, Brendan, you haven't seen Hinemoa all day?'

'No. I left early this morning.'

'Geez,' he said, with a distinct note of sarcasm, 'she moved that gear into the room all by herself. She's keen.'

More disturbing than even his strength or madness was Kane's intelligence.

The afternoon dragged on; prematurely the sky darkened and the rain poured; with terrible violence lightning hit the sea. For several weeks now the Gold Coast had been at the centre of ferocious evening storms. Every night they promised to bring an end to the drought that had been ravaging Queensland. But the storms were mostly electrical and brought little rain; what did fall dampened only the sand.

I sat in my bedroom and worked, watching the lightning unmask the neighbouring high rises in the dark and hoping, somehow, that everything would resolve itself. Outside my door I could hear Kane pacing around the apartment as he continued his endless, hectoring, purposeless lament. Soon a knock came at my door; Kane showed himself in without asking. Standing over my desk he looked at me before announcing solemnly, 'Mate, I just wanted to tell you about how Hine's been telling lies about me.' With that he sat on the floor, leaning against the wall to make himself comfortable for a lecture that, when finished, would run to over half an hour.

'I've been paying the rent on this place for the last two weeks, mate,' he began. 'I'm tellin' you now: when I'm gone, you'd better start finding another place because she 'aint gonna be able to keep goin'.' The fact that we could have kicked out Hine and found someone else – someone who, for instance, didn't have a mad boyfriend – had not, apparently, occurred to him. His head began its distinctive dance. 'You know why she's locked my stuff in my room?' A dramatic pause. Kane blinked purposefully. 'To get money outta me. She won't give it back until I've given her a thousand bucks. And you know what she does with my money?' – with 'you' he pointed at me – 'She gives it to Johnny. So basically I'm paying so that fuckin' cunt can have a holiday.'

He grew angry. The talk dragged on, becoming increasingly incoherent and vituperative. After another fifteen minutes or so he suddenly changed direction. 'I'm gonna put Hemi on a plane next week so that he can go and live with my mother for a while.' He shrugged and made gestures with his hands, gestures that emphasised his own reasonableness, his own calm acquiescence to the cruelty of fate. 'But mate, be prepared' – he looked at me and pointed to the floor – 'because you won't have this place in two weeks.'

With that he stood up and walked out into the hall. I stayed in my room and continued to work. Moments later I heard the rattle of tools. Poking my head out of the door I looked down the hall to the foyer. On a thin granite table that stood under a decorative mirror, Kane was pulling various implements from his tool kit, plonking them down on the stone surface with calculated, percussive drops. Once he had extracted the necessary selection, he gathered up the tools in two big hands and turned back to the door of Hinemoa's room. Leaning on one knee with his face near the handle, he began to needle at the door jam. After using both a screwdriver and a chisel his patience wore thin. Picking up a hammer out of the red box he began instead to subject the doorknob to a series of direct blows. The steel issued several echoing cracks that resounded through the marble foyer and down the hall. I withdrew to my room and began to fidget: sitting down, standing up, alphabetising my CDs – petty distractions filling my hands in horrible anticipation of what was to come.

The doorknob hitting the floor made a series of noisy bounces across the slabs of marble. The bounces, like a steel tennis ball, grew in rapidity until they were a single metallic vibration with all the finality of a dead phone line. A tinkle of metal parts hit the stone floor and soon the door opened, hitting the magnetic doorstop with a fateful clunk. For a whole minute there was silence broken only by an episode of *Changing Rooms* playing on the TV in the living room. I went across the balcony and sat next to Jeremy and Lenore on the couch. We didn't look at one another, just sat and waited, watching a program that suddenly seemed like a conscious affront.

Now the howling began. Kane's screams were audible in the living room; the heavy stomp of his rolling walk came tearing down the hall. 'She's crazy! SHE'S FUCKIN' CRAZY!' He stood at the entrance to the living room. 'Do you know what she's done?' We all turned to face him. His eyes were like fried eggs. 'Do you know what she's fuckin' done? She's gone and taken all my fuckin' stuff. She's STOLEN IT! She's stolen all my fuckin' stuff!' As he screamed he swung his hands in the air and his head shook violently. 'Crazy! SHE'S FUCKIN' CRAZY!' He turned to me and pressed his fingers in a tight bundle against his chest. 'Look what she's done to me, mate! LOOK WHAT SHE'S DONE TO ME!' And with that, trailed by Hemi, he tore back down the hall and into Hine's room. Lenore, Jeremy and I faced one another. At her boyfriend's instruction Lenore disappeared behind the flimsy wooden slats of their bedroom. I looked at Jeremy. Worryingly, he appeared as scared as I felt. A crashing came from the hall. I looked down the passageway. Kane was cleaning out an old shopping trolley full of various ephemeral items that had been sitting in our foyer since he moved in. Plastic bags full of old clothes tumbled out and spilt their contents on the floor; broken bits of machinery and electronic equipment made clacking noises against the marble.

After he emptied out the trolley Kane went back into Hine's room. Some seconds later he emerged with an awkward, bow-legged waddle and a wide-screen television pressed against his chest. With some difficulty, and with much crashing of steel, Kane dropped the television into the trolley and then waddled back into the bedroom, only to emerge with a VCR. Normally this would have been no concern of mine, but none of this stuff actually belonged to Hine; it had all come with the house and now Kane was about to walk out the door with several thousands dollars' worth of electrical equipment and the lease was partly in my name. We had an inspection in two days.

I asked Jeremy what he thought we ought to do. He just grinned and gave a feeble giggle. I looked back up the corridor – Kane was balancing a computer game on the trolley and talking loudly to himself about the best way to move a bar fridge. All the while, Hemi danced around his father in a frenzied, barefooted corroboree. Jeremy's cowardice in this instance surprised me, but I put it down to a desire to protect Lenore. I was now faced with a choice, and it seemed that the burden of responsibility had fallen on my shoulders. Marching down the corridor I stood in the foyer and watched silently as Kane padded the appliances with Hine's clothes.

'Um, Kane,' I said quietly but not, I felt, given the circumstances, without a certain reckless firmness, 'you can't take all that stuff. It's not Hine's and we have an inspection the day after tomorrow.'

Kane turned to me and, for a moment, I thought I was going to die. 'You'll get *your* gear back when I get *my* fuckin' gear back!' he screamed, his finger drilling into my face. '*Understand?*' Kane's anger was now beyond mere outrage; it could only be described as inhuman, an impression emphasised as he flung his fists forward, level with his chest, to grip the invisible bars of King Kong's cage. I held up my hands and backed away. 'That's okay, Kane,' I said in conciliatory tones. 'Fair enough, mate.' My every instinct was telling me that this was the end, that I had pushed my luck too far. This was no longer a story for my entertainment – *I* was the entertainment.

'Look what she's done to me, mate!' He came out from behind the trolley and began to approach me. 'I mean, mate, I need this fuckin' stuff!' He flung his arm back towards the trolley like a ham actor.

'Yeah, no, fair enough,' I said, slipping back down the corridor, nodding my head all the while, Kane continuing to follow me, his arms spread wide, his palms out-turned in a gesture of Semitic resignation. 'I've got a kid that I've gotta pay for at Christmas, mate!' His eyes were like tail-lights in the dark. 'She's stolen everything I have! You don't understand. She's crazy. She's fuckin' crazy!' I backed out into the living room and stood by Jeremy who was still seated on the couch. Kane moved very close. He was still frantic but had now adopted an air of reasonableness: he said he simply had to take all our stuff; it was just the way the world worked; I had better not call Hine.

I agreed and he went back to loading the trolley.

By this stage Jeremy had disappeared into his bedroom – I followed suit. As I paced around my room listening to the noise of the trolley on the marble, my phone rang. It was Hine. 'How's things?' she asked in her stoner drawl, especially irritating given the current circumstances. 'Get over here right now!' I commanded in a forceful whisper. Although I had seen Hine on the receiving end of Kane's violence, I had also seen the power she exerted over him in these fits of rage: the dangerous game of chance she played as she brought his anger to the brink only to reel him in again, as though the violence itself was the medium for their bizarre brand of love. It seemed to confirm my hypothesis that she was a willing victim.

I explained what had happened. 'You have to give him his stuff back.'

'Fuck that! I'm just gonna call the cops.'

At this my alarm increased. The only phone left in the house was mine; Jeremy's was out of credit and our home phone had been cut off after Krystal had registered it in the name of Beyonce Knowles and run up $1000 in calls to New Zealand. It wouldn't be exceptionally unreasonable to conclude that I had made the call.

'No, no, no. Don't do that,' I pleaded. 'He'll think I've called them.'

'No he won't. I'm calling them right now.'

And with that she hung up the phone and I was left trapped in my room, fear rapidly turning to panic. I couldn't leave because it would mean passing Kane in the hall and in his current state he may assume anything. I had left it too late and there was nothing I could do now but hope that Kane would leave the flat before the cops arrived. I didn't care about the TV; my attempted intervention had made me part of the conspiracy against him, an impression that would only be confirmed with the arrival of the police. And so, for some twenty minutes, I waited and prayed; prayed that the incompetent reputation of the Gold Coast police would prove founded.

It was not to be. After half an hour there was a buzz at the intercom. I heard Jeremy answer it, his usual jocularity under strain. Kane, meanwhile, oblivious, continued to pack and repack the shopping trolley. There was a knock at front door. I poked my head into the hallway. Kane opened the door and I could hear the conversation of the police in the foyer. Kane seemed confused; he was opening his arms in disbelief. I ran into the living room and began to confer with Jeremy. The police brought Kane through. There were two, a man and a woman: clean-skinned and with bottoms that had seen more than a few police-discounted Egg McMuffins. The fact they both looked younger than myself hardly inspired confidence. Kane turned and stared at me, his eyes blossomed; his mouth, parted just far enough to reveal his teeth clamped askew, issued heavy breaths.

The police began to discuss the terms of the restraining order. Hine had obviously told them Kane was in violation of its terms. 'So who was the applicant?' asked the male officer.

'What?' asked Kane.

'Who took the restraining order out on who?'

'There's no restraining order,' said Kane, for he knew it to be half true.

'Well there *is*,' said the policeman antagonistically. 'So who did the bashing?' He folded his arms and smirked at his own cleverness.

'What *bashing*?' screamed Kane and, for a moment, I thought he was going to punch the cop and all our troubles would be over. The cop reeled back. 'Steady on, mate. Now, who bashed who?'

'I didn't bash anyone!'

After several minutes of this conversation, reminiscent of a Lewis Carroll nonsense poem, it was confirmed that Hine had taken the order out against Kane. With the establishment of this fact, Holmes and Dr Watson (as I was by then calling them), announced they were taking Kane down to the station to investigate the terms of the restraining order, while Hemi, in what I would have thought was a violation of some sort of procedure, was left in our care.

Lenore, Jeremy and I sat in the living room, discussing our options. The foyer was a pillaged wreck. Hemi ran like a deranged brown leprechaun through the flat, throwing things, hurling abuse at furniture and bashing his head on the desk.

Not long after, the cops returned with Kane. The male officer stood in the foyer and forced him to put back all the equipment while the policewoman chatted with Lenore and Jeremy – she was, of course, a New Zealander. The policeman returned to the living room. 'Well,' he announced authoritatively, 'I've told him that he can't take the stuff and he's putting it back now. But frankly, I think she's being a crazy cow. I feel sorry for him. She's being very unreasonable. You can't just take someone's stuff.'

'Are you going to make him leave?' I asked.

'Well, he says he pays the rent here, mate.'

I was incredulous. 'He does not. He's not on the lease and I want him out of here.'

'Well, the terms of the restraining order have been changed, mate. She's invited him up here and he's got every right to be here.'

'No he hasn't,' I said. 'This man is dangerous and he's in my home.

He has his own home to go to and I want him out of here!' The cop rolled his eyes and wandered back to the foyer – there was some muffled discussion. The McMuffin-bottomed policewoman wandered up the hall to join her colleague. Hemi crawled under the glass coffee table. Lenore, Jeremy and I sat in silence, staring at one another, feeling sick. Hemi arched his back and the heavy glass tabletop came crashing down on the steel supports. In perfect unison all three of us broke into shouts: 'Hemi – stop it!' Hemi crawled out backwards from beneath the table. He stood up and stared, his eyes full of resentment and hate. Silently he ran back down the corridor to be with his father.

The policeman reappeared. 'Mate, he says his other home doesn't have any power or blankets. It's cold tonight and he's got a child. Do you want to put a little kid out on the street?' I was astonished. I could almost hear the violins being played down the hall. If I had to admit one thing, then it was that Kane was good. 'Well, I'm sorry about that,' I said firmly, 'but that's not our problem. This man is not our friend, he is dangerous and I don't want him in my home.'

'Mate,' he said, as though I had just proposed that we savagely mutilate a dolphin, 'he's got a little kid here. Do you want to put a little kid out on the street?'

Hindsight: what a fabulously ironic quality: far-reaching, all-powerful and ultimately impotent. With hindsight I should have said, 'I don't give a shit. Call the Smith Family.' But grace under pressure is another thing I do not share with Hemingway.

'Well, um, no, but . . .'

'Well, there you go, mate. Problem solved. They'll stay here tonight and then tomorrow they'll make other arrangements.'

'But he's a paranoid schizophrenic!' I was frantic now. 'He's a drug dealer. He has 'roid rage. He's threatened all the previous tenants. When you leave, he's going to kill me.'

The cop snorted through his nose. 'I think you're overreacting a bit there, mate. I've spoken to him and he's just a guy that wants his stuff back. He says as soon as he gets it, he'll leave.'

'What? I'm not overreacting! This guy has eight previous convictions. I want him out of my house. *Don't you understand?*' With that the delicate pride of the policeman had been offended.

'Look, mate, we've spent enough time here tonight. Other people need us too, you know.'

Ironies: everywhere I went on the Gold Coast I found ironies, and they were mine alone to be savoured.

Without further ado the constabulary waddled down the corridor and, with a final goodbye and a warning to Kane not to re-enter Hine's room, disappeared through the heavy security door. I ran into my bedroom, closed the door and lay on my bed affecting a pretense of reading, waiting for the inevitable. Some minutes passed before there was a knock on my door – I delighted in the incongruity of that knock; it was undoubtedly something his mother had taught him, like washing his hands before meals.

'Go away, Kane!' I called.

'I'm not going to do anything to you, mate,' he said, his face appearing through the door frame, dismissing my concerns with an out-turned palm and a soft, paternal shake of his head. 'Don't worry, mate, I'm not gonna do anything to ya.' He stood at the base of my bed and I rolled off, shuffling towards the window – Kane to my left, an eight-storey drop to my right. I remembered the heroin addict who had fallen out a window and lived. He pointed at me from across the room. 'I just want you to know that calling the cops was a fuckin' low act.' He paused for dramatic effect. 'Because of you, I've been screwed for twelve grand, *mate*. That's everything I have in the world.' His manner was infuriatingly supercilious. 'For Christmas I have nothing, and I have a ten-year-old kid. I hope that weighs on your conscience.' This tender attachment to the spirit of Christmas was highly affecting. Somewhere in a grimy Dickensian orphanage Kane, dressed as Santa, was handing out presents to underprivileged children, the snow drifting gently to the ground past frosted window panes.

'I didn't call the fuckin' cops, Kane!' For a moment I wondered who was screaming: they must have been a very foolish person to scream at such a volume at such a patently unbalanced individual. 'Hinemoa called them!'

'Did you tell her I was taking gear?' His eyes goggled in his head like Cookie Monster's.

'Yes, well . . .'

'Well, see!' he exclaimed, throwing back his hands in resignation. 'You screwed me, mate.' How I wished he would stop calling me mate. 'You cost me twelve grand, mate, and that's all I've got in the world.' He shook his head in disgust. 'That was a low act.' He looked at me intensely, raising his index finger to the level of his eyes and shook it in a reprimanding gesture: 'I won't forget this.' With that he turned and walked out of my room, closing the door considerately behind him.

I sat on my bed and considered my options. I was breathing heavily and my vision was receding and contracting like a sixties psychedelic camera effect. I realised I was having an anxiety attack. I tried to think; my mind was hot mud. Kane would be sleeping on the couch in the next room for the rest of the evening and I had no idea what to do. Where could I go? I knew that, by now, the voices in his head were saying 'kill the writer' and I had no desire for him to act on those instructions in a 3 a.m. fit of pique and for the last thing I saw on this earth to be his giant bunch-o-banana hands as they made their descent to my throat. After some consideration, including the option of clubbing him to death in his sleep with a pair of binoculars, I decided that the best course of action was to flee. Burrowing under pillows to muffle my voice I rang my friend Amy and asked if I could stay at her place. 'I'll explain it all later,' I whispered.

Suddenly Jeremy jumped into my room from the balcony, giggling with excitement. Behind cupped hands he whispered that Kane had left the flat but would soon be back. It was all I needed. Throwing a change of clothes into a bag and grabbing my computer, I snuck out the door, down the fire stairs (I didn't want to risk bumping into him in the lift) and through the garden exit. Gingerly I pushed open the gate leading from the barbeque area to Elkhorn Avenue and leant my head out into the unseasonably empty streets. I hung a right past the Prada boutique and came out from beneath the undulating awning of the Moroccan into the drizzle and straight into Kane. Fortunately he was hunched over the public phone, his back turned to me, deep in conversation with most likely Hine or, possibly, a bunch of mates who would be around soon to kill me. Sneaking back in the other direction like a cartoon thief in white sneakers, I made my retreat from the phone booth and then literally ran in the direction of the sea. On the other side of the block I jumped straight into a cab and asked to be taken to Miami, the suburb where my friend lived and where, ironically, Kane still had an apartment. The driver had a heavy Aussie–Chinese accent that in its lyrical modulation had an unexpectedly soothing effect. 'Wha' wrong wit you, mate?'

I guess I was still shaking. I explained.

He sympathised. 'Oh, mate. This sit-ee, full of bad people: everyone out to rob you; everyone out for a scam. I drive a cab here eight years and all the time I meet people who get their things stolen: their passport, all their money. Can't go back to their country! Is terrible. People here, they are dishonest; always look for money. No one know where you come from here, mate. Everyone just come and try to make something off someone.' He finished his piece and sat for some minutes in contemplative oriental silence, the lights of the Gold Coast Highway flying past us in a sparkling prismatic blur. Then he shook his head slowly in angered resignation before adding: 'The Gold Coast! What a hole.'

Nineteen

★

Escape from Pleasure Island

ON PAPER, THE GOLD COAST bus system sounds fantastic. It is the only twenty-four hour public transport service in Australia and with such a linear geography one might assume that all that might be required is for the cheerful yellow vehicles to trundle up and down the strip picking people up and then depositing them at various town centres. In reality, the Gold Coast Highway is almost continually choked and the city, fattened much further to the west than anyone might have predicted, is constantly outgrowing the current provisions for public transport. The result is that buses might as well be arriving and departing to a timetable psychically divined that morning by the reading of chicken entrails rather than any logical construction based on models of population growth or traffic density. This meant that a now tired and distressed writer, uncomfortable with the sun and easily burnt, stood baking under the intense solar radiation beside the roaring highway in a suburb named after a city in Florida while he attempted to conjure an identikit image of the kind of idiot who would have built a group of apartments in the form of a Greek fishing village beside such a hideous strip of road.

I had woken up that morning on the floor of Amy's house and, after eating some breakfast, gathered my things and walked some blocks to catch the bus. Amy herself had not been at home when I phoned the previous evening so she rang her flatmate and arranged for him to let me in: his apparent normality and kindness like a runic cave painting left by some long-forgotten civilisation as evidence of a more gracious time. Now my brief moment of security was over and I stood by the side of this appalling highway, thirsty and slimy as a sea slug, contemplating my uncertain future at the hands of a schizophrenic body builder who wanted to use my severed head as a hat. While waiting, I formulated a plan for my immediate future. Knowing Kane would be at work until at least two o'clock, I decided to return to the unit, grab some clothes and hightail it to Brisbane where I could stay with my friend Greg and, hopefully, arrange some alternative accommodation on the Gold Coast. To make matters even more absurd, we were due for an inspection the next day and, to my knowledge, no one had done anything about cleaning up the previous evening's disaster.

Just as I was about to either hail a cab or turn into flesh-coloured salt crystals, a beige van pulled up beside me and Hinemoa leaned out of the window. 'You wanna lift?'

The Gold Coast: big city problems, small town coincidences.

In the driver's seat was Aunty Judy who introduced herself as I climbed in the back of the van. I squeezed myself in between a teenage cousin and Drakkar, strapped into his baby seat, the position made doubly uncomfortable as I was forced to bend over to accommodate a huge iron cot in the back. Fixed in this position, Drakkar began to hit me in the face. 'Bray-yan! Bray-yan!' he cried in imitation of my name. 'Fack me! Fack me!'

I turned and peered behind me. The back of the van was full of toys and various electronic items, including Kane's black computer. This, as it turned out, belonged neither to Kane nor Hine but was actually the property of Kane's housemate, a prostitute who had once lived with him in Miami but who was now serving time on drugs charges. Kane, who had taken the computer in lieu of what he claimed was unpaid rent, had given it to Hine as a present (or so she claimed). I pointed to the equipment. 'Are you going to give his stuff back to him now?' I asked hopefully.

'Fuckin' no. He owes me heaps of money and shit. I'm gonna keep it and sell it. He 'aint getting nothing back.'

I tried to reason with her, but in the face of her almost hieratic imperviousness to argument, soon gave up.

'I feel so sorry for your poor housemates,' said Aunty Judy, a kindly and soft-spoken woman. 'It's like living in *Jerry Springer*.' Hine giggled. The cousin hooted with laughter. 'Fack me! Fack me!' screamed Drakkar, twisting my nose and grinning and laughing at his own cleverness.

Arriving back at the unit we lugged the steel cot up in the lift and Judy and Hine went to work assembling it in the bedroom. Lenore was in the hallway, vacuuming in preparation for the inspection. I grabbed a scrubbing brush and began to clean the bathroom. Two policemen soon arrived to discuss the terms of a new restraining order that Hine had promised she was to serve. One introduced himself as Henry; he was a Samoan from Rotorua and he knew Lenore's family – their brothers had both worked at the same timber mill. 'Hey, this place is pretty good,' said Henry, settling down on the couch. 'Wadda you fellas pay for it?'

Henry was not happy when we told him about the shoddy performance by his colleagues the previous evening. He promised to talk to them and reassured us Kane would no longer be allowed in the unit. The possibility of a new restraining order was discussed; one that would incorporate the whole building. This gave me some comfort, and I wondered whether I might be able to stay after all.

After chatting with Hine for some time the police made to leave but not before Henry's partner gave her a warning: 'He'll never change, you know. Just get him out of your life. But you have to be strong about this because I'm telling you now: I've seen it all before, and he'll never, ever change.'

She just nodded distantly. 'You fellas wanna drink?'

They declined and left.

With the bathroom scrubbed and the broken doorhandle held in place with a precarious application of Blu-Tack, I went downstairs and waited in the blinding afternoon heat for a bus to Nerang Railway Station: from there I could take a train to Brisbane. The bus was late and my distress in the heat grew, fuelled by semi-irrational fears that Kane may spot me on the corner. Eventually the bus arrived and I joined the backpackers and the kids returning from their daytrips to the beach. As I sat back in the seat and watched the towers roll by I was overwhelmed by a feeling of calm and security that only then did I realise had been missing from my life for the last couple of months. Slowly I felt my pulse rate fall, my face cool. I looked at my ticket. Never did the very word *Brisbane* seem to represent such an oasis of calm, such a pinnacle of civilisation, such a welcome respite from the horrors and mundanities of life. *Brisbane*: it might as well have been Constantinople or Timbuktu. *Brisbane*, where Kublai Khan a stately pleasure dome decreed . . .

I gazed out the window as we passed the site of the ninety-storey tower, watching the ocean flicker between the buildings. Even the beach it seemed was part of the conspiracy against me. 'Say what you will about the Gold Coast, you can't fault the beach.' It was the sort of thing I was used to hearing, even from people who didn't like the Gold Coast. All I could see, however, was an interminable, featureless strip of blue and white, its entire claim to 'paradise' resting on little more than its sheer length. It isn't even a particularly ideal swimming spot, plagued as it is by strong currents and rips. Why people would clamour desperately for a view of this banal strip of granulated silicon and water, the monotony broken only by other apartments full of other people clamouring for the same banal view, was beyond me. Of all the thousands of beaches in Australia, why this one?

Like everything else in this town the beach was a symbol – an *idea* of beach in the same way that fake snow in a shop window is an idea of Christmas. Nothing on the Gold Coast was without a message. Everything was a promise of a better, brighter world, but all it really seemed to offer was a chance to surrender your sense of self to a series of experiences – to the sun, to a lifestyle – and let your ego run wild. So many people, so many problems: all of them running away, as though a new set of circumstances would change everything; as though the problems were due to a lack of resort features rather than something from within. The Gold Coast was like the scene from *Pinocchio* in which all the boys have skipped school and gone instead to Pleasure Island (was it a coincidence that this had been the name of the first theme park on the Gold Coast?), only to realise too late that they have changed into donkeys. This city, once so full of light and energy and eccentricity, now seemed like little more than a dangerous exercise in narcissism.

I thought of some of the people I had met: an artist who told me the interactive CD-ROM of his terrible paintings would 'change the face of education'; a famous real estate developer who insisted in the face of all arguments to the contrary that the Gold Coast was as cosmopolitan as New York; the woman who ran the meter maid business handing out photocopies of her mid-'80s appearance in *Penthouse*; a retired golf pro who could recite every five-star hotel he had ever visited; Benny and his plans to take over the world Internet pornography market; the red-headed porn star and all the 'fun' he was going to have; the prominent real estate agent who had said 'Nobody has the knowledge I have,' and when I asked of what, replied, 'Of everything, mate.' Like Dorothy clicking her heels three times, the Gold Coast resident had only to believe that he or she had the power. Delusion was the mortar of this city and the void of the ocean, the blank blue expanse that all those buildings faced with such duteous absurdity was nothing but a reflection of the void within. My taxi driver had been right; the Gold Coast was a hole, literally.

The drive through the western suburbs was a dreary affair . . . row after row of pastel boxes, some facing golf courses, some facing canals. Finally we arrived at Nerang Station. It was big and new and had obviously been built in anticipation of a busier future. On the platform I waited in the shade, a pleasant breeze arriving with the late afternoon sun. The train pulled in and I boarded, making myself comfortable. For some time I sat and did little more than watch the passing bush, studded with factories and houses that soon would thicken to make Brisbane and the Gold Coast one gigantic, indivisible megalopolis. The suburbs seemed to stretch indefinitely but I found their banality comforting – like watching home shopping at three-thirty in the morning. Just as we began making the stops in the outer suburbs of Brisbane, I got a phone call.

'Hey, bro, guess what's happened?' It was Jeremy. I could hear the bells of the Clock pub chiming in the background. It meant he was on the street. 'I've just come home and Kane and Krystal are sitting in the lounge room like nothing's happened. He just walked in and she made him dinner.'

'What the . . . ? Oh, *fuck*.'

'They've eaten all my food,' he added mournfully.

'Oh, God . . . Oh, no.'

'Yeah, I know – they ate all my Tim Tams.'

'Look, Jeremy, forget about the Tim Tams. What do you mean he just "walked in"? Did she let him in?'

A group of girls across the aisle began to impersonate my frantic lamentations. 'Oh, fuck, Oh, fuck,' they whispered to one another in squeaky voices.

'Yep. And get this: she's moved all his stuff back in and Kane just came up to us and apologised like nothing happened. He just said, "Sorry about all the shit that went on last night, mate, it won't happen again cause me and Hine are back together now and it's all straight." Then he pulls me aside and says, "Listen, mate, between you and me, I'm gonna get some of the boys around with balaclavas and baseball bats and we're gonna break that fuckin' cunt Brendan's legs so fuckin' bad he'll never be able to walk again."'

'Oh, fuck.'

'Oh, fuck,' tittered the girls.

'Don't come back to the house, bro, no matter what you do. Lenore wants to leave too. I'll call later and see if we can work out a plan.'

The girls got off the train, giggling.

It seemed a funny moment for a revelation but it was only now that I realised just how Catholic was my worldview. I say this because for Catholics, the sincere expression of repentance and a desire to change is far more important than the actual history of a person's actions. This is why we make such good criminals. Perhaps if I had been raised a Protestant I might have kicked Hine's skanky arse out of the apartment a month ago. But something in me needed to believe in human goodness. Whatever the case, I had other problems. The good traveller, as I had continually reminded myself throughout various exotic mishaps, is always calm. And yet, try as I might, the knot in my stomach grew; the sudden and literal desire to shit myself remained unabated. The threat of physical violence has always terrified me, and not merely because I'm not good with pain. Kane's violence appalled on a deeper level; it brought me face-to-face with a universe in which the illusion of control and civilisation had been stripped away and all that was left was raw power and its consequences. As the kind of kid who had medicine balls tossed at his head, or couldn't do cross-country because he had a heart condition, or was forever disappearing in the middle of gymnastics because he had a nosebleed, I was desperately ill-equipped to deal with Kane's brand of lunacy.

I began now to formulate a plan of escape. There was no question of ever returning to the flat, but there were complications. For starters, I was going to lose my bond. Then there was Betty, whom I liked a great deal, and who was facing a blacklisting for fraud for letting Jeremy and Lenore have the room under her name. What's more, the Kiwis were facing homelessness. All these questions would have to be resolved later. For now all I could do was ignore the various horrible anticipations conjured by my subconscious and get in a cab to meet Greg.

Greg was a lighting technician by trade and had come to Brisbane to work with his sister Carrie, a choreographer, who was staging a production. The performance was in the suburb of New Farm at the Powerhouse, an old power station and now an arts centre on the banks of the Brisbane River. The area had once been a slum for junkies and aged alcoholics and was now, like inner-city cesspits the world over, in the middle of an apartment boom – the demand for such accommodation fuelled primarily by the thousands of bright young things who had fled the suburbs in the hope that, if they squinted, they might just be able to convince themselves that Brisbane was New York.

At the venue I found Greg. He said he would see me after the show so I went outside and waited by the river with the rest of the audience. The show had been billed as a 'promenade', which meant we were to be led through various rooms on some sort of *Magical Mystery Tour* of modern dance. My alarm at this prospect only increased as I surveyed the audience: sour art-school students; lesbians with canvas food co-op shoulder bags; art yuppies in linen pants. The twenty-or-so people gathered outside was almost double the number expected. For a work that had received a substantial arts grant, this was considered a grand success.

The performance began and we were led from the banks of the river through a series of rooms playing host to a variety of baffling tableaus; what any of them meant I cannot really say but I'll bet someone used words like 'context', 'identity' and 'discourse' on their Australia Council application form. In one particularly affecting sequence we were forced to stare for one whole confounding minute at nothing but a spot-lit square of green turf, and then without explanation, herded out by the ushers. The lesbians were visibly angered by this anticlimax as they had just managed to disrobe themselves of numerous backpacks, shoulder bags and various other Sapphic accoutrements in order to settle their haunches upon the floor.

In the final room a group of three women balancing tea cups in their palms danced around small, colour-coordinated piles of dirt. The dancing stopped but the music kept playing. By the time people began solemnly inspecting the dirt, I figured the show was over. I looked around me and wondered whether it might be possible that Kane had murdered me in my sleep the previous evening and that this was hell. There seemed few other plausible explanations for the preposterous incongruities of my day. Even for its moments of beauty this art seemed desperately irrelevant to a world only a suburban train ride away where the only thing that mattered was love, greed, hate or want – a pat on the head or a punch in a pregnant belly. It was a good reminder of why the Gold Coast did not 'need some culture'.

It was almost midnight when, while sitting in a pizza joint with Greg, I got a call from Jeremy. 'Hey, bro! Guess what?'

'What?'

'A dozen cops just came into the flat and arrested Kane.'

I was ecstatic. As it turned out, Kane had not been let in by Hine but had in fact broken the door down. She, eager to keep him calm, took him in and cooked him dinner. Just as he had settled into a late evening torpor, Hine had grabbed Drakkar, put on her best thongs (the ones with the big, white plastic daisies on the toes) and tottered down to the Surfers Paradise police station to dob him in. An hour later twelve policemen turned up to the flat. They encircled Kane where he lay on the couch and forced him to lie on the floor, after which he was handcuffed and literally carried out of the unit like a large bag of concrete. He was, so far as Jeremy knew, still being held in the Southport watch-house.

I thanked Jeremy and hung up my phone. With great pleasure I ordered another round of beers. It was the first time I had felt able to genuinely enjoy myself in a month. There was, however, a twinge of guilt for having doubted Hine and, once again, in my imagination, she became the plucky little strumpet with a heart of gold. I felt certain she had finally worked it out, that she had kicked the Kane habit. But then I remembered Hemi and my jubilation soured. Both his parents were in prison now and I wondered which hotel he would wind up in next.

Escape from Pleasure Island

*

My elation was somewhat premature. Kane was released without charge not long after his arrest. He was, however, forced to move his things out of the house and return to Miami. Thankfully, the terms of the restraining order had been increased so he would be allowed nowhere near the building or on the footpath outside, making it illegal for him to use the public phones. The Moroccan security guards had been issued with photos of Kane and instructed to call the police the moment he was spotted. On the strength of these measures Jeremy and Lenore had decided to stay. Kane, however, still blamed me for his misfortune and had reiterated to Jeremy his promise to have me killed. Despite this, Jeremy was very keen for me to come home. He reassured me that the 'friends' Kane had organised to beat me consisted of a single member of the scaffolding crew who thought Kane was a fuckwit anyway. I decided to give the issue some more thought while I spent another day in Brisbane.

After a pleasant afternoon spent buying books and visiting art galleries, I could think of nothing I wanted less than to go back to the Gold Coast: bamboo toothpicks under the fingernails, hot pokers to the genitals, a twenty-four hour, non-stop Gwyneth Paltrow film festival . . . all were considered and all deemed preferable to my *Return to Pleasure Island*. My decision to move back to the Moroccan might then seem a little mystifying. The way I saw it, I had been fending off bullies most of my life – Kane was just my biggest challenge. And there was another reason for going back: I wanted to find out whether Hine's baby really was Kane's. She had hinted to us on a number of occasions that the child might not be his and there seemed a good chance this might be true. To run away now would be not only a humiliating admission of defeat, but an eternal frustration for a curious mind.

Getting into a cab I told the driver to take me to the train station. The driver was young, very thin and had the chihuahua-nerves of a professional nightclubber. His teeth were brown, his skin taut and around his elbow he had tied a damp tea towel to keep his arm from burning on the door: it only added to his general air of seediness.

'Where're you off to from Roma Street, man?' A tape of jungle techno was playing, very loudly. I told him I was living on the Gold Coast.

'Know it well, dude; grew up there. I think I've lived in every suburb.' He listed about fifteen. 'But I finally escaped.'

The cabbie was a true Coastie. He had seen Nirvana support the Violent Femmes at Fisherman's Wharf; he had lived in a Scandinavian share-house; he had even gone to the sentencing of Miles Buisson's killer. I said I had little desire to return.

'Man, that place is fucked.' He shook his head. 'Everyone on the Gold Coast is on the make; everyone's got an angle. I virtually got chased out in the end.'

'Funny you should say that. What happened?'

'Well, the final straw came when I was living with a bunch of speed freaks and this one guy used to buy his fantasy off this other guy – not really a friend, but a friend of a friend. I tried to keep him at a distance, but . . .'

I paused. 'Fantasy is another name for GBH isn't it?'

'Yeah. Body builders like to take it – usually the morning before a comp. It cuts into you,' he gestured, slicing his arm. 'It makes all your muscles really defined. It also gets you high. I've never tried it myself – I was more into speed and pills – but this guy used to turn up at our place to sell his Fantasy. He was always off his face on speed and he'd be crashing on the couch and shit. I'd be sitting there and he'd walk in going "Ghhhhh, ghhhhh". He puffed himself up and made Darth

Vader breathing noises, his eyes staggered in their sockets, his head rocked like a Balinese dancer. 'And I'd just be like, "Whoah, Kane, what's going on?" His eyes, dude . . .'

At this point the cab pulled over and I got out. From behind a large, strategically placed bush appeared a smiling man clutching a clipboard and wearing a hairpiece and loud necktie. 'Brendan Shanahan,' he said, approaching with an outstretched hand, 'you're on *Celebrity Crank Call*!' With growing incredulity I soon realised that standing around me was everyone I had met on the Gold Coast: Ren, Betty, Hine, David, Jeremy and Lenore, even the man with no shoes on the bus to South-port, dressed now in a blue polo shirt monogrammed with the logo of a television station. They laughed, they grinned and they slapped their knees. Kane approached, extending his right hand, and then tore at the rubber mask that came off with a suck and snap to reveal my friend Greg, sweating but delighted in a foam rubber suit. 'Surprise!' they all cried in unison.

My mouth fell open and the words fell out in tangles.

There was laughter; there were tears. The psychic gave me a big bunch of flowers: '"Get out of the apartment." Ooooh, spooky!'

I laughed and wept for relief. I looked around. The Brisbane CBD reappeared around me. The host, the cast, Greg in the foam suit, all dissolved into an undulating haze and the tinkle of dream-sequence chimes.

'Hang on, what did you say his name was?'

'Kane – big Maori body builder guy. Fuckin' maniac, dude.'

'Kane Rosenberg?'

'Yeah, that's the dude.'

I told him with spluttering incredulity about my own situation. I described him physically.

'Yeah, that's him.'

I don't know which was more surprising – the coincidence, or his reaction. He shrugged his shoulders. 'Yeah, it wasn't just Kane. It was the drugs, too . . . and a couple of other people. But really, it was just the Gold Coast, man. I couldn't take that place any more. I mean, Brisbane is great: good pubs, great bands, chilled-out people. The Gold Coast is just a place you go if you don't have anything else to do. People there are all looking for the same shit: drugs, money, the beach . . . whatever. I'll never go back.' We arrived at the station. I paid him his money and he began to root around in his tray for the change. Looking up he dropped a pile of coins in my hand and said, 'Are you sure *you* really want to either?'

Back at home the estate agent's inspection had gone well. The only hiccup occurred when Hine's Uncle Daryl turned up midway through, brandishing a set of nunchakus, declaring that he was going to beat Kane to death. Uncle Daryl was Aunty Judy's husband and had been particularly incensed because Kane, while moving his stuff out of the apartment, had taken a swing at her. Luckily, the punch had failed to connect but he had managed to push her to the ground on his way out the door. At the arrival of Uncle Daryl the agent didn't bat an eyelid, but instead asked us to pay particular attention to the bathroom.

Hine was most excited by this latest development. 'You remember Uncle Daryl – he was the one with the missing teeth at the barbeque. Well, he's my mum's brother and there's ten of 'em! And they're so angry they're just gonna go round there and bash the shit outta him!'

'I'm in the middle of a Maori tribal war,' I said.

Hine almost wet herself laughing. 'Put that in your book.'

Apart from the imminent death of Kane, life in the Moroccan

returned to a state of relative, albeit uneasy, calm. Hinemoa had gone to her mother's where she was spending an increasing amount of time in the weeks before the baby was due. It was a measure of the closeness I now felt to Jeremy and Lenore that I agreed to lend them $1800 from my book advance to help them buy a car (I was also motivated by the rather more cynical hope that the money would guarantee Jeremy's physical support in any confrontation with Kane). As it was, the pair didn't have much money, and they already owed me two weeks' rent, but Jeremy assured me that with a car he would get a great deal of work he was currently missing out on due to a lack of transport. With a car, he might even be able to get a job as a greenkeeper. What's more, Lenore had a guaranteed job at a hockey clinic beginning in January. With their combined income they would soon be able to pay me back. I agreed and handed the money over the next day.

That morning we decided to investigate the Chateau's breakfast buffet. Jeremy and I went ahead while Lenore stopped at the payphone to call her family in New Zealand. Jeremy waded his way through steamers full of dripping sausages and frazzled bacon while I settled on a bowl of tinned fruit and a cup of watery coffee. Just as I was starting on my third cup, Lenore returned from the phone. 'The funniest thing just happened,' she said. 'I could have sworn that while I was talking to my mum I could hear Kane on the line talking about his flatmate – you know, the prostitute – and about how she'd stolen a whole lot of money from him.' After some discussion about the likelihood of getting a crossed line with the only person we had cause to avoid in a city of a million people, the mysterious conversation was dismissed as merely a case of mistaken identity. The lesson I had yet to learn was that even on the Gold Coast, you couldn't dodge destiny.

Twenty

★

I See Dead People

MY BIRTHDAY IS a particular misery. As a frequent traveller I have spent this supposed day of celebration in a variety of seedy bars or slovenly youth hostel dormitories in lonely parts of the world, more often than not in the company of strangers. Going on a bus tour of the Gold Coast hinterland, therefore, seemed as exciting a way to spend the occasion as any; and after the drama of the previous days, I was looking forward to seeing something pleasant.

The mini-van arrived at 7 a.m. driven by Jack, the tour guide. The rest of the group consisted of three single men. I scanned their hopeful, imploring faces and was reminded of the party scene with the cardboard guests in Steve Martin's *The Lonely Guy*. I wondered if it was their birthday too.

Driving northwards across the bridge, past the fake palm tree, we arrived at a barren spot in northern Southport where a mother and her teenage son were waiting by the highway. She was in her mid-thirties with an open, angular face emphasised by a severe blonde ponytail and a superficial tan glowing like the rind on a fragrant slice of gouda cheese – an unmistakably northern European look. Her son was dark and looked to be about twelve or thirteen, but his body was stocky and he had the coordinated gait of a man. The family ignored the others and walked up the aisle to sit on the back seat, chatting and laughing in an unidentifiable language.

The bus wound its way through the western suburbs. It wasn't until after about half an hour that the houses thinned and we began to climb a steep hill into the bush. To the accompaniment of piped New Age muzak our tour continued past some hobby farms and through two elderly towns dying of thirst in the drought. Finally we arrived in the middle of some dense bushland, the location of a jungle training facility for the army. It looked rugged, prickly and uninviting; it was not the sort of landscape I had expected. The bus wound on slowly. Jack had begun to speak into the microphone. He was a pleasant, doddering character with a fondness for inconsequential detail. 'Soon we'll be arriving at the alpaca farm,' he intoned. 'They have a cafeteria there where coffee can be purchased for $2.50 and anzac biscuits for $1.50.'

Our journey would take all day; after a stop at the alpaca farm we were going to drive through Lamington National Park where we would visit an eco-resort known as O'Reilly's. After this we would descend the mountain to stop at an area outside Mount Tamborine where we could have lunch if we wished: 'The café has a wide variety of excellent sandwiches, milkshakes, coffee and even fruit juice.' Our day would end with a visit to a waterfall.

By the time we arrived at the alpaca farm I had introduced myself to the other three men: a smiling Pole, who videoed every step of the journey, a glum Spaniard, and a leering Singaporean. Only the woman and her son remained a mystery. At the front of the farm we were led to a small enclosure where one of the animals had been tethered for the benefit of the group. Obediently we queued to rub its neck. The creature stood at its post, enduring the fondling with the kind of stoic mortification exhibited by an elderly hospital patient having his genitals inspected by a team of visiting medical students. Under the silent reproach of the alpaca's gaze we were herded back downstairs to the cafeteria where Jack could be heard reminding us that 'coffee is $2.50 and anzac biscuits $1.50'. Once seated outdoors we were encouraged to ask questions about alpaca farming. I affected a token curiosity but was soon dragged back into conversation with the leering Singaporean. It wasn't the fact that he was trying to pick me up that annoyed me, it was his dullness; his presence only seeming to confirm my theory that all the interesting people in Singapore are in prison.

'I wish you could come and see my beautiful country,' he said.

'I've seen your beautiful country,' I replied. 'It's a fascist hellhole.' Rising from my position at the picnic table while he was still in the middle of a passionate defence of Singapore, I wandered back to the café where the European woman was talking to the tour guide. 'I'm so scared of the insects,' I heard her say.

'You shouldn't worry,' said Jack.

Her son pointed an accusing finger at his mother: 'She's already spent $200 on insect repellent.' The woman nodded and laughed guiltily. 'I haven't slept since we arrived two weeks ago,' she said desperately.

I laughed and she smiled at me.

With that we climbed back on the bus and drove further up the mountain. It was an essentially uninteresting drive through a stretch of tepid bush denuded of the promised wild koalas but offering a beautiful view in a shade of watery lavender to the extinct volcanoes on the horizon. The view aside, I was starting to worry that this trip was unlikely to get any more interesting, but once we entered Lamington National Park my mood altered markedly. Almost immediately the vegetation changed, the scrubby bush giving way to something dank and elemental. Here the trees were so tall that the topmost branches could not be seen without craning your neck from the window. Their huge trunks were supported on podiums of tangled roots so limb-like it was as though, like enchanted creatures from a Norse fairy tale, they might at any moment lift themselves from the soil to scuttle across the forest floor. Dotted across the surface of the trunks grew giant bloomless orchids and slick green ferns sweeping upwards in elegant sprouting arcs, while between the branches hung an intricate weft of vines so thick that one could only see a short way into the forest before they drew across to shroud the distance in a veil of tangled gossamer. It was astonishing to think that this dense, ageless jungle sat here, less than an hour from the Gold Coast I knew. And now I was listening as Jack spoke the names of plants into the microphone: staghorn, elkhorn, orchid, pandanus. Here in the forest was a vegetable map of Surfers Paradise: an unexpected moment of poetry in a city with none.

 O'Reilly's is a private property and eco-resort in the centre of the national park. The main attraction is a beautiful treetop walk swaying tens of metres above ground. To reach it we went on a short trek through the bush. Jack showed us the strangler fig that grows in the topmost branches of a tree, creeping down over a period of hundreds of years to gently envelop the trunk and finally kill it. After another several hundred years or so the tree rots away to leave a cavity within the fig as smooth and round as a brick chimney up through the centre of which (soaring hundreds of feet high) you can see a perfect circle of atmospheric sapphire.

The treetop walk was indeed impressive, our legs shifting on the delicate swaying bridge as we traversed the forest canopy below. Jack pointed to the boards. 'See those plaques? The silver ones are for people who donated ten dollars and the gold for people who donated fifteen . . .'

Making our way down from the creaking bridge we turned and waked back through the shade of vines and scrub. A few metres into the bush Jack spotted a little kangaroo-like creature lying in a patch of sun. With its brown eyes, Womble-nose and iridescent pink ears, it had the kind of face that makes Japanese tourists lose bladder control. As it stood up we could make out a perfect miniature sitting in the pouch. The Polish man lay on the ground with his camera like a jungle guerilla. Jack told us that this animal was a female pademelon, a type of wallaby. 'What happened to the father?' asked the European woman.

'Oh, he's long gone,' said Jack.

'Huh! Same as in Holland.'

I was the only one who laughed. She smiled appreciatively.

After some parrot feeding which saw the Dutch woman almost collapse in convulsions of fear below the flapping of scarlet wings, we returned to the bus and wended our way back through the rainforest. I took the opportunity to sit next to her and strike up a conversation.

Her name was Mandy and her son's was Bonito, which, or so she explained with a ruffle of his dark coarse hair, was not her first choice; she had wanted to call him 'Benito', as in Mussolini, but his father had insisted on the Spanish form. Bonito was a handsome, stocky boy, his sense of preternatural maturity emphasised by his oversized hands, strong tan and a brilliant pair of purple eyes that roamed and then caught your gaze with an unnerving intensity. On his thick fingers he wore wide silver rings, one engraved with a pentagram; on his arm was the ghostly shadow of an old henna tattoo, long since flaked off. He looked nothing like his mother, although he had inherited her Flemish overbite. 'I had to quit my job to come here,' said Mandy, 'but now I think I might have to go back early because I am so scared of the insects.' She paused, before adding, 'Oh well, all part of the adventure.'

I asked what she did for a living. She said she had been a social worker but quit after becoming too depressed by the appalling heroin problem in Holland. She got a job in a casino but unfortunately they wouldn't give her time off for an Australian holiday, and now she would have to find another job upon her return to Maastricht. I asked about their curious language; normally I could recognise Dutch. 'Yes, our language is different,' she explained. 'We are from the German–Belgian border – not too far from France – and there we speak our own language. The other Dutch think we are idiots. I once went for a job as an airline stewardess and my regional accent was so strong that they wouldn't give it to me.'

Mandy had no self-pity but she did have a fear of Australian insects that bordered on a diagnosable disorder. Every night she would spray her body and sleeping quarters with a couple of hundred dollars' worth of poison in an unctuous nocturnal ritual of dubious efficacy. Yet still she could not sleep for fear of the cockroaches. When I asked if she planned to go anywhere other than the Gold Coast she said she would like to but did not want to spend the night away from her friends for fear of encountering wayward arachnids. That it was entirely illogical to attach such a talismanic faith in the ability of her acquaintances to keep insects at bay was of no concern to her.

We arrived for lunch at a strange tourist strip of craft stores and candle shops built in kitsch Bavarian style called Gallery Walk. 'Was this originally a German community?' I asked our guide.

'No, it's just a look they're going for.'

As we entered the café I attempted to persuade Mandy that the benefits of seeing other parts of Australia far outweighed the threat of being devoured alive by coordinated hordes of swarming vermin. She shook her head, unconvinced, although not entirely unaware of her own silliness.

We had only been seated for a minute before Bonito withdrew a golden packet of Benson & Hedges and lit up his first cigarette.

'How old are you, Bonito?' I asked.

'Twelve,' he replied, and ashed his cigarette. 'Mind if I smoke?'

Mandy became a little frantic. 'I know, I know,' she said. 'He's too young to be smoking. But at his high school already there are drinkers and pot smokers and all of that. So, just so long as he smokes, I don't mind . . . and you're supposed to ask *before* you light up, Bonito.'

'I never smoke pot,' said Bonito with total assurity. And I believed him.

'How many do you smoke?' I asked.

'Here, not so much, but back in Holland, I was on a pack a day.' He was neither proud nor remorseful.

'He always wanted to smoke,' explained Mandy. 'Even when he was five or six he'd say, "I'm going to take up smoking." My mother said to him, "If you don't smoke by the time you're sixteen, I will buy you a moped." He said, "Keep the moped."' I laughed and as the waitress came to take our order, an expression of barely repressed disgust spread across her face.

I asked how long they were to stay on the Gold Coast.

'Well, we are supposed to be here for three months. But now I think we go home early . . .' She trailed off. 'We are having problems with the people we are staying with. And the insects.'

'Do you like the Gold Coast?'

'Oh, yes! The beach is nothing like I have ever seen! So beautiful. Never have I seen a beach like this: like a dream. But, tell me,' she asked gingerly, 'is Sydney more of a proper city?'

'Well, it's more sophisticated. The Gold Coast is more like the Australian Costa Del Sol.'

She nodded. 'Yes, it is. We used to live in Spain.'

I thought I might hazard a guess. I nodded in Bonito's direction. 'Is his father Spanish?'

'No. A gypsy,' she said firmly. Bonito rolled his eyes and muttered. 'Bonito is not proud of his heritage,' she explained, turning to face him and waggle a finger. 'But he should be. The gypsies are a strong and proud people.' Bonito did a little pantomime of his mother's well-worn speech. I laughed and turned to Bonito. 'What do you like to do in your spare time?'

'I collect horror movies. I own almost 500. I have every movie and the sequels: *Jaws*, *Halloween*, *Friday the Thirteenth*, *The Omen* . . .'

'We had to travel to America because we were missing one of the *Halloween* sequels,' laughed Mandy, as Bonito lit up his second cigarette. 'I could never watch *The Exorcist*,' she continued. 'I was totally terrified. But when he watches it I hear him laughing!'

'It was so *fake*,' said Bonito dismissively.

'He wasn't raised a Catholic.'

'No, exactly,' said Mandy. Her tone changed. 'I was raised a Catholic. Bonito likes witchcraft and magic and all this kind of stuff, but I don't like him thinking about these things because in Catholicism this is not good. It upsets me.' She went quiet, before adding, 'And my mother.' Bonito grinned, pleased with himself.

'You know,' I said to Bonito, 'I have a horror movie story. Have you ever seen *Candyman*?' His eyes lit up. He certainly had. 'Well, you know how in *Candyman* in order to call the ghost you have to say "Candyman" five times into the mirror? And you know how the ghost is always accompanied by swarms of bees?' He knew all these details. He had even tempted fate by repeating the cursed word five times into a mirror, but nothing had happened.

I continued. 'Well, I saw that movie for the first time a couple of years back. Then, three nights later, I had a dream that I was calling the Candyman. There I was, standing in front of the mirror saying, "Candyman, Candyman, Candyman, Candyman . . ." then I distinctly remember I was about to say it the fifth time when my conscious mind took over and I said to myself, "Don't do it, Brendan. It's not worth it. Why take the risk?" At that point I woke up very suddenly.' Mandy was smiling excitedly. 'And then, when I looked around – and I swear this is true – my entire room, my floor, my bedcovers, my window sill, all of them were covered in dead bees.'

Bonito's mouth fell open and smoke drifted out from between the large gaps in his big Dutch teeth. 'Whoah. Really? Did that really happen to you?' I confirmed the truth of it. He nodded with the look of someone who is not easily impressed; suddenly he was a little kid again. Mandy's expression was hesitant. After a short silence she leant in close to my face and said quietly in her soothing, singsong Dutch accent, 'You know, when Bonito was younger . . .' Bonito cut her off sharply. 'Mum, have you gotta tell everyone?' A pregnant silence fell over our table.

After a minute or so Bonito turned and said, quite matter-of-factly, 'When I was young, I could see things.'

I stopped and thought. 'Did you see a ghost?' I asked. Bonito was not given an opportunity to reply before Mandy began. 'The moment we walked into that house I knew something was wrong. He was only two and he looked up at me and said, "I don't like this place, Mummy. I don't want to live here." I said, "Don't be silly, Bonito" and just ignored him.' She shook her head. 'I think part of the problem was that the people who had lived there before were Indonesian, and they had cast spells on the house.'

'What happened?'

'He could see them. He could see all of them. I would be standing in the kitchen or something, and there he was, only two years old, and he would point beside me and say, "Who is that woman, Mummy?" I was so disturbed. I said, "Bonito, don't say these things. You're scaring me." But he knew. He could see.' Her voice cracked slightly. 'It got very hard. I took him to see a doctor and then a . . . how you say in English? A doctor, with herbs?'

'A naturopath.'

'Yes, and he said, "Take peppermint." But it didn't work. Bonito kept seeing things. He would talk to them. He would say, "Guess what the ladies told me today, Mummy?" I was so frightened. People said to me, "You must stop this." My mother said, "If you keep saying these things people will think you and your son are crazy and they will take him off you." So I tried not to say anything to anyone. But it was hard. We lived in that house for a few years but it became too much. Bonito kept seeing them, the people who had died there. He has a gift, but I couldn't take it any more.'

'Like the kid in *The Sixth Sense*,' I said.

Bonito recoiled. 'I hate that movie.'

'I'm scared by that movie!' said Mandy and laughed nervously. 'His father had the same power. But he never did anything with it. When we first started going out he would point at a space on the wall and say, "Do you see those two people?"' She laughed. 'I thought he was joking but then I spoke to his family and they all said, "No, no. He can see. He has a gift." They were very serious.' She paused. 'But he never did anything with it.'

I sat quietly and sipped my lemonade. Under the radiant yellow umbrella the sun beat down through a violet sky and all around us a soft breeze blew through the groves of dwarf palms. As the wind rose and fell the branches whispered among themselves. We got up to pay.

'We're all together,' Mandy said to the cashier.

'Mandy, I can't let you pay for me.'

'No, no, no,' she insisted. 'It's your birthday. Enjoy it.' I demurred, embarrassed, and thanked her as we left for the waterfall.

Thanks to the drought, Curtis Falls was nothing but a delicate white spout of foam pissing out over a grey-green rock shelf into a black, reeking swamp. To reach it we had to trek to the bottom of an 800-metre path winding down through a baleful tropical jungle that caught at our clothes and terrified my Dutch friends with its insectival buzzings. Still, the Polish man videoed and I photographed Mandy and Bonito in front of what was left of the attraction before turning with the rest of the group to trudge back up the hill.

We got back onto the bus tired and sticky. I let the airconditioning blow on my shins and settled in for the steep and silent descent to the coast.

'Do you still see your father, Bonito?' I asked.

'No,' he said resolutely. 'And I don't *want* to either.'

'Bonito's father left just after he was born,' explained Mandy dispassionately. 'We never see him any more.'

'Does he still live in Spain?'

'No, Belgium ... I think. Maybe some times, accidentally, we bump into him and say hi. But we never make an effort.' Bonito nodded and changed the subject. 'Will we be in your book?' he asked excitedly. I was going to tell him that there was every possibility until someone spotted a koala on the side of the road and any previous conversation was immediately forgotten in the scramble to peer into the brown distance for evidence of the animals that had returned after the recent bushfires.

By the time we pulled into Southport Bonito was crumpled in sleep against the hard grey cushion of the seat. 'Here's my number,' I said to Mandy, as she roused her son and gathered their bags. 'If you want to go to the beach or the movies, or if you need a hand finding a new place, call me.'

'Thank you. I will,' she said. And, as we waved goodbye through the glass, I found myself hoping very much that she was sincere.

When I got home Jeremy told me he had put some credit on his phone. That evening Kane rang to tell him that when we had gone to breakfast at the Chateau the previous morning, he had been able to hear every word of Lenore's conversation to her parents. In evidence he repeated, almost word for word, the entire phone call. Lenore confirmed the accuracy of Kane's testimony. Kane explained that the police had bugged his phone and the one in front of the Moroccan, causing a crossed line. 'I hope you know I'm not lying about Hine now, mate,' he said and rang off.

Together we sat in stunned silence. After some minutes our words returned, but there seemed little we could add. Perhaps the phone really was bugged? He was a drug dealer, after all. But would the police bug a public phone? It sounded an awful lot like a schizophrenic delusion, but then again, it did seem an awfully big coincidence. Could it be, I ventured, that Kane was so insane he had bugged the phone himself? We could not agree; the only consensus was that a growing sense of paranoia had begun to infect us all and I was starting to wonder whether any story was worth the risks I was taking.

Twenty-one

★

Bonito Sees Death

MANDY AND BONITO and I went to a movie. I remembered thinking it was an odd choice of film because I had already seen it and thought it was terrible. It was a horror movie set on a cruise ship during the 1940s, featuring a particularly gruesome opening sequence involving a dance floor of soon-to-be phantasms and a length of booby-trapped metal cable. A jazz band played as the couples danced until, suddenly, the cable made an evil whipping noise. Everyone stood stock-still until, slowly, one by one, their bodies began to slide apart and fall in chunks to the ground, cut in half by the singing, gore-dipped cable. Before he died, one man looked down with surprise at his toppling legs and spilling guts and at the sight of this Bonito sniggered evilly. I recoiled from him in the dark.

After the movie Mandy and I caught a train. It was the late 1930s or '40s and I think the war was on. The world was black and white now. Together we sat facing one another in an old-fashioned carriage, the sort found in early Hitchcock films, travelling from Prague to who-knew-where, the snow-dusted landscape racing by outside. For some time I sat and felt the rocking of the carriage, watching the light through the window grow low and the details of Mandy's face fade until she was nothing more than a grey mask ringed by a faint halo of light.

'You know,' she said, 'Bonito saw something. But he doesn't want to tell you.'

I didn't say anything, just stared at the snow that was falling heavily now.

Mandy leant in and the light cut across her nose. 'Bonito sees death. He sees it all around you. But he does not want me to say.' She shook her head and sat back against the high-backed leather seat.

We arrived in Milan and I left the carriage. It was early evening in the snow but I did not feel cold. No one else got off the train and the platform was deserted. Alone I walked through a soaring wrought-iron train station of great beauty; an amalgam of a dozen such stations. Slowly I grew disembodied and my vision panned upwards through the elegant iron vaults to watch myself walk alone towards an unknown destination, a small, grey, lonely figure.

I suppose it would have made better dramatic effect had I received my first death threat the morning after this peculiar dream. But it wasn't until the next day that an unlisted number flashed on the screen of my phone. I answered.

'Haaaay, motherfucker. You better get out or else you're gonna die. 'Cause I'm gonna fuckin' kill you.'

Before our home phone had been cut off, we had been receiving these threats for some time and, lately, Jeremy and Lenore had been getting them on their mobile. Although the voice sounded unfamiliar it was almost comically obvious who was behind this campaign of intimidation. This was the first instance, however, that the threats had been directed specifically at myself and this disturbed me not only because I thought Kane perfectly capable of murder, or because it meant someone had given him my mobile number, but because the dark forces of fate were conspiring against me. Far more unnerving than the dream was the fact that I believed it.

Twenty-two

★

Kane and the B3 Nightclub Spectacular

THREE DAYS EARLIER, on the day of my dream, a 23-year-old boy had gone for a late-night swim in a Gold Coast lake and never came back. The suggestion that he had drowned while drunk was later disproved with the discovery of his body; a shark had torn off a huge piece of his leg. The air seemed full of bad portents. That day I was due to see Phil. In the weeks since I had met them at the second bondage party, Phil and Rachelle had become my good friends. Already I had visited their home for several boozy barbeques and also accompanied them on an excursion to a new wildlife sanctuary where the owner, an IT millionaire, had bought two elephants that no one wanted (one had killed a man) and was wondering whether Rachelle might be able to fill the position of handler. During the course of these social engagements I discovered that, between them, Phil and Rachelle knew every single person on the Gold Coast, or so it seemed. From Miles Buisson to Craig Gore, I had only to mention a name and Phil would hand me a phone number or, if he didn't have it, would call a guy who would make a call to a guy who would.

Phil was third-generation Gold Coast and Rachelle second; they were the closest I had come to meeting indigenous Coasties. Both were from notable local families; in his day, Phil's father had been a notorious Gold Coast entrepreneur and hard man, an Australian martial arts champion with connections to biker gangs and other underworld organisations. Rachelle's father was a war hero and had a park named after him. Both had been deeply scarred by their parents' divorces and so, even though they had been together since high school and had a child, they had never married.

Phil and Rachelle lived in a small house on the wrong side of the highway surrounded by their daughter's toys and dozens of animals. The living room alone played host to a talking galah, a tank full of tropical fish, two miniature turtles and a barrel-like blue-tongue lizard that would emerge occasionally from beneath its bark shelter to issue a series of irritable, reptilian snufflings which would never fail to startle. This afternoon, however, Phil was taking me on a tour of Rachelle's koala enclosure.

Meeting me in Surfers with his daughter Elizabeth in the back of the car we sped over the bridge and to the far north. At the lights, from a six-pack he had been keeping in the glove box, Phil cracked open a tinnie of bourbon and Coke. 'Want one?' he asked. I declined. Tinnies of bourbon and Coke are the official beverage of the Gold Coast and the only free alcohol I have ever refused.

Like everyone else in this city Phil was always concocting schemes of such ambition that the chance of their success could only be calculated by dividing the number of guarantees made for their eventual realisation into the total number of bourbons consumed during their formulation. As we drove he began to describe the often complex technicalities of a real estate deal he was planning. 'I'll have made a million by the end of this year – guaranteed,' he said, bashing at the steering wheel and sending a little arc of rum through the air.

We drove for some distance before we arrived at the nature park. After eating lunch to the accompaniment of a cork-hatted man on an electric guitar who sang a surprisingly deafening version in Cantonese of 'I was Made for Loving You' to a group of extremely appreciative tourists, we went off and met Rachelle at the koala enclosure.

She was very upset because an entire herd of kangaroos was to be shot after their dominant male had attacked two Taiwanese tourists. The removal of this animal had destroyed the structure of the herd and a chaotic power struggle ensued. Now the only option was to kill the animals that could not live in an unstructured society and would surely die in the wild. Phil thought this terribly funny and began to tease her. 'Shut up, you bastard,' snapped Rachelle, before breaking into laughter. 'Animals are dying. We have to be serious.'

As an Australian, the imagined familiarity of the koala has precluded any serious consideration of these creatures. Yet to take a long, objective look at one of these things is to realise that, far from being familiar or cuddly, they are a freakish deviation of nature's divine plan. As she wedged branches between the fork of a tree, Rachelle began to explain some of the little known facts of the koala. A persistent myth about them is that the eucalyptus leaves get them stoned, which is why they're so sluggish. The truth is koalas sleep a great deal only because the food is such a poor source of energy that the volume of leaves and the intestinal effort required to digest them allows little room for anything else. Essentially all of a koala's evolution has been focused on the job of being able to digest the tough sugars of the eucalypt, a process that begins when baby koalas eat their mothers' faeces in order to develop the rigorous chemicals of their gut. (Sometimes one can't help but wonder whether such creatures don't simply *deserve* to be eaten by cats.)

Koalas are incurably horny – sex being their only other major activity aside from eating. Rachelle revealed some of the quirks of their rich sexual life.

'The other day we had a photographer in and I was holding Teddy.' She pointed to the offender. 'And he began to extend his penis and the photographer kept rubbing him on the back and I was saying, "Don't do that! He'll ejaculate all over me!"'

'Have they ejaculated on you?' I asked.

'Yeah, all the time.' Phil had learnt to detect the smell.

She continued. 'Koalas have a very nasty barbed penis. When they mate with the female the penis withdraws and it actually rips them open – same as with cats. The pain is what tells the koala to begin sending out ovum. Koalas don't ovulate continuously like humans do so they need to know when the sperm is there.'

But there's more!

'Did you know that the excretory system and the reproductive system of the female koala is all in the same hole?'

Oddly enough, I didn't.

'So the male koala has an opening in exactly the same place as the female. Unfortunately what happens is that when we put two aggressive males together, come morning, the stronger one has raped the weaker one, and they cause a lot of damage.' She began to shake with laughter.

I was dumbfounded. Rachelle turned over her hands. Her wrists were scarred with the legacy of numerous attacks.

With the revelation of this unimagined viciousness came *Day of the Triffids*-style nightmares: human beings blinded by a meteor shower groping their way through the streets of Surfers Paradise, the helpless victims of the koalas' coordinated attacks. Gum leaves – a likely story. Kill them all while we still have the chance, I say.

Unbeknown to many, the Gold Coast region is the most biodiverse in the country, but unbridled development has meant the displacement of many native animals. Rachelle said that developers were supposed to report animal communities and hand over displaced specimens to wildlife parks. In reality, however, most simply pretended they weren't there. Occasionally, though, Rachelle would receive a gift of an irritated koala or some other distressed creature. One particularly peculiar story was that of an illegal American tortoise that had been found at a building site and handed into the wildlife park where Rachelle had worked formerly. Once they had ascertained that the animal was a violation of quarantine, it was placed in a special tank in the office where it sat patiently awaiting execution. But quarantine never arrived, and there for years the death-row tortoise sat in perpetual limbo and, so far as she was aware, sat still.

Leaving Elizabeth with Rachelle, Phil and I began the long drive to Movie World where he worked, on occasion, creating special effects. Today he just needed to pick something up. We drove through the tollgate and onto the back lot. A film of *Peter Pan* was being made at the studio. On the concrete driveways outside the shining hangars ran dozens of bare-chested children, their faces painted, feathers in their hair, playing hand tennis or munching on sandwiches. As I sat and waited for Phil I watched the kids and listened to the screams coming from the roller coasters. When Phil returned we bundled back in the car and took off for home. As we drove along, Phil's father rang. It was the second such call that afternoon. For some time they spoke, Phil talking on the phone with one hand, balancing his can of bourbon and steering with the other.

'Okay, see you later, Dad. Take care,' he said before hanging up.

'Well, at least you're still close to your father,' I said.

Phil laughed. 'Do you know what he was ringing for?'

'No.'

'Drugs. Just wants to get his hands on anything I can hook him up with.' He sighed. 'It's pathetic but that's what happens to old hippies on the Gold Coast.'

In the next hour his father rang another four times.

'So, how's your flatmate situation?' Phil asked.

I told him the latest.

'Oh, he deals Fanta, does he?' Phil always had hip names for drugs I had never heard of. 'You ever hear about an incident at the B3 nightclub in Broadbeach?'

'No, I don't think so. What happened?'

'Well, twenty people collapsed on New Year's Day out the front of the club. They'd all taken Fanta when it was still a very new drug. Nobody told them that they couldn't take alcohol with it! I think it was '95 or '96. Anyway, some died . . . I think. It's a famous incident, Gold Coast legend. What's your flatmate's name?'

I told him.

Phil gave a short burst of maniacal laughter. 'Oh, shit!' He laughed again and leant forward over the steering wheel. 'Do they call him Kane Rane?'

'I don't know, but it wouldn't surprise me. His surname is Rosenberg.'

'Then it was probably him who was dealing it. How old is he?'

'Thirty-two.'

'Easily could have been him. My mate was a DJ that night. He said Kane Rane was the dealer. I'll see if I can get you in touch with him.'

This was too much. Kane wasn't a man; he was a presence.

*

The story, like all local legends, had been exaggerated in the telling. The B3 nightclub disaster was not, for starters, on New Year's Day; it took place at six-thirty on a Sunday morning after an average Saturday night in early October 1996. The common but specious assignation of New Year's adds a certain mystique to the event and speaks of a strong desire to subsume it into myth. The mortality rate was also considerably less dramatic. People of all walks of life on the Gold Coast, from cab drivers to surf instructors, remain convinced that at least some people had died – one cabbie going so far as to claim twenty fatalities. In reality, only eight to ten people were hospitalised (the number varies in news reports) and there were no deaths. Still, the image of dozens of young clubbers cracking their heads on the pavement, their bodies laid waste like victims of the Jonestown massacre, was a powerful one.

At the time of the incident (disaster seems somewhat hyperbolic for an event in which no one died) GBH was still a legal drug in Australia. B3 changed that. The then Queensland minister for police, Russell Cooper, flew into action: 'The Gold Coast rave party which resulted in the emergency hospitalisation of nine young people this weekend has shocked the State and revealed a panorama of problems associated with the so-called youth drug culture. I can assure the House that I share community concern about these so-called rave parties and associated drug taking preying on impressionable and vulnerable young minds.'

Here was the popular image of the drug dealer as the Child Catcher from *Chitty Chitty Bang Bang*, tempting rosy-cheeked scamps with poisoned lollies. The evils of the 'so-called rave parties', not to mention the 'so-called youth drug culture' went no way to recognise the evils of ordinary society: far easier to ignore the fact that people take drugs because they like it or because they're unhappy or because their parents did it. Far easier to blame some nameless caricature of wickedness than to recognise that drugs are a logical product of a society in which choice and new experience are the two reigning virtues.

Twenty-three

★

Rod and Todd

JUST AFTER CHRISTMAS Kane rang Jeremy and described to him in alarming detail a number of changes we had made within the apartment since he had been banished from its confines. How he knew none of us could say and the suggestion that he had been making surreptitious excursions into our home set us all on edge. Add to this the steady diet of death threats and the attendant fear that Kane might at any moment break down the door and kill us all, one might reasonably have assumed that we lived in a state of almost constant panic. But perhaps because we had grown accustomed to the atmosphere of dread, life in the Moroccan seemed to return to a state of comparative stability. It was possible that I had begun to enjoy the game of cat-and-mouse I was playing with Kane.

Other than Kane's threats Christmas came and went almost without incident. The population of the city had grown to about a million people and the activity was feverish. Across the street, the Chevron Renaissance had risen to its full height; so keen were the developers to see the building occupied before the peak season that they had been moving in furniture at night-time. It had yet to rain, however, and every day the local council made desperate pleas to the citizenry to conserve water.

At New Year's some friends of mine from Sydney, including one who had just been inducted into the Australian Federal Police, came and joined a small party in our apartment. The evening was remarkable only because a policewoman bearing a significant resemblance to the one who had turned up the night Kane tried to steal our things appeared on the national news having been filmed dousing the face of a man with capsicum spray in what looked like a massive overreaction. In response there was community outrage and the Gold Coast police garnered, overnight, a bad reputation. Jeremy was especially pleased by the prospect of seeing the woman suffer disciplinary action: she had once booked him for speeding on his bicycle. Hine, meanwhile, was still spending a large amount of time at her mother's. Kane, she told us, was having a 'psycho attack'. He had been threatening her mother and siblings and she thought that she might disappear to Brisbane for a few days until he calmed down. So, when she vanished a couple of days after New Year's, we thought nothing of it.

There had, however, been one significant black note. Over the course of the last month I had been swapping emails with David, who had returned home. These emails consisted mostly of his telling me how much he missed me while I offered in return sound paternal advice about the importance of study and the need for him to consider a future away from his home town. The tenor of some of this correspondence had, however, begun to concern me. His tone had grown from merely plaintive to distinctly unstable. What's more, the details of some of his stories were hazy; his actions had become contradictory. In one very confusing incident he said that he had agreed to meet with his ex-boyfriend at the pub, despite telling me that he had been jailed. The correspondence grew more and more unsettling until one day I received a disturbing letter in which he claimed to have been the victim of a sexual assault. The details, once again, were sparse. In response I counselled him to remain calm and referred him to the appropriate authorities. I had, I felt, done all I could for David. Although I was still very concerned about his mental state and the possibility he might attempt to hurt himself, I began, quite consciously, to neglect our communication. As a result, his letters became less and less frequent until our correspondence dissipated into a couple of single-line updates. By early January I had not heard from him for several weeks. 'You are so lucky to be on the Gold Coast,' he had written in his final letter. 'Remember, I envy you!'

More than ten days passed and still there had been no word from Hinemoa. She was not answering her mobile phone and her rent was almost two weeks overdue. It had occurred to us that she might have had the baby, but it seemed unlikely; we had been in contact with one of her cousins who worked in the local supermarket and she had not heard from her either. In an attempt to track her down, Jeremy and I ransacked her bedside table for phone numbers. We found nothing but we enjoyed the snooping. The contents of the drawers were like a curious time capsule of my stay on the Gold Coast: paintings by Drakkar, social security statements, advertisements for rival phone sex companies, a hepatitis pamphlet and another detailing the dangers of steroid abuse, a phone sex 'time sheet' with various credit card numbers, a dramatic photograph by firelight of Kane in his days as a dancer on the islands, and a letter from Hemi's mother written in a fat, round script that reached the full height of the line: 'Remember that mummy will always love you and misses you very much.'

Our search fruitless, we flopped back down on the couch where Jeremy began to regale me further with the Thousand-and-One Nights of Kane. With every instalment the stories only grew more wretched and bizarre. This week at work Kane had been bragging to Jeremy about taking Hemi to the beachfront at Surfers where, as though the child was a pit bull, he would bet other fathers that his son could beat theirs in a fight. An incident that was merely peculiar by comparison had occurred the previous day when some of the boys from the building site had gone swimming. Undressing on the sand, Kane took off his shirt to reveal a torso covered in a vicious lattice of welts and contusions. Running down his back in two symmetrical rows, starting at his shoulders and ending at his pelvis, were six huge circular bruises. When questioned about his injuries Kane told them that a woman had paid him to suspend him from the ceiling and beat him across the torso with a large piece of wood. The circles on his back were from the suction cups she had attached to the hoist mechanism.

I made the observation that this 'woman' was possessed of an almost supernatural strength. Jeremy began to laugh. 'He is so full of shit. You know, he never even played squash! And he told me that he'd been picked for the State rugby union team but had to say no because of the steroids. He also says that Hine's baby isn't his. Oh, and he talked to me for about half an hour about how he's going to kill you.' For all his efforts, Kane's boasting, it seemed, had done little to endear him to the other men at the site. 'They were all calling him a dumb coconut 'cause he couldn't read the site map,' said Jeremy, laughing. 'He didn't know which end was which!'

The suggestion that Kane might be illiterate seemed to pass Jeremy by.

Just as Jeremy settled down to his evening meal of four pork chops, cooked dutifully for him by Lenore, there was a buzz at the intercom. A pair of grinning faces announced in American accents that they were 'here to take the room'.

'What room?' I asked.

'Um, the one someone called Hi-knee advertised at the flatmate agency.'

Rod and Todd's real names were Tim and Chastity (it was Jeremy who decided to name them after the characters of Ned Flanders's children from *The Simpsons*). Rod and Todd were both twenty-one and from rural Kansas. The pair, who were engaged, had attended the same high school where their parents had met. Rod and Todd had arrived in Sydney from the States only three days earlier and planned to be in Australia for six months. When a stranger they met on the steps of the Opera House told them the Gold Coast was 'where it was happening' they decided immediately to move.

Over the next few days, Rod and Todd were to prove so artless that at times one might have been forgiven for mistaking them for cavemen frozen during the last ice age, thawed now and at large in modern society. They refused to try a mango; the bats flying by the window sent them into such paroxysms of fear they would run shrieking from the balcony; Chastity had to spell out S-A-T-A-Y in order to ascertain that it was edible; and when I once mentioned Auschwitz Tim smiled sweetly and said, 'What's that?' Despite, or perhaps because of, their barely credible ignorance, Rod and Todd had a certain hillbilly charm. He was small and fragile, softly spoken with a shining slick of thinning golden hair. She was a wiry brunette with a pinched face, muscular buttocks and a voice of such shrillness and intensity that it could only be described as like listening to Liza Minnelli belt out 'Maybe this Time' on a balloon full of helium. When she spoke pained dogs in backyards everywhere began to run in circles.

The pair had an utterly co-dependent relationship. She was strident and cunning, he dimwitted and utterly compliant. (One afternoon, when they thought we weren't home, Jeremy, Lenore and I had sat in the corridor suppressing our hysteria as we listened to her relentless demands for sex: 'Tiiiiiiim, I want it nooooow.')

Chastity pointed to Jeremy. 'You talk funny, but in a different kinda funny,' she said, confirming my suspicion that she was the brains of the outfit. I explained that Jeremy was not an Australian but a New Zealander.

'Is New Zealand different to Australia?'

Jeremy launched into one of his patented spiels. 'Let me tell you why New Zealand is a fuckin' shithouse place: number one' – he counted on his fingers – 'we were the first to give women the vote. That, for starters, was a fuckin' idiot move. Number two: we've had not one but *two* female prime ministers, and Helen Clark is the ugliest mutt you've ever seen in your *life*! But – get this! This is the worst! – we are the only country in the world to have a transsexual in parliament!'

'She's still better looking than Helen Clark,' added Lenore.

By the time Jeremy had begun to make jokes about September 11, Rod and Todd could only look at one another with fixed smiles, their wind-seared mid-western faces frozen into a rictus of fear.

There was another buzz at the intercom. It was Hine.

Sitting down in the front bedroom she apologised for not having told us she had decided to move back to her mother's. I didn't know whether to be angry about her inconsiderate behaviour or just cut my losses and be grateful she was finally leaving.

While she and her cousin lugged garbage bags full of clothes down the hall I mentioned that I had been getting death threats from Kane and that he had, apparently, either been inside the house or been speaking to someone who had. 'Have you heard from him?' I asked.

'Yeah, I just tell him to fuck off,' she said wearily.

'I'm worried that he might break down the door.'

'He can't come near the building.'

'You have great faith in the power of restraining orders... Besides, I'm still worried about his mates.'

'Brendan,' she said with the barest hint of exasperation, 'the guys in the balaclavas don't exist.' She tapped her temple. 'They're in his head. He's beaten up every friend he ever had. No one even likes him enough to help him. Not even Bradley.' At least I had found out the Gimp's real name. With that she picked up the final pile of baby clothes and disappeared out the door.

Chastity sidled up beside me. 'Who's Kane?' she squeaked.

A few days later I awoke in agony. The pain stretched from my left shoulder to my right, down my arms to my fingertips, all the way across my chest and down my back to my pelvis, which felt as though it had been split in two. A couple of days prior I had gone to a party at Phil and Rachelle's. During the course of a conversation about my efforts to ascertain whether Kane had been the dealer at B3, Rachelle had casually offered the information that during high school she had dated the man known as Kane Rane. I asked her at what point she had been planning to tell me this. 'Sorry, I forgot,' she said.

'Well, it's very important that you remember.' I described Kane physically.

'Yeah, that's him.'

'Was his surname Rosenberg?'

She frowned. 'I dunno... It was a long time ago.'

With that I decided to get very drunk before falling asleep on a bed of stuffed animals in the spare room. The next morning, on their way to Southport, Phil and Rachelle dropped me off in Surfers. Phil stopped at a red light and I jumped out of the car. After giving them a quick wave I slammed the door shut and spun on my heel straight into the path of an oncoming bus. To the accompaniment of screeching brakes my body went flying to the ground, spreading across the hot tarmac in the posture of a fallen hurdler. It had occurred to me in the brief moment in which I turned to see the relentless yellow juggernaut move towards me, that this was to be the fulfillment of the prophecy made by Bonito in my dream. But after rising to my feet to give my frame a cautious pat down, and in the absence of any obvious injuries or bright tunnels in the immediate vicinity, I soon concluded that I would live to drink again. I turned and made a disgruntled gesture of explanation towards the driver. He just shrugged his shoulders and wound the bus around me to continue his route. At the time it had seemed a lucky escape, and it was. It had never occurred to me, however, that the pain might take a day to manifest.

After about an hour of futile shifts and wriggles, a buzz at the intercom forced me to rise. Bill, the producer of the porno, had arrived with the movie, as promised. He seemed keen to meet with me which struck me as odd because I couldn't do him any favours. It occurred to me that perhaps he didn't have many friends. I slouched over to the door like Igor in a Frankenstein film and bade him enter.

'What happened to you?'

I explained.

He laughed. 'That must have been fairly embarrassing.'

Together we sat on the couch and watched the video. The opening sequence was a collage of Gold Coast stock footage: Indy cars, horse racing, surfing – a notable absence of drunken horny teenagers throwing up on their brand new Nikes. Then the title flashed up: *Swing Party Down-under!* The voiceover was a morning radio weather report: 'It's another beautiful day here on the Gold Coast, sunny with a top of thirty-three degrees...' Cut to Construction and Twinkle, the bashful newlyweds searching the Internet for sex partners. After some protracted negotiation, Abattoir and Red arrive at the front door of the Broadbeach mansion. Somewhat reluctantly, they agree to be filmed by their hosts.

The orgy went ahead much as I remembered with one notable difference: the stars were almost unrecognisable. The men had deteriorated considerably. Construction was a shapeless white blob motioned by hispid thighs while Red, with his milky skin, essentially disappeared every time he walked in front of a wall. Twinkle and Roxy, meanwhile, with their glossy skin and pert bosoms, looked like fully-fledged porn stars. But the most extraordinary transformation was that of Abattoir who, although by no means attractive, was really quite passable, albeit in a 'last hour before closing' kind of way. Not once did Red's penis appear on camera.

I congratulated Bill and told him it looked very professional. He thanked me and said that 'amateur' and 'swing' porn was to be his chosen market, one that he felt had been greatly neglected. I asked if he had ever made porn before.

'Just once; with a mate of mine in Canberra.' He paused. 'But we got into all kinds of shit.'

'What kinds?'

'Well, um, put it this way: porn is very heavily protected by organised crime.'

'Why did you decide to make porn, Bill?'

'I told you, mate, it's just a niche. There's a demand for porn made in Australia, especially on the Gold Coast.' He paused and shook his palms in a gesture of refusal. 'I don't have a single porno in my house. It's not something I even get into.'

'Do you have a wife?'

The colour of his face deepened. 'Well, er, yes, actually, I do.'

'And she doesn't know you make porn, does she?'

'Um, no, she doesn't, mate.' He was red by now.

'What do you tell her when you're on the Gold Coast?'

He shrugged. 'I just tell her we're shooting a commercial.'

That morning as Bill feebly protested his innocence, I looked over at *Swing Party Down-under!* and then at the ubiquitous blue ocean in the distance wondering whether the whole scenario might not be construed as some sort of convenient metaphor for the Gold Coast, a city, like an ugly woman under hot lights, that strove always to convince us that somewhere out there – be it Shangri-la or in a high rise in Queensland – life was better.

Twenty-four

★

Fish Roulette

AND, JUST LIKE THAT, Kane was gone – no more calls, no more phantom buzzes at the intercom, no more threats. There were few reminders that he had ever existed, save an orange typewriter on the desk in the living room and a curiously effeminate sunhat doubling as a lampshade. What had happened to him, I did not know. Perhaps he had made good on a boast he made to Jeremy about moving to Sydney to sell ecstasy. Perhaps he was merely biding his time. Whatever the explanation, I was grateful for the peace. And yet, as though my happiness was contingent upon the presence of tension and fear, I fell into a deep depression.

My attempts to find out whether Kane was indeed Kane Rane had proven futile: Phil's DJ mate had disappeared to Melbourne and changed his name; a couple I met for dinner who had been present that night at B3 had inexplicably interpreted my assertion that the Gold Coast was the fastest-growing city in Australia as a slight on their home town and left; a third person gave me a fake phone number.

But it wasn't just my feeling of failure. It was the suggestion of having being lulled into a false sense of security, of having cheated fate. My time on the Gold Coast had not ended dramatically; it was winding down into a slow, inevitable torpor and now I was desperate for some signal, some sign that I was on the right track, that my project had purpose. The death knell had sounded a few days prior when, only two weeks after their arrival, we awoke in the morning to find a note from Rod and Todd explaining they had left to pick fruit at an undisclosed location in the hinterland. I was angry, but it had not been unexpected.

'Good,' exclaimed Jeremy indignantly. 'I'm glad those rednecks are gone.'

'Er, Jeremy,' I said, 'do you realise there are a lot of people who'd describe you as a redneck?'

'What?' he cried, incredulous. 'I'm not a *redneck*. I'm from Christchurch! That's the *third*-biggest city in New Zealand!'

We had yet to hear from Hine about the possibility of her subletting the room again. With Rod and Todd gone she was now a week overdue on her rent and I was beginning to suspect that I would never see my bond again. I didn't really care; without Kane I had no story and without a story I had no reason for being. Jeremy sat beside me on the bed, stroking my shoulder. 'Come on, bro! What is it with you?' He bent down and prodded my side before hoisting a reproachful finger: '*I* never get depressed!'

I got out of bed and shuffled into the living room. An angry stench of eggs filled the air. I went to open the balcony doors but Jeremy insisted they remain closed; insects were everywhere, he argued, just waiting for the opportunity to sting him, lay eggs under his skin or crawl into his urinary tract. I decided to leave the unit to check my email and visit my friend Jules.

Jules was a Goth: the same one I had seen walking through Southport some months before. He was tall and thin and the palest person I had ever met, so sallow and wan that he verged on translucence, an effect only emphasised by his uniform of black and a tangled nimbus of sooty hair. Here on the Gold Coast he looked utterly absurd, like a character from a black-and-white film who had wandered onto the set of *Baywatch*. Jules worked in a crushingly decrepit 1960s corridor arcade that ran between Orchid Avenue and the highway that, although hideous, greatly appealed to me.

The shops and shopkeepers in Jules's arcade were one of the last remnants of genuine eccentricity in the wasteland of downtown Surfers. They served as a living link to the older Gold Coast, the land before Starbucks; a time when John Paterson, aka 'the Mutton-bird Man' (so-called because he wore a pith helmet with a stuffed mutton-bird perched on top) would roam the beachfront in a decrepit Rolls Royce spraying people in his own brand of tanning liquid; a time when Dutch couple John and Trudy Maas ran a highly successful restaurant dressed in Dutch peasant outfits, singing with great force the songs of Edith Piaf for which Trudy would demand absolute attention; and when Ted Louey ran Ted's Garage, a service station and bikini car wash featuring a miniature train ride, a carpet python, a stuffed crocodile and a giant turtle kept prisoner for children's rides in a canvas wading pool. All were gone now but echoes still remained.

At one end of the arcade sat a morose Japanese man sipping green tea soft drinks and staring into a forest of coloured surfboard fins. Despite having lived in the city for thirteen years and owning his own surf shop, he would hint that he longed to return to Japan: he was divorced, too old to ever be a better surfer and the Japanese food on the Gold Coast was awful. At the other end was a transsexual by the name of Tracey who sold denim hotpants and other dance party accessories she made herself. Her father had been a rugby league star in the 1960s and she had once juggled in her own circus with a performing ox. She had led an interesting, picaresque life; unfortunately she would never allow anyone to forget it. Other tenants of the corridor included an eerily empty barbershop, a disorderly Internet café run by a voluble Korean and, in the middle of it all, sat the headquarters of the Country Women's Association; its window hung with a long line of knitted baby booties and cardigans in pink, yellow and blue wool.

Jules worked next door to the Japanese surfer. The shop sold body jewellery, kitsch T-shirts, bongs, pipes and other generic items of 'urban tribal' paraphernalia. The room was always conditioned to a temperature just above freezing. I found Jules that morning blowing up rubber gloves, drawing faces on them and then attaching speech bubbles made of paper: 'Hi, Jules, I am Grokon, the freestyle rapper. I your friend. Kill your parents.' He sticky-taped the glove to the glass counter over some photographs of a man being lifted off the ground by steel rods passed through his pectoral muscles. 'We never get any customers here,' he said, noticing my inspection of the glove. 'I get very bored.'

Jules had been born in Wales and now had one dream in life: to move back. 'I think I blend into the background in Wales. It's cold, miserable, the people are miserable, and I get happy from their misery.' He sighed and selected from behind the counter an enormous bowie knife with a grotesquely ornamented handle. 'I have to get out of here – now,' he said, stabbing with the knife at the inflated fingers of the rubber glove. 'A doctor once said that I was borderline schizophrenic and I'm afraid I might be about to make my first killing on the Gold Coast.'

'When are they going to knock this arcade down?' I asked.

'Soon, I hope,' he said, tearing Grokon to ragged shreds, 'with me in it.' We made ourselves a cup of instant coffee and headed out into the corridor, where most of the owners sat all day on benches in front of their shops. Tracey the transsexual, sucking on a cigarette, waved hello from her seat. On one of the walls behind the benches someone had drawn a graffiti tag with what looked like blood. 'I think it must have been done with a tampon,' said Jules, inspecting it closely.

'Lick it,' said Tracey.

'God, I hate this fucking town,' said Jules, turning in his seat and banging the back of his head against the wall repeatedly.

I would miss Jules; his steel-coated resistance to the charms of Paradise and his despondent yearning for escape had thrown into high relief my own desperate malaise. It seemed that there was little left for me in this city. The time to leave had come.

I farewelled Jules who was by then running around the shop chasing flies with the bowie knife. 'I try to get them mid-flight,' he explained, lunging past my head with the blade. I drew back. 'It's all right,' he said reassuringly, 'I've only ever sold one knife that's appeared on the evening news.'

At the Internet café I received an email from Ren explaining that, with a minimum of bother, Julian had come out to his mother (his father had died while he was still young) and then moved him into their home in Oslo. I sent my congratulations to Julian and my condolences to his mother. Emails from David, however, had ceased. Idly I opened an old one he had sent. It contained a picture of him sitting on his bed, smiling. 'Here's one of me,' he wrote. 'I hope it doesn't scare you.' I sat and looked at the picture. On the one hand I pitied him, but on the other his neediness irritated me. But, when I was really honest, I could only admit that it was because I saw some of the same neediness in myself – a loneliness that perhaps I had been denying by coming to the Gold Coast in the first place. And I wondered if I cared for him a great deal more than I liked to admit.

Back at home Jeremy had left for work and Lenore was still asleep. I opened the curtains and doors to let out the persisting smell of eggs. The stench didn't dissipate but rather seemed to arrive in waves with the changing winds. I hunted around the room for its source. After prolonged investigation I realised it was coming from the fish tank. I put my nose over the edge and flinched back violently, gagging. On top of the water, swollen and leaking, floated the final fish. I scooped it out with a jam jar and flushed it down the toilet. The tank reeked and needed to be cleaned. It had been Hine's but she had left it when she moved out, promising she would come by later to pick it up. As I went to lift it off the cabinet, a single fish darted out from its hiding place behind a rock. I put the tank down and stared at it through the glass. Fat and silver and apparently oblivious to its own good fortune, it flitted through the stagnant garden. The water needed to be emptied but I felt bad about flushing the last fish down the toilet, as though it had won an aquatic version of *Survivor* and deserved to be compensated. I netted it with a colander and transferred it to a plastic milk jug, leaving it to stand on the bench. After pouring the water down the bath I sat the tank on the balcony to air. Without the tank the room looked bare, so in its place atop the cabinet I positioned the broken orange typewriter. I had only just noticed its decorative qualities; it was, in its own way, a handsome object.

I was scrubbing out the last of the stinking algae when my phone rang. It was Hine's mother. A baby boy had been born that morning.

The day Hine brought the new baby over the *Gold Coast Bulletin* ran an irate story complaining about the results of a report that had found federal politicians thought the Gold Coast tacky and without character. I did not know which I found more absurd, the idea that the citizens of the Gold Coast didn't realise *everyone* thought their town tacky and characterless, or the notion that 'character' was not a quality inherent in every object, but rather an independent entity that might have been skimmed off, freeze-dried, turned into flakes and sprinkled across the city like salt.

I arrived home from a morning outing to find Hinemoa standing in the foyer in front of the mirror, turning her head to inspect her backside. 'Hello,' I said. Seeing her in jeans was a jolt. I hadn't realised how tiny she was.

'Heyyyy.'

'You look great.'

She gave me one of her reptilian grins. 'You see why all the boys down at the club call me lil' Beyonce?'

We walked into the living room. Sitting on the couch, perched on Lenore's knee sat a huge baby boy . . . a Maori child of Chilean origin and exceptional beauty. Which would have been great – had it happened. But it didn't. As it was the kid was the spitting image of Kane, complete with wide, staring eyes and rocking head, held tenderly now between Hinemoa's thumb and forefinger. At ten pounds he was the size of most six-month olds. I looked at his big pouty mouth, his staring eyes. He looked back unblinking, his head lolling and his tongue sending a little string of spit to the front of his tight, pink pyjamas.

'My God, he's a giant,' I said.

'Yeah, I know. He was hell to get out.'

'Must have been all the steroids,' I joked, in reference to Kane's habit. Lenore laughed. Hinemoa looked at me, narrowed her eyes and turned away.

'What are you going to call him?' asked Lenore.

'I'm not sure yet. I really like Stratos . . . but I also like Ridge, you know, from *The Bold and the Beautiful*.'

'Is Stratos a perfume?' I intuited.

'Yeah,' she seemed mildly impressed. 'Blue Stratos.'

It must have been Blue Stratos that I could smell in the air the day I hid in the cupboard. 'Have you heard from Kane at all?'

'Yeah, he keeps calling me all the time, asking for me to leave mum's and come back to him, but I just hang up.'

Hine's mother had already told me that they were back together. Listening to Hine now I could think of only one other instance in which I had seen someone tell such a bald-faced lie: it was a friend from high school, a heroin addict who had told me she was clean and then died of an overdose five months later.

'What happened to Hemi?' I asked.

'He's still with Kane . . . I think.'

'What about Kane's mother? He'd said something about sending Hemi to live with her.'

She let out a little disdainful snort. 'His mother's in a mental asylum in Sydney. She's been there since he was a kid.'

'So, what are you going to do about the room?' I asked, changing the subject.

'Well, I think I might just give the real estate agent a call and ask 'em if we can break the lease.'

I didn't argue. Lenore had decided to return to New Zealand; her coaching position had fallen through and she was growing fatter by the day. Although Hine was two weeks behind in the rent, and I knew I would lose my bond, we had all made the decision to leave.

Hinemoa set the baby down on the couch and began to rummage through some of the odds and sods that had been left behind in the kitchen drawers. She tipped out a glass jar full of keys and began to sort them. Holding up one jangling bunch for the unit she called out, 'Whose are these?'

Lenore and I shrugged.

She looked back down at the bench, her brow knitted in thought. 'Oh,' she said suddenly, 'these are the keys that I had . . .' She glanced sideways and paused. 'I mean, that Kane must have had cut.' Without breaking her stride she bundled them up and dropped them into her handbag.

I knew I had remembered to lock the door that day.

I sat back down on the couch and picked up the baby. He lay in my lap, his head at the end of my knees. Here he was: little Stratos or Ridge or Puff Daddy or whatever other ridiculous moniker she would inflict on him forever, as though he wasn't a child but a boat or a dog. I stared at him: at those empty eyes, that tongue like a feeding clam, and gradually I was overwhelmed by a sensation which, after some examination, revealed itself as a kind of repulsion. It was an illogical response, cruel perhaps, but it was not one that I could ignore. Floundering like a beached sea creature, lolling under his own weight, staring at me with blameless eyes, it was as though he was some sort of devil-baby, his sole purpose to continue an endless cycle of madness and chaos, and I wondered if it would ever end.

'So, what are you going to do now that you've had him?' I asked, handing him back to Hine as she settled onto the couch. 'Oh, I dunno, live with Mum for a while.' She paused. 'There's an apartment in Palm Beach I wanna get.' She looked away dreamily, her eyes full of *Perfect Match* fantasies of life on the sunny Gold Coast. 'I'm gonna apply to get Tejahn and Isaac back from their dad. He doesn't look after 'em properly. I'm gonna get 'em to come and live with me in Palm Beach.'

Lenore looked around her. 'I suppose it's a pity we have to give up such a nice flat.'

'If you guys could get a tenant for the front room you could keep it,' replied Hine.

'Let's get Kane to move back in,' said Lenore, laughing.

Hinemoa opened her eyes wide, cocked her head and said with no discernible trace of irony, 'What would you guys think about that?'

Lenore and I looked at one another, stupefied, like two people who have just had the same dream. God, I felt such a fool. All this time I had cast Hine in a series of literary clichés – the plucky battler, the hooker with a heart of gold – or seen her as merely selfish, but now I knew it went way beyond that. She was an empty vessel looking to be filled; her identity was entirely externalised. Hinemoa was nothing more than the reflection of the world around her and the fact that she had chosen violent men to animate her into existence was merely an accident of fate – today it was Kane but it might as well have been heroin. Leaving him was as likely as her chopping off her own leg.

I left the girls talking and went downstairs to the mall where I ate lunch in the shadow of a full-sized plaster replica of Michelangelo's *David*. After eating I dropped $2 in a fortune-telling machine and put my palm against the handprint. The contraption made a noise like a pinball machine and I waited for the print-out of my fortune. Nothing happened. It was broken. Enraged, I punched the sparkling box, hurting my knuckles and incurring the wrath of a passing granny.

Back upstairs Hine was complaining to Lenore about Kane, about how much she hated him and how he kept begging her to come back and, girl-to-girl, didn't she think that was pathetic? Lenore glanced away from the conspiratorial huddle and blinked out r-e-s-c-u-e-m-e in morse code. Over on the bench, the jug with the fish in it was gone.

'What happened to the fish?' I asked.

'I flushed it down the toilet,' said Hine.

'Fush, fush, fush!' screamed Drakkar and belted me in the knee.

'Why did you do that?'

'What d'ya want that fuckin' fish for?' She looked at Lenore and laughed.

Poor fush. With luck it would grow to enormous size in the sewers of the Gold Coast and return to wreak revenge on all those who had treated it with such callousness.

After what seemed like a stretch of time measurable only in tree rings, Hine ceased her complaints and made to leave. I said goodbye to Drakkar and he gave me his one-fisted wave before kissing me on the cheek for what would be the last time. In this republic of the false, the spontaneity and sincerity of his affection had felt simple and true. Hine said he often asked for me. It felt like my only real achievement on the Gold Coast.

Once she was safely out the door, Lenore and I collapsed onto the couch, exhausted by the effort of entertaining her limitless capacity for calamity. I couldn't hate her, she was too pathetic; but I was glad I would never have to see her again.

Lenore looked at me, laughing. 'Do you know why she got pissed off when you made the steroid joke?'

'No.'

'Because she told me she'd been injecting with Kane while she was pregnant.'

Twenty-five

★

Kane Rane

OUTSIDE, THE STREETS were cast in grey. Real rain had finally come to the Gold Coast, raising the level of the dam and breaking the drought. Down on the streets the meter maids in their satiny gold bikinis continued to do the rounds. Now, however, they had matching gold umbrellas which they held precariously above their oversized cowboy hats, giving them the appearance of extras in the Hollywood harem of an absurd oriental potentate as they tripped their way daintily across the wet pavements, washed clean now of the previous evening's vomit. The boutiques had been flooded and in each window display sat brightly coloured plastic buckets positioned to catch the trickles that ran through the cracks in the ceiling. Earlier that day, while we were busy bundling his stuff up into garbage bags, Kane had rung after several weeks of silence. 'I heard you were trying to fix me up with your cop mate in Canberra,' he chided.

It was interesting to hear the pathology of his schizophrenia: the all-powerful cop mate who was going to 'fix him up'; Canberra and all its associations of central control; paranoia within paranoia and all of it leading in a straight line from him to me.

'Bad move, mate,' he added.

'Kane! It's good to hear from you again.'

'You're fuckin' dead!'

The line went silent.

Although he had reappeared, Kane had been reduced to the status of a nuisance in my life. Lenore, however, had had enough. One night he had rung her and screamed such savage abuse that she had burst into tears and, two days later, returned to New Zealand, vowing never to return. The next day, Jeremy told the men at work what had happened. Upon hearing the story, one of the smallest members of the crew, Jeremy's friend Jimmy, dropped his tools and ran up to Kane. Barging him with his chest he stood teetering on his toes, boring his finger into Kane's face and screaming until he was red. Jimmy said that Kane was a 'psycho' and a liar. He said that he was sick of Kane harassing his friends, that Kane had no mates and nobody liked him. By that stage a small crowd gathered round the melee. Some cheered and applauded.

Kane stood back from Jimmy to address the horseshoe of men, his voice faltering. 'It's Hine,' he said, the sparkle of tears welling in his eyes. 'She hates me. She doesn't want me to have any mates. She always tells lies about me.' With the word 'lies' his voice cracked and he began to sob. Some of the men began to laugh. Jimmy walked away and picked up his tools. The crowd dispersed and Kane left the site, dabbing at his eyes with his singlet. He never came back.

Was it possible that the seeds of sympathy in me had taken root? A couple of days prior, one of Jeremy's friends from the site had been complaining to me about Kane's lies and irrational behaviour. 'Well, he is a paranoid schizophrenic,' I had reminded him.

'Yeah!' he had replied irately. 'He's a total schizo!'

It was only at this point that I realised most people spoke of schizophrenia with the same derisory intent that a twelve-year-old might have reserved for 'spastic'. That this was a real disease with debilitating symptoms had, it seemed, never occurred to them.

Jeremy and I took the garbage bags and the rest of the junk and threw it down the communal garbage chute in the hall. The typewriter spun around, hitting the sides several times as it fell the eight storeys to the steel bin in the basement, making a satisfying crash. I threw the sunhat down after it.

'He still talks about that hat,' said Jeremy. 'He's always asking me to give it back to him.'

After the hat I dropped the broken electrical appliances and after them a stack of Ren's pornographic magazines that had been sitting in the desk since he left; as they fell down the black void they made a pleasant fluttering noise that seemed to melt away all my anxiety and fear over the last four months.

Lying at the bottom of Kane's box of junk was a photograph of a little girl, barefoot and in a pink dress, standing by some rose bushes. She had Kane's unmistakable features. On the back of the picture someone had written the words 'Can I have a hug?' I was going to send it down to meet the rest of his mismatched detritus, but decided to pocket it instead as a melancholy reminder of my adventures in the Moroccan.

'I would still like to find out whether Kane was the dealer at B3,' I said as we returned to the apartment.

'What was that?'

I told Jeremy the story.

'Kane Rane,' he exclaimed. 'I know him. He sells speed to all the boys at the construction site. He sells them their GBH down at the gym, too.'

'Who is he?'

'He's Kane's drug buddy... he's half-Maori as well. I know where he'll be right now if you wanna go.'

Together Jeremy and I got in the car and drove to a motel in northern Southport. 'He lives up there,' said Jeremy, pointing to the second storey of a decrepit 1960s building folded around a stagnant swimming pool. 'Do you want to go in?'

For some time I sat in the car, watching the grey door and considering my options. It looked like the kind of motel where Quentin Tarantino characters went to hide out and polish their silencers. 'No,' I said eventually. 'I believe you. I think this story has gone on long enough.'

Twenty-six

★

Farewell to Paradise

CALL ME KINKY, but I have always had a fondness for Canberra — any city so many people hate was bound to inspire some affection in me. It was now a few days since I had left the Gold Coast and had arrived in the capital to visit my policeman friend, the one with the connections to the various spy satellites that were currently listening to Kane's every word. Today the city appeared to be in the grip of some sort of cultural festival. During the day a string quartet in tuxedos had played in the central square, and by night people sat around a public movie screen nestled in jumbo-sized beanbags (provided by the local government), sipping red wine and watching a free screening of *Casablanca*. The previous day I had gone to the National Gallery where I met a woman who had worked for a minister during the Menzies era. Together we stood in front of *Blue Poles* and talked about Brancusi and Lucian Freud. Her husband had been an ambassador during the Petrov Affair.

It was as though Alice had stepped back through the looking glass.

Farewell to Paradise

If a city could be judged by the quality of its people then this was (officially) the best-educated, most intelligent, wealthiest, healthiest, most politically aware city in the country. And these days in pre-autumnal Canberra (the trees developing a faint blush of apparently natural orange) were like the final lines of a high school creative writing assignment: '... and then I woke up and realised that it was all a dream'. At parties people would look at me and say, 'What do you mean you *lived* on the Gold Coast?' as though the air there was poisonous and the ducks flew upside down. But I could understand their mystification; so different did the world seem outside Pleasure Island that even I had begun to feel there had been something hallucinatory about the experience. Had all those extraordinary coincidences really happened? Did I really meet those absurd, disturbed people? Was Bonito's prophecy anything more than a bad dream?

My last night on the Gold Coast had been spent at Palazzo Versace where I threw a party for the people I had met during my stay. As the new epicentre of all that was desirable in a Gold Coast lifestyle, Palazzo Versace had seemed an appropriate venue; and even though my suite faced the airconditioning unit of the Marina Mirage, I had certainly not been disappointed by the kitsch value of the complex, embracing as it did a glorious mismatched baroque amalgam of everything from Moorish Palace to late-eighties bank foyer. With its fake marble pillars, dark purple corridors and the giant chandelier that had once hung in the State Library of Milan, it looked like the Vatican might have if Michael Jackson had been Pope. That all this was sandwiched between a fading mall built by Christopher Skase and a shack housing a fish wholesaler was a testament to the triumph of delusion over reality that the Gold Coast had made into an art form. The frumpiness of the Sheraton Mirage across the street suddenly looked like a salutary *memento mori* for this grand usurper.

Palazzo Versace was another of the Gold Coast's mini-utopias; a hermetically sealed world of privilege and luxury for men and women with tans like rotisserie chicken. In the foyer was a shop, haunted by dozens of desert-mummy women (better dressed than the crowd at the mall, but featuring nevertheless that same aura of the crypt), where, like a more expensive version of Craig Gore's Aurora, you could purchase everything to create what the hotel literature referred to as 'the Versace lifestyle', including beds, rugs and a $2000 soap dish. (The Aurora parallel became even more pronounced when I discovered that some of those who lived in units within the Versace complex had forked out millions of dollars to have their entire apartments outfitted in top-to-toe Versace, prompting one to wonder why they didn't just hang out in the foyer during the day and get some nice discount Ikea for the evenings.)

My friends Amanda and Luke turned up from Brisbane in the afternoon followed by Phil and Rachelle in the early evening, the latter bringing with them a menagerie of their friends: strange, grizzled men with juiceless skin and speed-corroded teeth; their families had lived in the hinterland for five generations. As they filed through the door I grew suddenly conscious of the sign in our suite informing guests that everything in the room had been accounted for and that all missing items would be billed: including in this category the $500 cut-glass tumblers, the several hundred dollars' worth of pillow cases and the $80 teaspoons. Rachelle told me not to worry: these were her mates and they would never rip me off. No matter how many times I heard that on the Gold Coast, it still made me laugh.

The gathering had been a fairly last-minute affair and as we sat down and cracked open our first beers I realised that there were people whom I had either forgotten to invite or hadn't given the full details: Benny and Danger, Jules the Goth and my journalist friend Amy. There were others I wished I could have invited: Ren and Julian, Rod and Todd, Betty, Mandy and Bonito, HUSLER – even the repulsive Leonard might have been fun. For the hell of it I had even considered giving Kane and Hine a call, but quickly decided against it. Then I thought about David. The previous week, in a fit of guilt and consternation, I had written him an email saying I hoped he was all right, but received no reply. With his sudden silence, the memory of those scarred wrists had begun to play on my conscience and I grew anxious. In my idle hours morbid tableaus of bodies – hanging, bleeding, floating – had begun to pollute my thoughts.

The night grew increasingly opaque. Sitting in the spa between Rachelle and her friend Nikki, a former biker moll, I drank champagne from a shoe and left my beer in the soap holder. Later we went on an abortive trip to the beach, avoiding the surreptitious rustling of the men in the bushes only to return to Marina Mirage and go to the nightclub. An unexpected moment of poetry came in the form of a tour of 'Australia's smallest zoo', an aviary inside Marina Mirage. We stood in the middle of the forest listening to the low cooings of the birds while a big white owl swooped over our heads and Rachelle pointed to the fat bundles that sat sleeping on the branches, naming each one.

Back at the hotel, by 4 a.m. I had fallen asleep on the double bed between Nikki and Hugo, another of Rachelle's friends. My friend Luke lay slumped across my feet. The last I had seen of Jeremy was his huge form wandering down the low purple corridor at 3 a.m., looking disoriented.

Quite unlike Hunter S. Thompson I spent much of the next morning in a fit of guilt, cleaning up broken beer bottles and setting cushions artfully over cigarette burns. In the sober light of day I began to panic that I might be about to receive a bill for several thousand dollars after what we had done to the furniture but as I checked out, nothing was said. I was so grateful to be leaving the Gold Coast that I even paid without complaint the several hundred dollars' worth of drinks that Phil had thoughtfully charged to my account. Loading my bags into the back of Amanda's car, we drove back out through Main Beach, past the radio palm tree, across the bridge, through Southport and on towards Brisbane, the towers of the Gold Coast growing small in the rear view mirror, and the last four months turning to memories and the laughter of relief.

Then there I was in Canberra, watching *Casablanca* on the big screen in the dry night and wondering why I ever thought moving to the Cold Coast might have been a good idea. If the Gold Coast was the future of Australian society – which it was – then it was a vision of a two-tiered dystopia every bit as sinister as *Metropolis*. But this gave it no cause for superiority or complacency; the Gold Coast might have been the first city in the country to be created purely out of a yearning for pleasure, but at the beginning of a new millennium its promises were as ubiquitous as the sun that beat down on the mummy women who lined the beaches. The entire world, to paraphrase Billy Joel, was in a Gold Coast state of mind.

The following is a scene I witnessed in Sydney not long after leaving the Gold Coast. An obese homeless woman, clutching at dozens of plastic bags, struggled through the centre of town – she could be smelt from several metres away and people crossed the road to avoid her. Draped over her frame, like a dress, hung an enormous Pepsi T-shirt (clearly a discarded freebie from some recent advertising campaign) emblazoned in foot-high lettering with the slogan 'Live Life to the Max!' This image gave absurd form to one of the most insidious myths offered by the notion of lifestyle – that it is democratic, that everyone has the same shot at the brass ring, that 'lifestyle choices' are in fact choices at all. For example, my 'choice' to have four children before my mid-twenties, to binge drink while pregnant and to court dangerous, mentally ill boyfriends was a decision based on careful consultation of the available literature rather than, say, my general fucked-upness. In the new world order of lifestyle a select group were busy fortifying themselves inside child-free, security-patrolled, burnt sienna Super Apartments, disappearing into the forest for Native American sweat lodges or experiencing the healing power of reiki as their rubbish was trundled away to be compacted into frozen cubes. Meanwhile Kane and Hine and all their ilk had been cut adrift, rootless and fractured, to navigate their way through a series of mirages and hollow promises. If living on the Gold Coast had served any purpose then it was to remind me that utopias are doomed – whether you're selling capitalism, communism or aluminium siding.

Meanwhile, back on Pleasure Island, a shark in a canal had taken and killed a second man. The rain was falling hard, flooding the canals and washing away the ground, destabilising foundations and causing backyards to drop off into the water. It was almost as if between them – the bats, the sharks, the lizards and now the floods – the Gold Coast was being slowly reclaimed by nature, washed away into the water and returned to the swamp on which it was built. Then, of course, Kane was still calling me. These days, however, I had become attuned to the patterns and rhythms of his threats and rarely answered the phone. His calls didn't worry me anyway: they were sad more than anything else. Sometimes I would try and chat with him, but he could never be drawn into conversation, always cutting me short before breaking into his mad scientist cackle, and hanging up with a portentous finality that was comical in its childishness.

Jeremy, who I kept in touch with, not merely because he still owed me more than $2000, had recently joined the same football team as Kane and even though the pair rarely conversed, was in close enough contact to inform me that Hine was now back living with him and the children (including, for the moment, Hemi, Drakkar and little Puff Daddy) in a townhouse in Palm Beach. And so would continue the wretched cycle, I feared, until either she found something more stimulating, or she or one of her children ended up dead.

As Bogey told Bergman they would always have Paris (why did everyone meet in Paris and never, say, Southport?) I still thought of David. The constant doubt that had been chipping away, defying me to ignore it over the last month, finally broke my resolve. I thought again of those scars on his wrists and those final mournful letters and knew now that something terrible had happened. 'Bonito sees death,' Mandy had told me in my dream. How like me to have assumed it meant my own.

The next afternoon, after a day of vacillation and against my better judgment, I looked up David's home phone number in the book. For hours I sat and did nothing, watching television, reading and wondering whether I ought to make the call or if I could face the horrible inevitabilities conjured by a guilty conscience. By nine o'clock I could stand no more and took the phone in hand. For some time the phone rang but when someone finally answered, I almost hung up.

'Hello?'

'Hello, is that David's mum?'

'Yes.' She had a slight eastern European lilt.

'Is David there?'

'No.'

I realised I might have woken her. 'Do you know where he is?'

'Well, David took an overdose of pills a week ago.'

I felt the pit of my stomach fall away. 'Oh, shit, no, really? Is he alive . . . I mean, is he okay?'

'Well, he had to go to hospital.'

'Oh, no, is he all right?'

'I don't know really . . . he's run away.'

'What do you mean? Where has he gone?'

'Who is this?'

'My name's Brendan. I'm a friend of his . . . from the Gold Coast.'

'Well, look, I have no idea where he is. I think he's run away to Adelaide.'

'Oh, I see.'

She said nothing.

'So you've not heard from him?'

'No.'

'Not at all?'

'I have no idea where he is.'

I sat in silence. 'Um, so you don't know where he is?'

She became a little exasperated. 'No, and look, I've got to go now.'

'Oh . . . all right.' I thanked her and hung up.

Four months ago I had drifted to the Gold Coast in a depressive fog, hopeful of escaping my problems and of giving my life some direction. Unfortunately, like so many thousands of others, I had not only taken my problems with me but watched them magnify in a land without limits. I had been too world-weary for happiness, settling instead for nothing more complicated than a good time, only to discover too late that good times were not independent from consequences. I thought again about Pinocchio's adventures on Pleasure

Island. The scene of the transformation of boys into donkeys has terrified a generation of children but it has always been one of my favourites in the history of film. I love it not merely for its formal beauty but for the almost Biblical simplicity of its message: be grateful for what you have and, above all else, be careful what you wish for.

Epilogue

★

THE MONTHS PASSED and I stayed in contact with Jeremy. In between reassurances that he would eventually pay back my money, he managed to keep me up-to-date with the endless romantic contortions of Hine and Kane. Despite Hine's mother being subject to a vicious campaign of intimidation (during which a number of bricks had been thrown through her windows and her car set on fire), she had apparently reconciled with the pair and could now be regularly seen cheering from the sidelines of her son-in-law's football matches, tinnie of rum and Coke in hand. Kane had also begun to boast that he had moved into pimping and was supplying three teenage girls with GBH in return for their sexual servitude. The chance of this being true seemed to me highly unlikely.

After a while Jeremy went quiet, refusing to answer his phone and, apparently, ignoring my text messages. I was beginning to grow anxious that I would never see my money again. One afternoon I rang his number and a man by the name of Alan, a member of the construction team with whom Jeremy had been living after leaving the Moroccan, answered the phone: apparently I wasn't the only one who was owed money. Unbeknown to me, Jeremy had been accruing debts across the length and breadth of the Gold Coast: everyone, including the local rugby club, had a claim to make. The debts had finally run out of control when – in what might rate as the most bizarre self-fulfilling

Epilogue

prophecy of my stay on the Gold Coast—a white-tailed spider had bitten him during rugby practice. Perhaps this was living proof that our fears alone are sometimes strong enough to guide our destinies. The bite had developed a strain of deadly flesh-eating bacteria and he was forced to have a large chunk of his foot cut out. Upon release from hospital, on crutches and unable to work, he sold everything, including the car I had paid for, and flew back to New Zealand. Lenore, as it turned out, had been pregnant the entire time we had been living in the Moroccan and gave birth to a baby girl only a couple of weeks prior to Jeremy's run-in with the spider. After a brief dispute over the child's paternity, Jeremy had decided to go and live in Rotorua where, to my knowledge, he, Lenore, the baby and my $2000 still reside.

When I rang Phil and Rachelle and told them what happened they were very consoling. 'Don't worry,' said Phil, 'it's not a true Gold Coast experience if someone hasn't ripped you off.' The pair, meanwhile, had experienced an unexpected windfall. Having sold their home at the height of the real estate boom, they made almost three times what they paid for it and with the proceeds purchased a huge house (complete with spouting concrete dolphins at the four corners of the swimming pool) several blocks further west of the highway. I'm not sure whether Phil's million-dollar Gold Coast dreams will ever come true but the concrete dolphins seem to serve as some sort of powerful visualisation technique.

In the world of pornography, Benny had managed the seemingly impossible and successfully launched his all-day 'strip cruise'. The web site, so far as I know, is still in the production stages. What became of Bill I do not know but *Swing Party Down-under!* can probably be found in the $5 bin at a sex shop near you. As for Leonard the Satanist, he never did produce his magazine. Meanwhile, the Brisbane police announced they were combing the sadomasochistic clubs of Brisbane

Epilogue

for leads on a brutal serial killer known colloquially to prostitutes in the area as 'the schizo'. He was suspected of having killed four women and was expected to strike again. After I read the news I remembered my night with the insomniac at the first bondage party and wondered whether I would ever be called upon as the star witness in some future murder trial.

In a move that surprised many, Craig Gore sold for a profit of almost $120 million the land on which Aurora was to be built and refunded the deposits of those who had purchased apartments. The new developers said that they were scrapping the 'adult community' concept. Despite having cried when he broke the news to his employees, Craig explained his actions to the press by saying that 'at the end of the day I understand the responsibility that we directors have to our shareholders'. Craig continues to build developments on the Gold Coast and coastal New South Wales.

In May of 2003, in response to a public perception that schoolies had become out of control, the Premier of Queensland, Peter Beattie, announced a 'three-point plan' to make schoolies a safer event. Practical measures included more police with special 'move on' powers on the Surfers Paradise beach, improved lighting, and identification wristbands for genuine school leavers. In spite of the new plan, schoolies is still an unofficial event and it remains to be seen whether the measures will bring about any significant change.

As for the case of the tortured housemate, that was eventually resolved with the jailing of Eng Hou 'Thomas' Mah who pleaded guilty to charges of torture, deprivation of liberty and grevious bodily harm. His victim was an autistic man whose mother had left him alone while she went to work in Melbourne. Mah was jailed for six years.

In early September I experienced a rush of panic as I spotted from the corner of my eye images on the TV news of an Islander

Epilogue

woman sobbing on the front lawn of her home in the aftermath of what was described as 'an horrific triple murder of three children and the attempted murder of their mother and brother at an outer Gold Coast suburb'. It was not until a few days later that the name of the family was released and I could be sure that it had not been Hine and the children. Still, the possibility that such a thing might one day happen I cannot entirely dismiss.

The only unresolved passage of my Gold Coast journey was David. Several months after he had run away I rang him again. He had returned home and when I asked how he was doing he said he was fine, but would tell me nothing of why he had tried to kill himself again or why he had run away. The conversation was full of excruciating silences and, by the time I hung up, I knew we would never speak again.

Despite having sworn never to return, I began, with the passage of time, to find myself growing inexplicably nostalgic about my sojourn on the Gold Coast. Unlikely as it may seem, I can concede that I experienced moments of happiness there. With fondness I recall the nights dancing in Melbas, watching the expressionless Norwegian girls grinding away like marble maenads on some ancient temple frieze; or the day spent nursing Drakkar, while watching the Gauguin women at the children's birthday party. Odd things too have stained my memory: certain old signs, like the one attached to a hotel on the highway of a mermaid pouring water from a conch, her tail bent like a hairpin and a scarlet hibiscus behind her ear.

I suppose the palliative of history had allowed me to recall without prejudice some of the things I had enjoyed, perhaps even admired, about Pleasure Island: the gleeful nihilism of digging a canal, whether the fish wanted it or not; the thrill of watching your giant Chinese pagoda/mock-Greek fishing village/Bavarian schloss stretch

Epilogue

its shadow further and further across the sand until it blocked the sun completely; and the notion that there was a place where anyone could get a second chance. By the time I found myself checking the evening news to see what the weather was like on the Gold Coast I realised that, whether I liked it or not, the city had become a part of me.

I acknowledge the absurdity of my position. I cannot deny that I met more unhappy and troubled people on the Gold Coast than in any other place I have ever lived. Neither can I deny that I regard it as a failed experiment – a harrowing glimpse into a future of growing social inequality. What I also cannot deny, however, is the fact that even a failure, no matter how spectacular, requires an effort in the first place. The Gold Coast is not a virtuous place but it has virtues, primary among them that people who go there do so because they want, in whatever crazy, illogical, screwed-up way, to be happy. It is a city of aspirations and dreams, and that these are so rarely realised, or that human beings can be so utterly misguided in their endeavours to achieve them, is more an indictment of society (and possibly the universe itself) than of the people who populate it. Of all the bad behaviour I witnessed on the Gold Coast, little had been malicious. Loneliness and disenchantment can make people so unhappy that, sometimes, like starving refugees at a food drop, they can forget everything else – even the welfare of those closest to them.

After speaking with David for the last time I rummaged through the bag I had taken with me to the Gold Coast. I was still using it and had never cleaned it out properly. Hidden away in numerous pockets and linings were various souvenirs and pieces of incongruous debris that seem to stick to my person like lint. On previous travels I have returned with sculptures, textiles or strange new music; my Gold Coast trip had yielded a small mound of banalities: a meter maid

Epilogue

stubby holder; a 1960s coffee-table book, its pages full of too-bright photographs of sun bathers in a world before skin cancer; my mask from the bondage night; the picture of Kane's little girl in the garden. They were not attractive things, nor made with great care or craft – no ambassador of the French court ever genuflected before the King of Siam to hold aloft a stubby holder. Yet they were, in their own way, an important reminder that, while we may never find north on the compass or sneak our way back into the Garden of Eden, we were forever bound to try; which means that, sometimes, lifestyle is just another word for hope.